MANAGED BY THE MARKETS

MANAGED BY THE MARKETS
How Finance Reshaped America

GERALD F. DAVIS

OXFORD

UNIVERSITY PRESS

2009

OXFORD

UNIVERSITY PRESS

Great Clarendon Street, Oxford OX2 6DP

Oxford University Press is a department of the University of Oxford.
It furthers the University's objective of excellence in research, scholarship,
and education by publishing worldwide in

Oxford New York

Auckland Cape Town Dar es Salaam Hong Kong Karachi
Kuala Lumpur Madrid Melbourne Mexico City Nairobi
New Delhi Shanghai Taipei Toronto

With offices in

Argentina Austria Brazil Chile Czech Republic France Greece
Guatemala Hungary Italy Japan Poland Portugal Singapore
South Korea Switzerland Thailand Turkey Ukraine Vietnam

Oxford is a registered trade mark of Oxford University Press
in the UK and in certain other countries

Published in the United States
by Oxford University Press Inc., New York

British Library Cataloguing in Publication Data

Data available

Library of Congress Cataloging in Publication Data

Data available

Typeset by SPI Publisher Services, Pondicherry, India
Printed in Great Britain
on acid-free paper by
CPI Antony Rowe, Chippenham, Wiltshire

ISBN 978–0–19–921661–1

1 3 5 7 9 10 8 6 4 2

PREFACE

In the fall of 2008, financial institutions in the United States underwent a period of upheaval not seen since the wave of bank failures that led off the Great Depression. Dozens of private mortgage companies had gone under during the previous year, when the housing bubble burst. Now the trouble had spread throughout the financial sector, and the US government was on a takeover binge to prevent failing financial grants from bringing down the rest of the economy. Fannie Mae and Freddie Mac, the corporations standing behind half of the American mortgage market, were placed under the control of the Federal Housing Finance Agency in early September. The following week the Federal Reserve acquired 80% of AIG, the nation's largest insurance company. A few days after that Washington Mutual, America's largest savings and loan, became the biggest bank failure in US history when it was seized by the Office of Thrift Supervision and sold to JP Morgan Chase.

In the meantime, investment bank Lehman Brothers had gone bankrupt—the largest bankruptcy in US history—while its distressed competitor Merrill Lynch sold itself to Bank of America. Goldman Sachs and Morgan Stanley, the two remaining major investment banks, converted to bank holding companies under the supervision of the Fed. And in October the Treasury Department compelled the nine largest US commercial banks (which now included Goldman and Morgan Stanley) to sell stakes in themselves to the government, drawing on a vast new bailout fund authorized by Congress a few days earlier. In a period of just over a month, a conservative presidential administration devoted to free markets and financial deregulation had engineered a level of direct government control over the nation's financial institutions undreamed of by V. I. Lenin a century before.

The frequent comparisons of the economic crisis of 2008 to the Great Depression of the 1930s were not misplaced. Like the first Great Depression, GDII was a crisis of economic institutions, not simply a financial crisis, because finance permeated the economic lives of American households. From college and retirement savings invested in equity mutual funds, to monthly credit card payments tied to LIBOR, to refinanced mortgages and lines of credit that allowed homeowners to extract cash from nominal changes in the value of their dwellings, Americans' economic security was lashed to financial markets to an unprecedented degree. The crisis itself had been precipitated by an unlikely nationwide bubble in housing prices. Demand for "safe" mortgage-backed securities among global financial institutions had turned homes into a peculiar form of stock option, increasingly available to buyers with sketchy documentation of their income. This drew speculators, who found that the returns available from buying and flipping houses surpassed those available on the stock market, and without the downside risk—if the house declined in value, one could just walk away from the mortgage. The result was a run-up in prices unprecedented in American history.

The housing bubble had partially masked weaknesses in the real economy, from the long-term stagnation of wages to the death throes of much of the manufacturing sector. Homeowners had extracted hundreds of billions of dollars in equity from their homes, much of which went to finance personal consumption that outstripped their wage income. The bubble was thereby responsible for many of the new jobs created in housing and retail. Meanwhile, the deindustrialization of America gathered steam for its final push, as more than 4 million jobs in manufacturing evaporated during the eight years of the Bush presidency.

With home prices in free fall and credit tight after the housing bubble burst, consumers avoided major purchases. The result was an existential threat to the American auto industry, a keystone of the production economy. It appeared that without a government bailout, one or more of the "big three" (General Motors, Ford, and Chrysler) would end up in bankruptcy, or perhaps even liquidation, along with dozens of their suppliers. The financial crisis was like the meteor that wiped out the dinosaurs—in this case, America's largest remaining manufacturers.

The financial crisis further accelerated the decline of the peculiar American system of social welfare, in which health care and retirement income were tied to corporate employers. Economic pressures had led many firms, such as GM, to abandon their commitments to health insurance for retirees and their families, and now financial distress was causing employers to cut back on coverage for their current employees. Retirement security was also threatened by collapsing stock prices. For two decades, companies had shifted employees from company pensions to individual 401(k) plans invested in the stock market. Workers had been encouraged to think of themselves as investors responsible for their own economic destiny. Millions had taken the bait, leading to a nation in which half the population had their economic security tied to the stock market.

Finance had become the new American state religion. Its converts adhered to a shared creed: Index funds were a safe and remunerative place to put your savings. House prices always went up, so it made sense to buy the biggest one for which you could get a mortgage. And most importantly, trust the market: it speaks with wisdom greater than any of its participants. Even the way people talk had been transformed. Getting an education became "investing in human capital," and getting to know your neighbors was "investing in social capital." A home was not so much a tie to a community as a tax-advantaged option on future price increases. Shakespeare wrote, "All the world's a stage, and all the men and women merely players." Now, all the world was a stock market, and we were all merely day traders, buying and selling various species of "capital" and hoping for the big score.

The mortgage meltdown and the resulting global financial crisis shattered the creed of the new investor-citizens. American stock indices at the end of 2008 were well below where they had been a decade before, meaning that average investors would have been better off putting their funds into a government-insured savings account than into the stock market. Perhaps one-quarter of homeowners with mortgages—and half of homeowners in "bubble" states like Nevada—found themselves trapped by houses worth less than they owed, and many of them were compelled to abandon their homes and move on. Entire neighborhoods from Southern California to Florida to Detroit were dotted with empty houses in foreclosure. Meanwhile, villagers in Narvik, Norway, found that their municipal budget had been sacked by collapses in the value of bonds that their local government had bought from Citigroup, backed by mortgage payments owed by American property speculators. Citigroup in turn had to seek capital from the sovereign wealth funds of Abu Dhabi, Kuwait, and Singapore due to its own multi-billion dollar losses and ultimately required a vast Federal bailout.

Banks around the world found themselves holding securities that were effectively impossible to value because their markets had disappeared. And their governments tried a variety of methods to deal with the problems that American mortgage securities had precipitated in their local financial sectors. The UK, facing a similar situation to the US, adopted a bold bailout plan that partially nationalized three of its biggest banks—Lloyds TSB, Royal Bank of Scotland, and HBOS (slated to be acquired by Lloyds), with the latter two losing their CEOs as a result. The fifteen members of the Eurozone collectively agreed to a similar plan. And leaders of the G20, which included both rich countries and large emerging markets such as China, India, and Brazil, met in Washington to create a coordinated response to the global economic crisis.

Observing the financial crisis unfold was like watching a game of cricket: the action didn't make any sense, it never seemed to end, and it was impossible to keep track of all the players. Who was to blame—bonus-obsessed Wall Street bankers, an overly cautious Federal Reserve, rapacious mortgage brokers, lax regulators, greedy speculators (some of which were pension funds or Norwegian villagers), homeowners who borrowed too much? Indeed, who was *not* to blame? And how were we going to get out of this mess?

***

The early years of the previous century had also seen large-scale economic upheaval and financial crisis. The United States at the turn of the twentieth century was in the midst of a generation-long transition from an agrarian to an industrial economy. Industry was becoming concentrated in a few dozen manufacturers, railroads, and utility companies, and a handful of New York banks held privileged positions in the new corporate power structure. Through a massive merger engineered by Wall Street in 1901, US Steel became America's first billion-dollar company, to be joined by other giants such as General Motors, General Electric, and AT&T. Big companies had the jobs, the assets, and the power; their executives and bankers were in charge. In this new corporate system, populists knew whom to hold accountable—J. P. Morgan, John D. Rockefeller, Henry Ford. To understand the plotline of American society, one had to understand the newly corporatized economy and its workings.

My grandfather's life encompassed the shift from an agrarian to an industrial society in the early twentieth century. After growing up on a family farm in Indiana and mustering out of the army in 1919, he migrated to Detroit to work at Ford Motor Company's Highland Park factory making Model Ts. He moved on to be a welder at the River Rouge, Ford's massive complex in Dearborn, where he worked at various points until the 1960s—retiring with a gold watch, a company pension, and health care coverage. His home in Dearborn—Ford's company town—was a storehouse of Ford products, from cars and old tractor parts to Ford Philco radios, kitchen appliances, and a color television. For him, Ford was not so much a company as a way of life, reflected in the local custom of calling the company "Ford's." He and his colleagues had all seen old Henry on the shop floor at one point or another.

The Rouge was an entire industrial economy in two square miles, bringing iron ore, coal, rubber, and sand in one end and sending cars out the other. In the 1930s over 100,000 people worked at the Rouge in the most vertically integrated factory the world had ever seen, with its own fire department, police force, and hospital. A factory tour I took as a child was both terrifying and enlightening, as I saw slabs of glowing orange steel rolling out to be pounded into door panels for Ford Mustangs.

Today, the idea of moving to Detroit to work for Ford as a young man—and retiring forty-five years later with a company pension—is as remote as the idea of carving a family farm out of the wilderness of Nebraska, or heading to Wisconsin to be a fur trapper. Most of the Rouge's components are now run by a handful of multinationals, not Ford, and its bankrupt steel mill was bought by Russia's SeverStal in 2004. The strategy of vertical integration has fallen into disrepute in manufacturing, as has the idea of a company town. Ford has since sold its Jaguar division to the Tata Group, an Indian conglomerate whose Tata Steel company still operates a company town around its primary plant in Jamshedpur. By 2008, the centenary of the Model T, the company that had invented the $5 workday was selling for less than $2 per share, and Ford's entire North American workforce was smaller than that of the Rouge during the Great Depression. Meanwhile, in January 2008 Ford had offered to pay off its remaining hourly workers to leave the company so that it would not have to look after them in retirement.

***

Sociologist C. Wright Mills wrote that "Social science deals with problems of biography, of history, and of their intersections within social structures." The sociologist was like a mapmaker, describing large-scale historical changes—such as the transition from an agrarian to an industrial society, or large-scale migrations from the rural south to the urban north, or the Great Depression—and the social structures through which they affected individual lives—say, large manufacturers like Ford and its Rouge complex. That was where individual biographies took place; that is how we can link one man's move from farm to factory to the larger currents of social change. In the mid-twentieth century, management theorist Peter Drucker observed that "In the industrial enterprise the structure which actually underlies all our society can be seen." In a sense, the Rouge was a map of the American economy, making the connections among the parts tangible and revealing how individuals fit into the larger enterprise of industrial society. Moreover, the Rouge's mass-production model for making cars had spread far beyond manufacturing: farms, stores, insurance companies, research labs, governments, armies, and even the Gilbreth family of *Cheaper by the Dozen* had adopted the operating logic of the Rouge.

It is clear now that the map of society represented by the Rouge no longer gives us an accurate view of post-industrial America. Most Americans do not live their lives through careers in organizations; far more work in retail and other services than growing food or making tangible objects like cars. What we need is a new map, a new way to understand biography, history, and their intersection in social structure.

This book is a sketch of such a map. Drawing on the past twenty years of my own and others' research, I aim to provide an understanding of how large-scale changes in the economy have influenced the organization of American society. My basic argument is that twentieth-century American society was organized around large corporations, particularly manufacturers and their way of doing things. It is now increasingly organized around finance—not just particular Wall Street banks, but finance as a model of how things are done. If the Rouge was a map of American society in 1950, then Nasdaq was a representation of American society circa 2000. And if the Gilbreths saw child-rearing as a form of mass production, today's sophisticated parents had come to see their children as an investment in their social capital. The consequences of tying the well-being of society to financial markets have become starkly evident due to the global financial crisis.

The argument unfolds over seven chapters. The first lays out the broad terrain in the shift from an industrial to a post-industrial economy. The second describes the hyperactive growth of finance over the past twenty-five years and the system of corporate governance that grew up in the US to guide its publicly traded corporations. I then describe how corporations grew to predominance in the US over the twentieth century and how they came to be social institutions, fulfilling many of the social welfare functions done by states in Europe. This model collapsed through the takeover wave of the 1980s and the subsequent triumph of the "shareholder value" movement; together, these two trends moved corporations toward a vertically dis-integrated network model that became widely adopted in both manufacturing and service. Chapter 4 describes how the financial services industry has been altered by a shift from the model of banking in *It's a Wonderful Life*—taking in deposits and making loans—toward a Wall Street model in which assets (mortgages and other kinds of debt) were turned into tradable securities. Banks largely became portals to financial markets, which changes their basic mode of operation and the nature of their connections to local economies. In Chapter 5, I argue that many governments have increasingly followed the lead of shareholder value-oriented corporations, by conceiving of their role as business service providers—"vendors" of laws—and through the widespread use of outsourcing, particularly in the US. Thanks to changes begun in the Clinton Administration and accelerated under George W. Bush, the American government has increasingly come to resemble Nike, relying on contractors for much of the basic work of government. Chapter 6 assesses the effects of post-industrialism, corporate restructuring, and the spread of financial thinking to households. Here I survey the effects of widespread stock ownership on people's perceptions of their political interests and analyze the causes and consequences of the mortgage crisis as examples of how finance has penetrated basic social processes. Finally, Chapter 7 gives a more speculative view of what comes next for American society in the wake of the financial implosion of 2008.

This is a lot of terrain to cover in one book. In a limited space, my hope is not to provide a detailed topographic map of North America, but something closer in spirit to the London Underground train (Tube) map. The Tube map strips away a great deal of detail and follows a few simple rules—most notably, all train lines are portrayed as horizontal, vertical, or diagonal lines. On the one hand, this level of simplification is in flagrant violation of reality, as the Tube's lines twist and turn in all kinds of unlikely ways. On the other hand, a Tube map is the single most useful piece of paper a visitor to London can have for navigating his or her way around a buzzing and complicated city. I hope I've succeeded in making a financial tube map for the contemporary United States that helps readers navigate our new economic and social terrain.

A note on sources

My aim in writing this book is to provide a text that is as reader-friendly as possible within the constraints of the subject matter. In many cases I am drawing on research areas with very large literatures. The reference section at the end of the book provides an entry point into these literatures. The attentive reader will note that a suspiciously large number of the works listed in the references are written by me and my co-authors, on topics such as corporate boards of directors, bank consolidation in the US, proxy voting by mutual funds, American Depository Receipts, corporate social responsibility among multinationals, activism by institutional investors in corporate governance, and so on. This is not because I single-handedly wrote 10% of the relevant literature, but because the literature reviews on each of these particular topics is generally contained in my prior articles. The intrepid user of search engines is likely to find many of these prior works available over the Web.

November 14, 2008   G.F.D

ACKNOWLEDGMENTS

Managed by the Markets has had a very long gestation. After almost a decade of mulling a book about finance and society, I wrote a basic outline while spending a sabbatical at the London Business School in early 2006 and managed to persuade a delightful editor, David Musson of Oxford University Press, that the idea for the book was good (true) and that I would complete it by March 2007 (false). Fortunately for the book, and unfortunately for the rest of the world, subsequent events have borne out the thesis of the book about the effects of finance on American society. As I wrote, banks failed, executives were fired, bankruptcies surged, home foreclosures skyrocketed, neighborhoods were blighted with newly abandoned houses, and unemployment leapt. There was broad agreement that the world was on the precipice of a second Great Depression brought about by financial excesses, and that only massive yet deft intervention by governments—including a new American administration led by Barack Obama—could avert global economic Armageddon. Presumably, the wisdom of my glacial writing pace is now evident.

My family has been an almost constant delight as I wrote the manuscript, and I thank my wife, Christina Brown, and our children Ben Davis and Gracie Davis for their endless support. I imagine there is a point when family members tire of hearing fascinating factoids while they are trying to do something else ("Yes, Dad, I know that Wal-Mart employs more Americans than the dozen largest manufacturers combined, that insurance contracts on the terminally ill can be securitized, and that Liberia's ship registry is actually a business in Virginia—but I'm late for practice"); fortunately, they did not let on too often.

I have been fortunate to work at the world's greatest university for interdisciplinary research, the University of Michigan, in a school with an unparalleled combination of collegiality and rigor, the Stephen M. Ross School of Business. My colleagues among the graduate students and faculty in Management & Organizations have provided a stimulating milieu for thinking deeply (or at least as deeply as I am capable of). Current and recovering students have been particularly helpful through their conversations about the ideas in this book: Adam Cobb, Natalie Cotton, Dan Gruber, Olenka Kacperczyk, Chris Marquis, Eric Neuman, Klaus Weber, Melissa Wooten, and Mina Yoo. And Rena Seltzer provided wise guidance on making enough time to complete the book without letting everything else fall apart.

I haven't managed to securitize my intellectual debts, so here is a partial repayment. Many people read portions of the book and gave useful comments. These include Ben Davis, Fabrizio Ferraro, Anne Bowers Fleischer, Mike Lounsbury, Joshua Margolis, Chris Marquis, Eric Neuman, Charles Perrow, Sarah Quinn, Cathy Shakespeare, Marina Whitman, Mayer Zald, and seminar participants at the University of California at Berkeley Sociology and Organizational Behavior departments and at IESE. I am especially grateful to Christina Brown and J. Adam Cobb for reading the entire manuscript end-to-end and giving me excellent suggestions for improvement.

All remaining errors are my own. In fact, for the more pedantic readers, I have purposely inserted a small handful of minor factual, grammatical, and spelling errors—its the least I could do to keep their interest up.

CONTENTS

1

The New Financial Capitalism

The American economy has undergone fundamental changes in the three decades leading up to the financial crisis of 2008. Some of these changes were visible to everyone—the explosion of information technology and the increasing globalization of trade, for instance. Other changes were initially subterranean but potentially more consequential. A revolution in finance has encouraged more people than ever before to participate in financial markets, from buying mutual funds to refinancing their home mortgages. It has also vastly expanded the domain of what can be bought and sold, from plain-vanilla stocks and bonds to mortgages, credit card receivables, student loans, payouts of insurance contracts on the terminally ill ("viaticals"), future lawsuit settlements, and opaque derivatives such as collateralized debt obligations and credit default swaps. As more things are traded on financial markets and more households participate as buyers and sellers, directly and indirectly, finance has seeped ever deeper into the fabric of everyday life. This book is about how the financial revolution has re-ordered American society through its effects on corporations, financial intermediaries, governments, and households. My core argument is that financial markets have shaped the transition from an industrial to a post-industrial society. For most of the twentieth century, social organization in the United States was shaped by the gravitational pull of the large corporation. It is now oriented around financial markets to a degree that was almost unfathomable until it was revealed by a global economic crisis.

Large corporations were the dominant social institution in American life for generations. From their abrupt emergence at the turn of the twentieth century until the takeover wave of the 1980s, a few dozen corporations came to control most of the nation's industrial assets and to employ a sizeable part of the labor force. Along the way, they re-formatted society in their own image, turning an agrarian society into an industrialized world power. At the end of the nineteenth century, nearly half of the nation's workforce was dispersed among 6 million farms. Five decades later, fewer than one in six worked in agriculture, while manufacturers— mostly corporations—employed almost half of the non-governmental workforce. The large industrial corporation had become the organizing structure for economic and social life, exerting a gravitational pull on the character of industrial society. The employment practices of these firms formed the careers and broader life-chances of individuals and households, their choices about how and where to expand shaped regional economies, and their charitable donations and community involvement determined the character of cities. *Fortune Magazine* drew out the political implications of this situation in 1952: "Any President who wants to run a prosperous country depends on the corporation at least as much as— probably more than—the corporation depends on him. His dependence is not unlike that of King John on the landed barons of Runnymede, where Magna Carta was born."

Yet by the early 1970s, the passing of industrial society was in sight, and with it the dominance of the large corporation. When sociologist Daniel Bell described the post-industrial society in 1973 as one in which "the majority of the labor force is no longer engaged in agriculture or manufacturing but in services," the US was the only country where this was the case—about 60% of Americans were employed in services. Today, the transition to post-industrialism is nearly complete in the United States. Agriculture and manufacturing combined account for a mere 11% of the workforce (and falling). Retail employment surpassed manufacturing by the turn of the twenty-first century, and Wal-Mart alone now employs more American workers than the dozen largest manufacturers combined. At the height of the real estate bubble in 2006, there were more real estate agents than farmers, more mortgage brokers than textile workers. The employment practices of large manufacturers and other bureaucratic firms, which once set the standard for middle-class life in America, are irrelevant for most of the population, and the idea of an organization providing a career of stable employment has been banished to civil servants and that sliver of academics with tenure. Many of the core firms of the mid-twentieth-century US economy—AT&T, General Motors, US Steel, Westinghouse—have either disappeared or substantially retrenched, and whatever influence on public policy they may have had is long gone.[1]

As large corporations have lost their gravitational pull on the lives of their members, another orienting force has arisen: financial markets. Fewer than one in ten households owned corporate shares at mid-century, and nearly half of those owned stock in only one company—often the household head's employer or the local utility company. Fifty years later, over half of American households were invested in the stock market, usually through diversified mutual funds. Corporate pensions that once paid specified benefits to employees upon their retirement from the company, thus tying them to a particular employer, had been replaced by portable 401(k) plans owned by the employee. The growth of stock ownership was particularly striking among the young: where one in eight households headed by someone under 35 was invested in the stock market in 1983, half were in 2001. If their parents had made a losing bet on a lifetime of employment at AT&T or Westinghouse, then this generation was not about to entrust their future to a career at Pets.com or Wal-Mart.[2] The bonds between employees and firms have loosened, while the economic security of individuals is increasingly tied to the overall health of the stock market.

The administration of George W. Bush sought to institutionalize this transition through a set of initiatives—labeled "the ownership society"—that became a centerpiece of Bush's second term agenda. The most notable effort was a plan to partially privatize Social Security by allowing individuals to invest a portion of their government-mandated retirement savings in the stock market rather than in the government's trust fund—essentially creating 401(k) plans for everyone. In his second inaugural address, the president stated: "We will widen the ownership of homes and businesses, retirement savings and health insurance— preparing our people for the challenges of life in a free society. By making every citizen an agent of his or her own destiny, we will give our fellow Americans greater freedom from want and fear, and make our society more prosperous and just and equal." As "agents of their own destiny," individuals would no longer rely on corporations or governments to vouchsafe their economic well-being: they would rely on financial markets. Just as the transition from feudalism to market capitalism had turned peasants into wage laborers, the transition from an industrial to a post-industrial society would turn corporate employees into shareholding free agents. This vision was particularly remarkable given that, as Bush spoke, the American household savings rate had turned negative for the first time since the Great Depression. Instead of investing their wages in the stock market, households had come to rely on increases in the value of their asset ownership—homes and stock portfolios—to fund consumer spending that outstripped their employment income.[3] As we shall see, when individuals come to see themselves as free-agent investors, the consequences for society can be dire. When home mortgages are regarded as stock options on a grand scale, for instance, entire neighborhoods can be dragged down by a few underwater mortgages.

This book is about how these trends are connected—about how financial markets have shaped the transition from a corporate-industrial to a post-industrial society in the US. I argue that many seemingly disconnected developments are shaped by the same underlying forces. The expansion of financial markets into ever broader domains has changed the organization of society in myriad ways, from the governance of corporations and states to the daily decisions of households. When Adolf Berle and Gardiner Means, a lawyer and an economist, announced the arrival of corporate capitalism in the early 1930s, they claimed that corporations were becoming the dominant institutions of the modern world, drawing the rest of society into their orbit. This imagery of a corporate-centered society held sway for decades and informed the understandings of social theorists and the larger public. But the shift to a post-industrial economy has displaced this familiar corporate order with one oriented toward financial markets and their signals.

The change is, in a sense, a Copernican revolution. Copernicus is credited with showing that the earth was not the center of the universe, and that the earth and the other planets in the solar system revolved around the sun. By the same token, from a social system orbiting around corporations and their imperatives, we have moved to a market-centered system in which the corporations themselves—along with households and governments—are guided by the gravitational pull of financial markets. As industrialism has given way to post-industrialism in the US, financial markets have re-formatted the institutions of the corporate economy and oriented corporations toward shareholder value as their guiding star. Moreover, the changes have spread from the corporate sector to the broader society, from choices about what kinds of housing will be built to how people perceive their economic interests when they vote. This shift is perhaps a generation old—its start might be dated to 1982, with the simultaneous advent of the first hostile takeover wave, the 401(k) plan, and the Third World debt crisis—and is not yet complete. But we can outline its emerging forms now. It tied the well-being of American society to financial markets to an unprecedented degree. With the economic meltdown of 2008, corporations, financial institutions, local governments, and households all found themselves whipsawed by financial forces beyond their control, and perhaps beyond their comprehension.

American corporations were the proverbial canary in the coal mine, as the takeovers of the 1980s and the shareholder value-driven "downsizings" of the 1990s hinted at what was to come. The corporation itself is ultimately a financing device, and a creature of financial considerations. As a result, corporations vary substantially among different countries according to how financing is organized, whether primarily by banks, markets, or some other combination. Because generations of companies in the US have relied on stock and bond markets for their financing, American corporations have long been in the vanguard of changes associated with financial markets. As Berle and Mean described, dispersion of corporate ownership early in the century brought about a shift in the nature of property—in their memorable metaphor, it had "split the atom of property"—and left the corporation's nominal owners holding merely a partial claim on uncertain future cash flows. During the restructurings of the 1980s and 1990s, the corporation was again transformed from a social institution to a mere contractual fiction oriented toward shareholder value. Through trial and error, those that ran corporations learned what the stock market values and what it disdains, resulting in a wholesale redistricting of the industrial map into a format tailored to the requirements of the market: manufacturing conglomerates, for example, became variously broadcasters (Westinghouse), casino operators (ITT), and banks (GE). Shareholder value—shorthand for being guided by what the market values—thus set the laws of motion of the corporate economy.

As financial markets extended their reach beyond the corporate world, more aspects of social and political life were drawn into their rhythms. From corporate shares to home mortgages to insurance and lawsuit settlements bundled into securities, ever more members of society participated in financial markets, directly and indirectly, as buyers and sellers. And as they did so, the thoughtways of finance became more widespread. What emerged can be called a *portfolio society*, in which the investment idiom becomes a dominant way of understanding the individual's place in society. Personality and talent become "human capital," homes, families, and communities become "social capital," and the guiding principles of financial investment spread by analogy far beyond their original application.

The portfolio society is in some sense the doppelganger or evil twin of Bush's ownership society. The term *ownership* evokes the family farmer working his ancestral land, patiently improving his patrimony for future generations. But portfolio ownership means something very different. Owning shares in a widely held corporation merely gives a fractional claim on future residuals and pointedly excludes real control. Portfolio ownership—through mutual fund shares and 401(k)s, the most common

6

pattern today—entails a fractional claim on a set of fractional claims held by an intermediary institution such as Fidelity or Vanguard. Moreover, some of these claims may be on things quite obscure to their ultimate beneficiaries—bonds backed by mortgages or toll road collections on another continent, or by David Bowie's album sales. "Property" and "ownership" in this context are those of the arm's-length investor, not the vested interest of the farmer or factory owner.

The disruptions that accompany rapid market expansion (or contraction) provoke changed ways of thinking about social relations. In Shakespeare's time, as the social implications of the market economy were being worked out, buyers and sellers were seen to be intrinsically in conflict, and markets turned their participants into actors in a theater of misrepresentation. Adam Smith argued, in contrast, that markets bring out the best in participants: in spite of themselves, sellers are led to provide things that buyers are willing to purchase voluntarily and to become more virtuous along the way, leaving them both better off. Karl Marx saw markets stripping away sentimentality and leaving people to perceive all social relations to be, at bottom, economic exchanges. Ultimately, everything was for sale. But transactions on financial markets are rather different from those on other markets, from what is sold to how prices are set. Capital assets are promises, claims on the future, and are marketed and evaluated according to peculiar rules. *Investors* are different from other buyers; *issuers* are different from other sellers. As more of society is securitized and more households became investors and issuers, willingly or unwillingly, more of social reality is drawn into the financial nexus.

Portfolio thinking has penetrated deeply into our social institutions. For "investors," the common sense of financial prudence—diversify and maintain adequate liquidity—spread to the many forms of capital in which they invest, including human capital and social capital. The prudent investor avoids concentrating his or her portfolio on particular asset holdings (jobs, homes, friends, communities). For "issuers," the requirements for appealing to investors acts as an invisible hand in creating conformity to the market's standards. For US corporations, this has meant creating a system of corporate governance purported to focus management attention on shareholder value as the ultimate scorecard. The market values visibility ("transparency" in governance and operations) and commensurability (that is, making things that are traded comparable to each other). Transparency is sometimes observed in both its meanings. Thus, corporations have shifted from social institutions to mere networks of contracts, and states—following the lead of corporations—have increasingly shifted from sovereigns to vendors competing in the marketplace of laws and contracting out tasks beyond their "core competence."[4]

The remainder of this chapter gives a glimpse of where we have been and where we are headed. The rest of the book provides a more detailed discussion of the trends outlined here, and what it means for American society.

The emergence of corporate society

The American corporate economy of the twentieth century, with large-scale industrial firms owned by dispersed shareholders, originated through a confluence of factors in the late 1800s. At the beginning of that century, incorporation was granted by state legislatures on a case-by-case basis to enterprises deemed worthy due to their benefits to the public—turnpikes, canals, and other such public works. Over the course of the century, general incorporation statutes spread widely among the states, allowing individuals to form corporations for essentially any business purpose. The need for large-scale investment encouraged railroad corporations to raise capital on stock exchanges, and they were largely responsible for the growth of American financial markets in the second half of the nineteenth century. Manufacturers, in contrast, played a relatively trivial role in financial markets prior to the end of the century. But a wave of industry consolidation at the turn of the century—driven by antitrust laws, managerial and technological considerations that favored massive scale, and financed by bankers with a strong preference for publicly traded corporations—created dozens of professionally managed oligopolists with dispersed shares traded on the stock market. Thus, the two distinctive features of the American corporate economy—grand scale and public ownership—emerged together at the turn of the twentieth century and decisively shaped its trajectory.[5]

Large industrial corporations quickly became a dominant economic force in the US, and after the First World War the principles of mass production spread widely, as even the new Soviet Union emulated the low-cost production methods of Henry Ford. The limits of vertical integration appeared quite distant. Ford's River Rouge plant in Detroit, for instance, employed 75,000 people when it reached scale in 1927, turning iron ore, coal, sand, and rubber shipped from Ford-owned mines and plantations on Ford-owned ships and trains into steel, glass, and other components, and ultimately into Model A cars.[6] The bureaucratic techniques developed to manage large-scale vertical integration were extended to allow expansion into related industries, and the creation of the multi-divisional structure ultimately led to the conglomerate in the 1960s and 1970s—a sort of *reductio ad absurdum* of the corporate growth imperative.

Dispersed corporate ownership was a less obvious development than large size. Early on, J. P. Morgan and other bankers served as corporate directors of the companies with which they did business, and Louis Brandeis's *Other Peoples' Money* in 1914 documented a "Money Trust" that dominated the corporate economy through tentacles spread among the top tiers of industry. Bank-centered corporate systems had arisen in Germany and other industrial economies as well. But within a few years, bankers in the US had largely withdrawn from the business of overseeing corporations, and ownership became increasingly dispersed as members of the general public flooded into the stock market during the 1920s. In their 1932 book *The Modern Corporation and Private Property*, Berle and Means described two trends that the new "corporate system" had wrought: corporate control was centripetal, accumulating in the hands of management, while ownership was centrifugal, becomingly increasingly dispersed among thousands of anonymous (and powerless) stockholders. As they portrayed it, both trends would continue through the indefinite future, leaving a relatively small class of professional managers in command of most of the nation's economic resources. This was "managerialism," a corporate system analogous to the medieval feudal system, with management as the new nobility.

In other nations, large firms were often owned or strongly influenced by governments. European states such as France had grown up long before the industrial corporation, and they were able to shape the developmental path of the corporate economy. But in the US, the opposite was the case. David Vogel points out that "Not until the late 'thirties did the annual revenues of the federal government rival those of the largest industrial corporation . . . . In the United States the professionally managed, oligopolistic, multidivisional firm literally exists for a generation without the modern equivalent of the state."[7] The autonomy of the large American corporation and its professional managers was perhaps unique in the world.

Without constraint from shareholders or from a weak Federal government, how would the new corporate nobility use its power? Berle and Means saw several possibilities. One was that the new professional managers would continue to pursue maximum profits—perhaps the least likely possibility. They might instead pursue naked self-interest, staffing the board of directors with compliant cronies that would provide them with rich pay and perquisites detached from hard effort. Alternatively, the professionalization of management might create a commitment to the corporation itself as an institution endowed with responsibilities to employees, customers, communities, and other stakeholders (as they would be called today)—in short, *noblesse oblige*. By the 1950s, academic commentators agreed that, for the most part, managerialism had followed this last path, even as the trends toward increasing concentration of control and increasing dispersion of ownership continued unabated. Economist Carl Kaysen described how the "soulful corporation," freed from the demands of shareholders for maximum profitability, had become an institution run by benevolent elites. "No longer the agent of proprietorship seeking to maximize return on investment, management sees itself as responsible to stockholders, employees, customers, the general public, and, perhaps most important, the firm itself as an institution." Moreover, "The whole labor force of the modern corporation is, insofar as possible, turned into a corps of lifetime employees, with great emphasis on stability of employment" and thus "Increasingly, membership in the modern corporation becomes the single strongest social force shaping its career members." And even critics such as sociologist C. Wright Mills agreed that finance had little influence on the modern corporation: "Not 'Wall Street financiers' or bankers, but large owners and executives in their self-financing corporations hold the keys of economic power."[8]

Thus, events around 1900—mergers creating large-scale, vertically integrated manufacturers, and the use of stock markets to finance them—set in train the development of the American corporate economy, with its distinctive contours and institutions, which reached its mature state by mid-century. The managerialist industrial corporation was, as management theorist Peter Drucker put it in 1949, "the decisive, the representative and the constitutive institution" of a new social order in the US.[9] But it was not a *permanent* institution, as its two bases— vertically integrated production and managerial indifference to financial markets—would quickly erode as the US transitioned from an industrial to a post-industrial economy in the 1980s and 1990s.

Post-industrialism and the decline of managerialism
Several interrelated developments in technology and trade ushered in an era of post-industrialism, and with it the decline of the vertically integrated managerialist corporation. Information and communication technologies (ICTs), including computers, the Internet, and mobile telephony, changed both the kinds of products that could be created and the cost profile of different organizational arrangements. These technologies expanded the feasible forms and locations of production and distribution and allowed trade in "weightless" products outside of traditional territorial boundaries. Behind even the simplest products, there are often global supply chains: a t-shirt might be made of cotton grown in Texas from crops bio-engineered in Boston, sent to China for milling, sewn in Mauritius, silk-screened in Mexico, and sold to the final consumer

at Wal-Mart, travelling at various times by ships bearing the flags of Panama or Liberia.[10] More complex products such as mobile phones or high-end fashions typically entail real-time coordination among components along the supply chain via the Internet.

Transactions that would have been protected within a single organization's boundary in the industrial era are more cheaply outsourced across organizational and national borders today. "Original equipment manufacturers" (OEMs) routinely subcontract for the design, manufacture, sale, and delivery of products bearing their brand, from computers to hot dogs. An entire sector of generic electronics manufacturing firms, such as Flextronics, SCI Systems, and Jabil Circuit, expanded in the 1990s to free OEMs from actually making things. Solectron assembled and distributed high-tech products such as routers, cable modems, and cellphones for firms like Cisco and IBM, and expanded by buying production facilities from Hewlett-Packard, NCR, Mitsubishi, and Sony and running them itself. Even the smallest tasks can often be outsourced to take advantage of specialization and economies of scale made possible by ICTs.[11] McDonald's hires remote call centers to take orders from drive-through customers at restaurants around the country and to convey them back to the kitchen over the Internet. The minimum-wage call center operators can be more effectively monitored for efficiency and disciplined than on-site employees.[12] Today, the value chain in Adam Smith's famous pin factory would undoubtedly span a half-dozen contractors across three continents.

New spaces are complemented by new products and new ways of consuming them. The digital technology that initially allowed music companies to sell compact discs for twice the price of LPs later enabled intrepid users to bypass purchase entirely and share music peer-to-peer over the Web, for later download to MP3 players. Internet pornography begat mobile phone porn. And entirely new categories of products have been enabled by jurisdictional legerdemain, such as Internet casinos whose parent companies are traded on the London Stock Exchange but operate in Gibraltar to avoid legal entanglements.[13] "Weightless" products are effectively placeless as well; nationalities and organizational identities are fungible.

The re-globalization of trade, following a long hiatus after the First World War, achieved multi-trillion dollar levels and elevated China to a world manufacturing center. Containerized shipping, a relatively simple technology, was largely responsible for this increase, as 90% of global exports travel by sea, and now half the retail goods sold in the US arrive by ship.[14] Cross-border trade and financial flows have changed the relations among states and corporations and the very meaning of "nationality." Corporations are able to fine-tune where they house their production to manage labor costs; their intellectual property and legal place of incorporation to manage tax rates; their securities for access to capital markets; and their headquarters for year-round access to golf.

In the industrial era, the corporate imperative for growth meant more sales, more employees, and more industrial "territory." This impulse was realized by Henry Ford in vertical integration all the way back to iron mines and rubber plantations; for the conglomerateurs of the 1960s and 1970s, it meant acquisitions in any industry that would help feed their expansion. But the size that matters for the shareholder oriented company is market capitalization, ideally achieved with as few tangible assets as possible. Information technology has greatly enhanced the ability to outsource various steps of the production process and to keep track of quality, from the design, manufacture, and distribution of products to human resource management. The hurdle for vertical integration is high, and external market comparisons are readily available, such that few functions within an organization are indispensable.

Information and other technologies, along with the globalization of trade and finance, have given rise to post-industrialism—a situation in which manufacturing and agriculture account for a vanishingly small part of the American labor force, in favor of services. But "post-industrialism" does not mean that nothing is manufactured or grown in the United States. Indeed, the US still leads the world in manufacturing value added: at roughly 24%, its share of global manufacturing has declined only minimally in two decades. Offshoring and the use of undocumented labor account for some of the declines in employment in these sectors. But more importantly, gains in productivity mean by definition that fewer people can produce more things, a trend showing every sign of continuing indefinitely around the world.[15] Put another way, it is hard to imagine circumstances that would bring back stable employment in large-scale manufacturers for a significant number of Americans.

The combination of these developments could have resulted in any number of different corporate forms. The Nobel Prize-winning economist Ronald Coase commented in 1937 that the telephone had enabled a vast expansion in the scale and scope of firms; by analogy, the Internet might have encouraged conglomerates to grow ever larger and more diverse, with GE, Westinghouse, and ITT battling for supremacy. Yet quite the opposite has occurred, as the concentration of assets and employment among large firms has declined since the early 1980s (Wal-Mart notwithstanding) and the modal corporation is quite industrially focused. The reason for this is the ongoing financial revolution.

Reflections on the revolution in finance

The new information and communication technologies that have transformed manufacturing and services have perhaps had an even greater impact on finance, and in particular on the ability to trade assets on markets. ICTs have enabled dramatic changes in how finance is done: more information is available to allow valuation of more kinds of securities; trade has expanded in scope, allowing individual investors to buy and sell securities from around the world through their mobile phones; and financial innovations are generated at a breakneck pace, greatly expanding the types of things that can be traded on financial markets— from shares of stock to home mortgages to natural disaster bonds to bundles of insurance contracts for the terminally ill. Economist Robert Shiller states that, thanks to information technology, economics today is "roughly where astronomy was when the telescope was invented or where biology was when the microscope was invented," and the ferment of innovation in finance is palpable.[16] If trading bonds consisting of bundles of insurance contracts for the terminally ill seems exotic, then the future promises ever-stranger possibilities. Many securities today are effectively incomprehensible and can only be valued with the aid of computers—or not at all, as became abundantly clear when the crisis of 2008 left financial institutions with balance sheets full of financial instruments that were impossible to market, and thus in principle without value. Even sophisticated institutions with well-paid staffs of mathematical savants were at a loss to figure out what this stuff was worth.[17]

A primary driver of financial expansion was cost. ICTs greatly reduce the costs of financial transactions and of valuation. Those over 40 may recall standing in line at the bank to deposit their paycheck and to withdraw cash, and the hours of preparation required to have currency on hand for foreign travel. Those under 40 are more familiar with airport ATMs that accept cards from anywhere in the world and spit out locally denominated cash at an appropriate exchange rate. They may also have online brokerage accounts to buy foreign equities, researched with the help of Google and on-line tools for making sophisticated assessments and comparisons. Thus, the cover charge for participating in financial markets as an investor has declined dramatically. For those uninterested in playing the market directly, the cost of investing in mutual funds has greatly dropped over the past decades, making them a relatively inexpensive destination for household savings, and the number of households owning mutual funds increased from under 6% in 1980 to nearly half by 2005.[18]

The entry charge also went down for issuers of shares and other securities. Roughly 3,000 US companies made initial public offerings during the 1990s. In prior years, issuers usually had something of a track record—revenues, say, or products. During the 1990s, however, new firms with no profits and minimal revenues had little difficulty going public. Biotech firm ImClone, for instance, first sold shares to the public over a dozen years before it had a product to sell, and dozens of other biotech firms went public with similar prospects—nearly fifty in 2000 alone. From some perspectives, the ease of going public may have lowered the bar too much. Pets.com raised $82.5 million through an IPO in February 2000 and spent nearly all of it to establish a brand name through costly advertising and discount offers for pet supplies sold online; within less than a year it was in liquidation, its credulous investors forsaken. Although the Sarbanes–Oxley Act increased the cost of being a public corporation, it did not entirely eliminate the enthusiasm for IPOs, and apparently had little impact on the sales of other corporate securities. Indeed, even companies in financial distress could access the capital markets by securitizing their receivables, whose credibility depends on the firm's customers rather than on the firm itself.[19]

Changing intermediaries

A consequence of the lowered cost of using financial markets was a shift in the composition of the most important players in finance. In the US, commercial banks held a predominant place in the corporate ecosystem throughout the industrial era, and their boards of directors were gathering places for elite chief executives from the command posts of the economy. The board of New York's Chase Manhattan Bank in the early 1980s included top executives from over a dozen major national corporations, including AT&T, Bethlehem Steel, Exxon, Pfizer, and Xerox. Outside the money center, regional banks held similar positions in their local networks. Bank of Boston's board had top executives from Cabot, Gillette, and Raytheon, all major firms in Boston; First Chicago had executives from Chicago's Amoco, National Can, and Quaker Oats; and Pittsburgh's Mellon Bank had directors from Alcoa, Allegheny International, and Westinghouse.[20] If not the controlling hydra of Brandeis's imagination, commercial banks were certainly well-connected to important sectors of the local or national economy.

All that changed in the 1980s and 1990s. In the simplest terms, the business of a commercial bank is to take in money from depositors, who are paid interest, and lend it out to creditworthy businesses, who are charged a higher interest rate. Profit comes from the difference between these two rates. But the banking *function* need not be done by organizations called "banks." Banks are in the information business, and their historical advantage in financing businesses was superior access to information. But corporations increasingly turned to lower-cost financial markets for debt, beginning in the 1970s and accelerating in the 1980s. Demonstrably creditworthy borrowers found that they could turn to competitive markets for funds at lower cost; few doubted that AT&T or GM would be able to pay back their debts, and by the mid-1990s the value of commercial and industrial loans held by US banks was equalled by the value of commercial paper issued by firms. Information technology simply lowers the bar for being "demonstrably creditworthy." Anyone can now get the kind of credit information formerly hoarded by banks, and the information benefits of a bank's proximity to its customers are less often outweighed by the costs. Thus, much of a bank's business could be automated and taken out of the fallible hands of human bankers. John Reed, CEO of Citibank at the time, predicted in 1996 that banking would shortly become "a little bit of application code in a smart network," while Wells Fargo CEO Dick Kovacevich stated that "The banking industry is dead, and we ought to just bury it."[21] (The mortgage crisis, which resulted in part from making "automated" mortgage loans through the use of computerized credit scores, ultimately ended up burying a large part of the industry—see Chapter 6.)

In response to their declining corporate lending franchise, banks began to move into fee-based services and, when regulations allowed, investment banking and other financial services. Moreover, thanks to the expansion of financial markets, banks found that they could re-sell business loans and other debt to get them off their balance sheet, just as they had done with home mortgages. Indeed, much of a bank's assets, such as credit card receivables, could be securitized: bundled together and turned into bonds that could be sold on markets. Rather than being a repository for loans, banks were simply "originators" that could briefly hold debt before re-selling it on the market—the functional equivalent of what underwriters had always done. Just as original equipment manufacturers need not manufacture anything bearing their brand, banks need not hold any of the loans they had made on their balance sheet.

Deregulation in the 1990s finally allowed the consolidation of the banking industry that had been delayed for decades by geographic and antitrust restrictions. As a result, a handful of regional banks grew to national stature. Charlotte, North Carolina, became an unlikely international banking center, housing two of the five largest banks in the US. Bank of America, # 1, was the entity that resulted from North Carolina National Bank's two-decade campaign of acquisitions, which culminated in its purchase of San Francisco's Bank of America in 1998 and Boston's FleetBoston in 2003. Its neighbor Wachovia Bank was # 4, also thanks to a massive acquisition spree begun by predecessor First Union; Wachovia in turn was acquired under duress in later 2008 by # 5, San Francisco-based Wells Fargo. And JP Morgan Chase resulted from the mergers of many of New York's (and the nation's) largest banks: Manufacturers Hanover and Chemical Bank in 1991, Chemical and Chase Manhattan in 1996, Chase and JP Morgan in 2001, and the combined firm with Bank One in 2004. At the end of this consolidation process, many cities found themselves without a significant locally based commercial bank, including Philadelphia, Los Angeles, and every city in Texas.[22]

Meanwhile, households had moved their savings from low-return bank accounts to money market funds and then, particularly during the 1990s, to equity mutual funds, and retirement savings shifted from corporate-managed "defined benefit" plans to employee-selected "defined contribution" plans largely invested in the same mutual funds. The number of US households with savings accounts declined from 77% in 1977 to 44% in 1989, while the proportion of households invested in mutual funds expanded from 6% in 1980 to roughly half by 2000.[23] "Savers," in short, became "investors." Mutual fund companies consequently gathered assets at a rapid clip, increasing from about $1 trillion in 1990 to almost $7 trillion in 2000. Most of the inflow of new investment went to a relative handful of "brand name" funds such as Fidelity, Vanguard, American, Putnam, and T. Rowe Price. As a result of the flood of new investment in the 1990s, mutual funds became the most significant corporate owners, and a handful of them amassed substantial ownership positions not seen since the days of J. P. Morgan a century earlier. Fidelity became the largest shareholder of roughly one in ten US corporations, owning more than 10% of several hundred companies.[24]

At the same time, deregulation enabled financial institutions to expand into diverse lines of business that increased their potential conflicts of interest. The mutual funds that owned shares on behalf of their investors were also selling benefit management services to the companies they invested in. Fidelity ran pension funds for hundreds of companies in which it owned (and voted) shares, and the company staked its future growth largely on managing health and retirement benefits and other outsourced human resource functions for corporate clients.[25] Commercial banks offered loans to companies (and their executives) that their investment banking arms were doing business with and that their analysts were recommending to their brokerage clients. Banks made personal loans totalling $1.3 billion to WorldCom CEO Bernie Ebbers to fund his personal acquisition of a shipyard, a half-million acre cattle ranch, a trucking company, and timberland, among other things. Citigroup alone lent him more than a half-billion dollars, while its Salomon unit allocated him hundreds of thousands of "friends and family" shares for firms about to go public (and experience the usual first-day run-up in price). At the time, Salomon was WorldCom's primary investment bank and, along with several other investment banks, earned millions in fees from WorldCom as Ebbers led a vigorous corporate acquisition program.[26] And investment banks provided merger and acquisition advice to firms in which their mutual funds held major investments. The market bubble of the late 1990s and the corporate scandals of the early 2000s were in part a result of the endless web of connections among financial service firms that created pervasive conflicts of interest in the finance industry.

Efficient markets and the theory of the corporation
Just as finance has undergone a revolution in practice, financial economics has seen a "Copernican revolution" in its theories of the corporation and their surrounding institutions. The center of this new

approach to institutions was the efficient market hypothesis—the claim that financial markets generally get it right when pricing stocks, bonds, and other financial instruments. Financial markets are a species of prediction market, able to incorporate broadly dispersed information in evaluating the future prospects of a company or other traded entity and to update prices quickly. The result was that a company's share price was the best available guide to the consequences of corporate policies, a compass that told those inside and outside the company whether things were going in the right direction. This doctrine provided a compelling rationale for the re-orientation of companies toward shareholder value. Financial markets knew things that individual executives or bankers could not; as such, it was best to defer to their judgment.

A theory of corporate governance was developed to describe the internal and external devices purported to discipline corporate management and to orient them toward share price. If share price was a compass pointing toward True North, then corporate governance was a global positioning system making sure that those driving the car paid heed. Shareholder-elected boards of directors selected and oversaw executives at the top of the hierarchy; compensation systems tied to share price aligned executives' interests with those of shareholders; and an external takeover market ensured that those who failed to build shareholder value were shown the door. Outside accountants audited the company's books and verified to investors that the figures added up; financial analysts dug deeply into the company's operations and rendered informed judgments; and stock exchanges promulgated standards for listed companies to keep them disciplined. In combination, according to the theory, these and other governance devices channelled corporations in the pursuit of shareholder value. In many ways, this theory was the reverse of the analysis of Berle and Means, discovering a matrix of mechanisms that functioned to compel managerial attention to shareholder interests— many of them self-imposed by those same managers. Corporate elites were not feudal nobility, indifferent to their shareholder-principals, but the voluntary servants of the stock market.

A distinctive feature of the new theory was that the corporation was no longer portrayed as a tangible institution with an inside and an outside, as in the industrial-managerialist days. Rather, it was a network, a "nexus of contracts," organized in such a way as to promote the creation of shareholder value. It had no moral commitments to various stakeholders. Its commitments were those explicitly stated in written contracts with buyers, suppliers, and customers, or implicit in its status as a for-profit enterprise. Those companies that deviated from this model suffered the consequences, at first merely in theory, but later in reality.

During the hostile takeover boom of the 1980s, nearly one-third of the largest US manufacturers were acquired or merged, as the conglomerates assembled during the 1960s and 1970s were re-configured into industrially focused parts. Companies that started the 1980s producing goods in dozens of industries ended the decade producing in only one.[27] Some ended the following decade so focused that they no longer produced in any industry at all. Sara Lee divested many of its production facilities in clothing and food products to focus on brand management, following the model pioneered by Nike and Coke. Dozens of electronics companies such as Hewlett-Packard followed a similar path, relying on specialized "board stuffers" (so named because they originally did the low-value tasks of attaching components to printed circuit boards) to produce and ship the goods with their brand name on them. As the practices of outsourcing matured, corporations came to look more like the shifting nexus-of-contracts described in financial theory than the sovereign institution of the mass-production economy, a transition that generally enhanced their stock market valuations. Sara Lee's CEO put it thus: "Wall Street can wipe you out. They are the rule-setters. They do have their fads, but to a large extent there is an evolution in how they judge companies, and they have decided to give premiums to companies that harbor the most profits for the least assets."[28]

The new theory provided both a practical guide and a moral rationale for shareholder capitalism. As managerialism was replaced by an orientation toward shareholder value, this theory yielded policy implications for those in companies and governments. For companies, share price reactions upon the announcement of corporate actions provided immediate feedback on the wisdom of those actions, allowing firms to quickly change course when necessary to avoid the damages foreseen by the market.[29] Because the market was smarter than any individual participants, it was wise to pay heed; in any case, by the end of the 1990s executive pay was so tied to share price that no further rationale was needed. Like a referee at the World Cup, the market's judgment was right by definition, and resistance was futile. For policymakers, a central policy goal implied by the theory was to make sure that corporate control was contestable—that managers who failed to heed the signals of financial markets could be replaced without their consent. And the theory provided a blueprint, a potentially exportable model of how to run an economy to achieve the miraculous economic outcomes of the United States. Nobel Prize-winning economist Douglass North stated that a central puzzle of human history is why some economies flourish and others flounder. Financial economics had discovered an answer: economies that managed to sustain large capital markets—to fund businesses and guide their decision-making through appropriate systems of corporate governance—grew faster than others.[30] If missionaries in prior centuries exported eternal salvation through the doctrines of Christianity, their contemporary counterparts exported temporal salvation through the doctrine of shareholder value.

Changing relations between corporations, financial markets, and states

Corporations oriented toward share price cannot exist without institutional supports. Thus, law and economics theorists further reconceptualized the institutions that surround the corporation, including managerial labor markets, takeover markets, and the law itself. According to these scholars, shareholder value was not just True North for the corporation, but also for the institutions in which it was embedded, guiding their actions in hitherto unsuspected ways. An essential job of governments in the economy came to be seen as creating conditions appropriate for shareholder-value-maximizing corporations to do what they do. Moreover, financial market reactions became an increasingly important guide to governmental policymakers as it was for corporate executives, from the Philippines to Bill Clinton's America.[31] Clinton was famously responsive to the bond market, following the advice of his first Treasury Secretary Robert Rubin, a former investment banker. Like a CEO anxious to see how his company's share price reacted to the announcement of his latest restructuring, Clinton was highly attuned to financial market reactions to his policies. The proliferation of financial news networks helped enforce this attentiveness; when Bush spoke on Wall Street to lay out his administration's response to the corporate scandals early in his first term, cable news networks helpfully ran an electronic ticker tape crawl at the bottom of the picture to show the market's reaction (which, in the event, was negative—the Dow Jones Industrial Average dropped 2% the day of the speech—presumably due to the inadequacy of Bush's policy response).[32]

The parallels between governments and businesses went beyond their mutual attentiveness to financial markets. States were, in a sense, in the business of providing laws and regulations, and the new approach to law and economics pointed out that states were not monopoly suppliers. Consumers of laws are more or less mobile, none more so than corporations. Thus, states had to provide laws and regulations that their shareholder-oriented corporate customers were willing to buy, or those customers would shop elsewhere. Within the US, competition among states as providers of corporate laws had gone on for well over a century. American corporations are chartered by the states, not the federal government, and firms can choose where to incorporate regardless of where they actually do business. In the nineteenth century, New Jersey became the most popular state of incorporation after it allowed corporations to themselves own other corporations.[33] In the twentieth century, Delaware won the bulk of the incorporation business, and the revenues from this business provide a substantial part of the state's budget.

As competition among states for various kinds of corporate business expanded, governments correspondingly became more like corporations—less a sovereign than a vendor of laws, competing with other vendors to attract corporate customers. This was particularly evident for corporate finance. Securities and other financial instruments are weightless products, and their issuers have great flexibility in where they choose to register them. New Hampshire-based Tyco International re-incorporated in Bermuda in the 1990s, along with Accenture, Cooper Industries, Ingersoll-Rand, and several other firms, to take advantage of a legal system designed by American insurance companies a few decades before. The South Pacific island nation of Nauru created an international banking industry almost overnight that served as an entrepôt for Russian mobsters, who availed themselves of the looting opportunities created in part by Harvard economists. Liberia, whose ship registry was created by American oil companies seeking to avoid US labor laws, diversified into the incorporation business, attracting firms such as Miami-based Royal Caribbean Cruises. As a "foreign" ship operator incorporated in Liberia, it was not obliged to pay US income taxes, an obvious advantage for Royal shareholders such as Fidelity (which owned 9% of Royal's shares in early 2005). And established ship registries such as Liberia and Panama faced new competition from cut-rate vendors like Bolivia, a land-locked country that nevertheless managed to bring in substantial revenues by registering hundreds of ships, no questions asked.[34]

Like corporations, vendor-states discovered the benefits of outsourcing. Liberia's corporate and ship registry was housed in an office park in suburban Virginia, while American entrepreneurs bought up the rights to Internet national domain names like NU (Niue) and TV (Tuvalu). States honed their skills at brand management: following Britain's lead to re-brand itself as "Cool Britannia," dozens of nations and municipalities retained marketing consultants to aid their efforts to sell themselves to corporate clients, complete with logos and bullet-pointed value propositions. And vendor-states listened to their customers in designing their products. American International Group executives helped draft many of the laws that turned Bermuda from a backwater of the British Empire to the "risk capital of the world," housing offshore operations of many of the world's largest insurance companies as well as intellectual property subsidiaries used to shield overseas income from US taxes. Meanwhile, the US under the Bush Administration emulated the best practices of OEMs, doubling annual spending on contractors to $400 billion for services ranging from operating cafeterias to allegedly interrogating prisoners at Abu Ghraib prison in Iraq.[35]

Securitizing society

Back at the household, Americans were instructed not to entrust their future to a company providing a career, but to think of their job as a setting to enhance their human capital while their financial capital accumulated. The 1990s provided a mass boot camp in stock market investing, and by the end of the decade over half the population had joined the army of shareholders. Tens of thousands of investment clubs sprang up across the country, and one of them—the Beardstown Ladies of Illinois, average age 70—parleyed their homespun investment wisdom into a bestselling *Common-Sense Investment Guide*, whose cover touted their 23.4% annual returns (later revealed to be 9.1%, as common sense apparently did not extend to correctly operating a spreadsheet). Members were drawn to the clubs by the prospect of attractive returns during the long bull market as well as by the low rates paid by banks and the uncertain prospects for Social Security and corporate pensions. The amounts that most households invested in the stock market were not especially large. Among US households invested in the stock market, the median portfolio was worth roughly $36,000 in 2001 and declined to $24,000 by 2004, far less than the value of the median family's home—or a new car, for that matter.[36] But the effect was highly disproportionate to the money at stake. People thought of themselves as *investors* and became far more attuned to fiscal policies (e.g. tax rates on capital gains) and financial market indicators such as interest rates.

Home mortgages also sensitized people to financial markets. The cost advantages of mortgage securitization meant that most mortgages were re-sold by their originators and bundled into bonds, perhaps to be purchased by overseas investors. Thus, as interest rates declined, almost half of the homeowners with mortgages refinanced them in the three years between 2001 and 2004, and a third of these borrowed additional funds to spend on home improvements, debt consolidation, and consumer goods (a phenomenon known as the "wealth effect").[37] Homeowners were betting the (three-bedroom) ranch on their homes continuing to increase in value—an expectation that was catastrophically shattered for millions during the mortgage meltdown.

The effect of home mortgages becoming financial market commodities was somewhat paradoxical. Generations have regarded home ownership as a stabilizing force for communities. Homeowners are more likely than renters to vote, plant flowers, know the names of school board members, maintain their dwellings, and have children that complete high school without becoming pregnant.[38] The societal virtues of home ownership were praised by a long line of presidents, from Calvin Coolidge ("No greater contribution could be made to the stability of the Nation, and the advancement of its ideals, than to make it a Nation of homeowning families") to Franklin Roosevelt ("A nation of homeowners, of people who own a real share in their own land, is unconquerable") to George W. Bush ("Just like that, you're not just visitors to the community anymore but part of it–with a stake in the neighborhood and a concern for its future"). Savings and loan associations in the US were premised on the theory that saving to buy a home was a school for civic virtue and moral rectitude: "A man who has earned, saved, and paid for a home will be a better man, a better artisan or clerk, a better husband and father, and a better citizen of the republic." And: "Thrift is a disciplinarian. It breeds virility. It strikes at sensuality, self-indulgence, flabbiness. It teaches the heroism of self-denial, temperance, abstemiousness, and simple living. It is the way to success and independence. It makes for happy homes, contented communities, a prosperous nation."[39]

Yet through multiple rounds of refinancing, and debt structured to take advantage of the tax deductibility of mortgages, homeowners increasingly saw their home as just another financial asset, a piggy bank to fund a new flat-panel television. Financially, this made some sense at the time: the essence of diversification is avoiding over-reliance on particular assets, and outright home ownership left one perilously under-diversified. But from the community's perspective, highly committed and relatively immobile homeowners were the kinds of residents that voted in school board elections and joined bowling leagues with their neighbors. Thanks to the securitization of mortgages and the consequent ease with which homeowners could now extract whatever equity they might have built up, home buyers came to see their house as the equivalent of a stock option, which could be cashed in if the price went up or abandoned if it went down. An analyst at one bond rating agency said, "It seems there was a shift in mentality; people are treating homes as investment assets."[40] A generation of home buyers had been turned from ants to grasshoppers.

Thinking like an investor can have political consequences. Republican theorists discovered in the late 1990s that shareholders were somewhat more likely to see themselves as Republican than non-shareholders were, and thus a host of policies were proposed that built on this effect—notably a tax cut on capital gains and the plan to partially privatize Social Security by allowing workers to invest in shares rather than only government bonds. This latter plan appealed to current shareholders, but Republican activist Grover Norquist pointed out a further advantage: if shareholders vote Republican, then privatizing Social Security would create more shareholders, thereby making the Republican Party "a true and permanent national majority." While dismissed by many Democrats as implausible, this theory built on a long tradition of political thought stretching back to James Madison's writings in *The Federalist* # 10, where he argued that different kinds of property ownership lead to different "sentiments" and perceptions of political interests. Thus, rather than changing the party to appeal to voters' interests, this plan would change voters' interests to fit the party.[41] After the 2004 election, the Social Security plan flopped spectacularly, but it was not without effect. According to the American National Election Studies, whereas 31% of shareholders identified themselves as Republican in 2000, 39% did in 2004; among non-shareholders, the proportion of self-identified Republicans held steady at 18%. Moreover, while just over 50% of shareholders voted for Bush in 2000, 56% of them voted for Bush in 2004.[42]

Portfolio thinking spread to how social theorists think of their subject matter. In an earlier era of market expansion, Karl Marx and Frederick Engels described how market relations had "stripped away the sentimental veil and revealed the family relation to be a mere money relation," and the economist Gary Becker filled in some of the details. Having children, for instance, was like buying durable goods such as cars or refrigerators. In the 1990s social scientists began to describe human relationships not as consumer goods, but as capital assets. "Social capital" became a dominant metaphor, turning one's family, friends, and community into investment vehicles, and joining "human capital" among the securitized categories of social life. Bowling in a league was not just a comradely way to spend an evening, but an investment that might yield rewards down the road. And joining the PTA was not just a way to build "social capital" with the teachers whose grades might validate the children's "human capital." Housing values depend on the neighborhood school's showing on standardized educational tests, and so real money was at stake in how well the school educated neighborhood kids to fill in bubbles on rote exams.[43]

The plan of the book

My broadest assertion is that the expansive use of financial markets has shaped the transition from industrial to post-industrial society in the United States over the past three decades. I have described this as a Copernican revolution: where industrial society orbited around large corporations, post-industrial society—including corporations—increasingly orbits around financial markets and their signals. The remainder of this book details the arguments and evidence behind this claim. The next chapter describes the unprecedented expansion of financial markets in scale and scope in recent decades and its implications for how companies are run. For companies to be traded on the stock market there need to be systems in place to maintain a kind of discipline. I describe these systems as a functionalist theory of corporate governance and examine its links to the efficient market hypothesis in financial economics. I also discuss the limitations of the analogy between finance and other kinds of technology.

Chapter 3 describes the rise and fall of the conception of the corporation as a social institution in the US. I focus in particular on changes in the corporation since 1980, including the bust-up takeovers of conglomerates in the 1980s, the rise of the shareholder value movement in the 1990s, and the ensuing corporate scandals of the 2000s. In broad terms, the corporation has changed from an institution, with members, obligations, and sovereign boundaries, to a nexus or network. If the conglomerate represented the corporate growth imperative taken to its logical extreme, then the contemporary corporation has moved in quite the opposite direction, to an ephemeral legal fiction.

Chapter 4 analyzes how the most significant financial intermediaries have shifted from commercial banks to investment banks and mutual funds, as household savings shifted from low-interest bank accounts to retail stock funds and portable pensions. I describe bank consolidation and how it has affected the social structure of corporate elites in American cities, and how the logic of securitization has changed the basic function of banks. This chapter also details some of the conflicts of interest facing de-regulated financial intermediaries, such as mutual funds that run corporate pension plans, commercial banks that also do underwriting, financial analysts charged with following the clients of their employers, and investment banks whose brokerages retail shares of client firms and in-house mutual funds. The deregulation of finance has breached long-standing boundaries among formerly separate players, creating seemingly irresistible conflicts of interest that resulted in a rich diversity of scandals.

Chapter 5 describes the new place of states in a post-industrial world and how states have come to look less like sovereigns than like vendors of law, selling a product to corporate and other customers. This transition is exacerbated both by financial markets and their influence on state policy, and by footloose firms that can shop for jurisdictions. The global shipping industry provides a cautionary tale for the potential consequences of competition among vendor-states, and the effectively stateless world of the high seas offers some perspective on the prospects for a world in which institutions are a choice rather than a constraint. As vendors in a post-industrial economy, many states have increasingly emulated the practices of "network" corporations.

Chapter 6 analyzes what this all means for individuals, with their roles as employees, citizens, and voters re-imagined as "investors" in human capital, social capital, and political capital. Shareholders tend to follow different sources of news and to have different perceptions of their interests, from how they evaluate national economic policies to the values they seek to inculcate in their children. And homeowners have been encouraged to see their homes as an investment asset rather than a durable tie to a community. Portfolio thinking is thus evident in a number of domains beyond finance and has potentially large political and social consequences. The mortgage crisis of the late 2000s illustrates some of the unintended consequences of inducing citizens to think like investors.

The final chapter summarizes the argument and evaluates it in terms of the evidence drawn together in the previous chapters. Here I speculate more broadly on the potential consequences of the broad spread of portfolio thinking. Although I draw on systematic academic research wherever possible throughout the book, this chapter is more frankly speculative and suggests areas that citizens and researchers would do well to attend to in light of the current economic crisis.

2

Financial Markets and Corporate Governance

As the American economy became increasingly permeated by finance during the 1990s and 2000s, a series of bubbles, scandals, crashes, and bailouts created a sense of economic vertigo. Dot-coms and telecoms worth billions in February 2000 were worth little or nothing a few months later. In the name of creating synergies, corporate executives built media and financial conglomerates that were later broken up in the name of creating shareholder value. In each case, the strategies seemed to justify eye-popping levels of compensation, often in the form of stock options granted at suspiciously low price levels. The enormous demand by institutional investors for "safe" mortgage-backed securities created a vast industry to make it easy for buyers to get mortgages that stretched their means, and for homeowners to refinance their mortgages to take advantage of the inexorable rise in the value of their house. Mortgage-backed securities, which pooled thousands of mortgages together into bonds, begat "collateralized debt obligations" (CDOs) which pooled together slices of those bonds. When housing prices reversed course, many of the largest commercial and investment banks went bust or were forced into acquisition. The casualty list from 2008 was a Who's Who of American finance: Bear Stearns, Lehman Brothers, Merrill Lynch, Washington Mutual, National City, and Wachovia, among others. Other financial institutions, such as the two government-sponsored (but shareholder-owned) mortgage companies Fannie Mae and Freddie Mac, were deemed "too big to fail" and were seized by the government in

September 2008, at a potential cost to taxpayers in the hundreds of billions of dollars. AIG, one of the world's largest insurers, was also effectively seized by the US government a week later. Meanwhile, millions of homeowners discovered that they owed more on their house than it was worth, and many found themselves having to access finance in novel ways—for instance, by selling the payoffs of their insurance policies to entrepreneurs in the "settlements" business, who would then bundle them together and re-sell them as bonds.

This chapter surveys the new world of finance and the institutions that govern it, broadly referred to as corporate governance. "Corporate governance" was a phrase rarely heard outside of law and business schools prior to the 1990s, but with the scandals that followed the burst of the market bubble in 2000, the topic gained widespread attention as both a problem and a solution. *Corporate governance* describes the systems that allocate power and control of resources among participants in organizations, particularly public corporations. Narrowly, it refers to boards of directors and their connections to shareholders, on the one hand, and top executives, on the other. But more broadly, corporate governance can be seen as the set of devices and institutions that address problems created by systems of financing–how it is possible to get money from households to businesses that need it, and then back again—particularly through financial markets.

In the United States, the main "problem" solved by corporate governance is the problem of accountability and control created when ownership is widely dispersed. In the decades following the emergence of the large corporation around the turn of the twentieth century, corporations grew concentrated into oligopolies, while their ownership became increasingly dispersed. The largest corporations, such as AT&T or US Steel, often had hundreds of thousands of shareholders, none owning more than a tiny fraction of the company's shares. In these firms managers, not owners, selected the board that nominally oversaw them, allowing management to become a self-perpetuating oligarchy accountable to no one but themselves, and using the company's vast resources for whatever purpose they saw fit—a situation that became known as "managerialism." They might use their position of control to line their own pockets and to build corporate empires, or they might be more responsive to their employees, customers, and communities than companies run by profit-driven owner/managers. In any case, with ownership separated from control, managers could largely ignore shareholders.

Financial economists and legal scholars in the 1970s argued forcefully that managerialism could not be the whole story. Investors are not fools—at least not the ones whose assets survive—and sensible investors do not hand their capital to companies whose managers ignore their interests, at least as long as there are alternatives. And companies that do not attract investors are unlikely to survive for long. If their share price drops low enough, then outsiders, such as industry competitors, will find it worthwhile to buy control of the company and manage it more effectively—a sort of Darwininian selection process favoring shareholder-oriented companies. Scholars in law and economics began to theorize other mechanisms that both responded to and reinforced an orientation towards shareholder value, including Wall Street firms (whose concern with their reputation prevents them from underwriting stock offerings from unworthy companies), self-regulating stock exchanges (which are similarly attentive to the quality of their merchandise), and labor markets for corporate directors (which reward good directors with more directorships and punish those that oversee poorly run companies), among others. Moreover, even self-interested managers cannot force investors to buy their shares, but must attract them with credible shows of their devotion to shareholder interests, by hiring rigorous auditors to certify their accounts, listing shares on a stock market with high standards, and incorporating in states with laws favorable to shareholders.

An array of institutions turned out to serve the purpose of orienting corporate managers toward share price, according to this approach. Much as sociobiologists of the time worked backwards from social practices to the reproductive functions these must serve, theorists in law and economics explained various economic and legal institutions in terms of the function these served in creating shareholder value. This was a Copernican revolution in thinking about the corporation: rather than the economy revolving around large corporations, as prior theorists had described things, it revolved around financial markets and the signals they generated. I refer to this approach as the "functionalist theory of corporate governance."

The institutions that evolved to address the problems of dispersed ownership may be broadly applicable in a world of expansive financial markets. Investors are increasingly distant from their investments, whether in emerging market companies or in bundles of asset-backed securities. The functionalist theory of corporate governance could be seen as a basic blueprint for enabling financial markets to work in situations where owners were distant or dispersed. Thus, aspects of the peculiar matrix of American institutions spread outside their domestic context to new applications.

This chapter describes how financial markets have spread and how corporate governance (at least in theory) deals with the problems of control this raises. It highlights the functionalist theory of corporate governance that has developed and describes how this served as the intellectual and moral bulwark for the shareholder value movement of the 1980s and 1990s. In a sense, finance is to economics what technology is to science, but the "finance as technology" analogy breaks down in ways that became evident during the recent bubbles and scandals. In subsequent chapters, I analyze in more detail the limitations of using financial markets as the flywheel of the economy.

Financial intermediation
Financial intermediation describes how money gets from savers (such as households) to those that can put that money to use profitably (particularly firms) and back again. Financial intermediation can be done in many ways. Informal groups can pool their savings into funds that are lent to members to start businesses. Individuals can put money in bank accounts, and banks can invest the money with entrepreneurs or companies that meet their standards. People can buy shares of stock directly,

or invest in mutual funds that buy company shares. Each method of intermediation has characteristic strengths and weaknesses, and each creates its own set of problems to be solved.

Political scientists have categorized advanced industrial economies into two main types based on their primary form of financial intermediation. *Bank-based systems* allocate capital through the decisions of particular organizations, while *market-based systems* allocate capital largely through stock and bond markets. In the first case, bankers hold a critical place as intermediaries, determining what kinds of projects and businesses are worthy of funding, while in the second case funding is dis-intermediated once the securities are brought to market. Thus, bank-based systems are intrinsically more susceptible to personal influences. Moreover, in some bank-based systems, the most important banks are owned or strongly influenced by governments, leaving their decisions open to political influence. Governments can use banks as levers of policy to guide business investment in particular directions. In South Korea, for instance, the state sought to grow the economy by focusing on particular keystone industries (such as steel, shipbuilding, and autos), which it accomplished by guiding bank lending to favored chaebols— family-run conglomerate groups that established leading firms in critical industries. In the other cases, such as Germany, banks are relatively autonomous actors in their own right, holding substantial ownership stakes in companies and often asserting their influence directly, such as by placing representatives on corporate boards.[1]

Market-based systems allocate capital through relatively impersonal processes, at least in theory. While banks are important intermediaries in bank-based systems, market-based systems lack centralized actors, and banks may be relatively unimportant. In the US, for instance, mutual funds own large stakes of the corporate sector, and investment banks act as brokers to bring stocks and bonds public, while commercial banks became relatively peripheral during the 1980s and 1990s, as it became cheaper for companies to rely on markets for both debt and equity.

Each system of intermediation allocates control differently, and each has a characteristic problem to be solved. When banks are gatekeepers for capital, bankers have a direct means to exercise influence over the companies they fund and to make course corrections when things go wrong. But bankers may be prone to "cronyism"—favoring the projects of friends and family, or those that are politically connected. Risky projects with merit may not be funded, and banks are prone to valuing tangible collateral (e.g. real estate and factories) over intellectual assets (e.g. the ideas of scientists at a biotech lab). Financial markets, on the other hand, are good at funding riskier ventures because they allow the risk to be priced and spread over many participants. But by spreading risk, they also dilute the capacity for influence. The separation of ownership and control that comes with dispersed shareholdings is the characteristic problem of market-based systems. It is also sometimes called the "agency problem" because agents—the managers who run the company—are detached from the principals that own the firm.

The separation problem was commonplace in the US but relatively rare elsewhere in the world, at least until recently. Most countries did not have stock markets, and in those that did, families, banks, or governments typically held controlling stakes in most enterprises. Since 1980, however, the number of countries with stock exchanges has doubled, as formerly Communist states set up markets to allow trading in shares of formerly state-owned businesses that were privatized, and low-income countries sought access to overseas investors newly interested in "emerging markets." Solutions to the separation problem—how to ensure returns on investments outside one's direct control—became a major growth industry in the 1990s as cross-border equity investment became legitimated and then rampant, and privatization became a popular mode of raising finance for governments around the world. As financial markets have grown in size and scope, so has the relevance of corporate governance.

The growth of financial markets
While commentators in the 1990s often spoke of the "triumph of markets," it was the triumph of *financial markets* that was most distinctive. International trade in goods surpassed levels seen on the verge of the

First World War, but financial flows reached an unprecedented volume, with trillions of dollars exchanged across borders daily. More than four dozen nations opened their first local stock exchange after 1980, including current and former Communist countries (China, Vietnam, Russia, Hungary); low-income countries in Latin America (El Salvador, Honduras) and Africa (Malawi, Swaziland); and nations in the Middle East (Oman, Kuwait) and the Caribbean (Trinidad, Barbados). Portfolio investment by wealthy nations in these "emerging markets" grew from almost nothing in 1980 to hundreds of billions of dollars in the 1990s, led in large part by dozens of new investment funds attracting the capital of institutional investors. Trading in company shares spread to almost every corner of the world—including Iceland, which opened its stock exchange in 1985.[2]

Investing in foreign shares was made easier by the practice of listing companies on non-domestic markets. Hundreds of companies from around the world listed their shares on Nasdaq and the New York Stock Exchange during the 1990s—including more than sixty Israeli high-tech companies and two dozen Chilean firms. By 2005, all but two of the world's twenty-five largest corporations were traded on US stock markets, regardless of where they called home. Sociologist Anthony Giddens states that "the current world economy has no parallels in earlier times. In the new global electronic economy, fund managers, banks, corporations, as well as millions of individual investors, can transfer vast amounts of capital from one side of the world to another at the click of a mouse. As they do so, they can destabilize what might have seemed rock-solid economies—as happened in the events in Asia" in the late 1990s.[3]

The range of things traded on financial markets has also spread well beyond plain-vanilla stocks and bonds. Stocks and bonds are capital assets—that is, ownership of claims on future cash flows. In principle, almost anything that has a cash flow associated with it can be channelled into a tradable capital asset ("securitized") if the price is right. Some flavors of securitization are widely known—for example, Fannie Mae in the US pioneered the practice of bundling together illiquid home mortgages and selling slices of these bundles as bonds (known as mortgage-backed securities). The rationale for doing this is straightforward: while holding any one mortgage may be risky because the homeowner may default or repay the loan early, large groups of them together are more predictable, and thus suitable for selling as bonds. (Chapter 6 goes into more detail on the market for mortgage-backed securities.) From mortgages, the practice of bundling debts together expanded in the 1980s to include auto loans and credit card receivables. In each case, the ability to make reasonable estimates of future payoffs meant that securities could be created to trade in these assets.

During the 1990s, securitization became increasingly baroque, thanks in part to advances in information technology and financial theory that allowed the valuation of more kinds of future income streams. In 1997, pop star David Bowie received $55 million from the issuance of 10-year bonds, to be paid from the anticipated royalties generated through future album sales. The entire issue was purchased by Prudential Insurance, and a unit of Nomura Securities subsequently established a division to specialize in creating such instruments to be backed by future revenues generated by music, publishing, film, and television products.[4] J. G. Wentworth, affiliated with Dutch financial conglomerate ING Group, bought the rights to insurance settlements from their beneficiaries—typically injured persons—that were normally paid out over the course of several years. These were then bundled together and re-sold as debt securities—in some cases, to the insurance companies making the payouts in the first place.[5] Similar schemes have been used to buy veteran's pensions and lottery winnings, in which the beneficiary receives cash now to sign away their monthly payments (often at very high interest rates). Distressed firms and others can securitize their receivables, based on the creditworthiness of their buyers. Entrepreneurs have sought to securitize property tax liens, lawsuit settlements, and college loans, among other things. Information and communication technology massively increased the ability to gather value-relevant information and therefore to create new species of securities that convert expected future payments into bonds with an agreeable face value. By the end of the decade, the value of securitized assets outside the mortgage market grew into the trillions of dollars.

An essential factor enabling the growth of securities markets is a technology for evaluating capital assets at low cost. What is the right price for a security? The value of a capital asset (such as a share of stock) *should* be equal to the value of all the future cash flows that come with its ownership, appropriately discounted to present value (that is, future payoffs are worth less than current ones, and uncertain payoffs are worth less than certain ones). If one summed all the dividends that a company paid out until it was liquidated, and discounted them to the present, that would give a good idea of what a share *should* be worth. The capital asset pricing model (CAPM) in finance specifies some of the details, providing a framework for setting prices for securities in markets.

Financial market efficiency

A central claim of financial economics is that the stock market is remarkably good at predicting a company's future and reflecting it in the share price—in other words, that the price on the market is quite close to what it should be. According to the *efficient market hypothesis* (EMH), the prices of traded securities (stocks and bonds) represent the best estimate of their discounted future value stream. When buying shares, you get what you pay for. More formally, the EMH claims that the market price of a security is "informationally efficient" in that it represents an unbiased estimate of its value based on all publicly available information. When new information appears, prices change accordingly. For instance, when a pharmaceutical company receives an important patent or has a new drug approved, its share price is likely to go up quickly, and conversely for rejected drugs. The speed of this reaction is an indication of the informational efficiency of the market.[6]

Financial markets therefore can be seen as a species of *prediction market* in the sense that the prices they yield are well-informed predictions about the future. Research suggests that prediction markets are often highly accurate at estimating quantifiable future events, such as the outcome of elections, or the amount of weekend ticket sales for a new Hollywood movie, or the likelihood of a business project being completed by a particular date, or who will win a sports event. Although there is occasional evidence of bias, the track record of several prediction markets (e.g. the Iowa Electronic Market, which predicts electoral outcomes—see http://www.biz.uiowa.edu/iem/) is quite good and generally beats other prediction sources such as opinion polls. In part this is because prediction markets can take into account all these other sources of information when generating prices.[7]

Prediction markets are particularly effective at gathering dispersed information—in this sense, markets "know" things that no individual participants in them do, and this is what gets revealed in prices. Summarizing their review of the research, economists Justin Wolfers and Eric Zitzewitz state that "The power of prediction markets derives from the fact that they provide incentives for *truthful* revelation, they provide incentives for research and *information discovery*, and the market provides an algorithm for *aggregating opinions*. As such, these markets are unlikely to perform well when there is little useful intelligence to aggregate, or when public information is selective, inaccurate, or misleading."[8] In other words, share prices may not be accurate in situations of executive deception. Notably, it is difficult to assess the accuracy of prediction markets when the truth is never known—the outcomes of elections and Hollywood film openings are observed, but the "true" value of a share, or a bundle of mortgages, arguably is not.

Claims for the efficient market hypothesis have occasionally been extravagant. Financial economist Michael Jensen stated in 1988 that "No proposition in any of the sciences is better documented" than the efficient market hypothesis—a remarkable claim for a hypothesis that had only been named two decades earlier.[9] But more importantly, if the EMH were true, then prices on financial markets provide an unbeatable augur of future events. The head of Israel's central bank put it thus: "Capital markets are capable of transforming all the future and all the past into the present. When individuals go to the market, they bring all their memories about the past and act on all their expectations about the future."[10] Share prices aggregate all the information available to all the significant players about a company's prospects. Unlike the evaluations of a founding family or a banker, the price that prevails on the stock market is stripped of sentimentality and reflects hard facts (or at least their consensus interpretation). Moreover, the market price adjusts remarkably quickly to new information, providing a minute-by-minute assessment of a company's performance, and thereby a guide to decisions. Managerial decisions are rewarded or punished within hours after they are announced, and thus mis-steps can be recognized and corrected quickly. If a company's share price declines after it announces an acquisition, then we not only know that it was a bad idea, but how bad it was in dollar terms.

According to enthusiasts, then, price accurately answers two questions: "What is it worth?" and "What will the future bring?" The efficient market hypothesis thereby solves many problems for managers, law, and public policy. For managers, it provides a relentless report card, letting them know how their performance measures up at any given moment. For judges and lawyers, price can provide a yardstick for measuring damages—indeed, one tax accountant received a 24-year sentence for fraud based on the drop in his employer's share price on the day that news of the fraud was revealed.[11] For policymakers, market movements indicate the wisdom of policy changes—Bill Clinton was famously responsive to bond market reactions to his policies, thanks in large part to the influence of Treasury Secretary Robert Rubin. And for outside observers, prices on financial markets provide a barometer to measure how an economy is doing and an informed indication of what the future will bring.

The centrality of smart prices is why financial economists place great emphasis on reducing impediments to market efficiency. If one takes seriously the idea that price provides privileged access to truth, then getting prices right is an important policy goal in itself. Accurate prices can justify market practices that some find unfair. Thus, short selling—betting that prices of a security will decline—has at times been illegal and is still unavailable to certain classes of investors, yet according to financial economists, it should be actively encouraged, the better to get prices right. If one can only bet on prices going up rather than down ("going long" by buying shares outright), then prices will tend to have a positive bias. Similarly, insider trading, although perhaps unfair to non-insiders, is nonetheless useful as a means to get prices right, because insiders have access to value-relevant information that can, through their trading, make prices more accurate more quickly.

The separation of ownership and control

Capital markets provide a means for matching investors with opportunities and yield informative prices as a side benefit. But capital assets are a strange kind of property. When you buy a pair of shoes, you can hold them in your hands and examine their qualities. Capital assets, in contrast, are virtual goods, and their elusive qualities lead buyers to require a different kind of quality assurance. A shoe buyer may have little sense of the conditions under which the shoes were made—whether by well-paid union laborers working under comfortable conditions, or by children in poverty. But buyers of capital assets will demand that structures be in place to protect their investment and ensure accountability. This is the domain of corporate governance.

Berle and Means acutely analyzed what the managerialist corporation, whose dispersed ownership had left management in command, had wrought for our conception of property ownership. They argued that the corporation had "destroyed the unity that we commonly call property" and dissolved "the old atom of ownership into its component parts, control and beneficial ownership." *Beneficial ownership* was subsequently defined in the law to have two parts: the ability to buy and sell one's shares, and the ability to vote.[12] But owners of shares on this account lack a large number of rights associated with other kinds of property. The finance company that (briefly) held your mortgage could not move some of its mortgage brokers into your spare bedroom, because what they owned was a claim on your future payments, not access to your house. Similarly, ownership of shares means only that one is a "residual claimant" entitled to whatever is left of the revenues after all the other expenses are paid (or, in the case of mutual fund shareholders, the residual of the residual that is left after the fund company deducts its fees for buying, selling, and voting on your behalf).

Shareholders do not have direct control of the organization or its property—they can't show up and demand a ride on the corporate jet, for instance. Moreover, in the US they don't get to vote on who will be CEO, and while they do elect the directors that select and supervise the CEO, it is extremely rare for them to choose which candidates end up on the ballot. In almost all cases, their only options are to vote in favor of a director candidate or withhold their vote, and a director receiving a plurality of votes (which in an uncontested election means at least one) wins.

Buying shares in a company thus entitles an investor to almost no real influence on how the company is run, or by whom. A vast territory of corporate policies is immune from shareholder oversight because most questions of strategy and operation are considered "ordinary business," under the sole direction of the board of directors. Even if almost all shareholders voted in favor of a particular policy (e.g. in the case of one restaurant chain, demanding that the company not discriminate against gay employees), the board could legally ignore them, as such shareholder votes are merely advisory ("precatory"). In short, in a company with dispersed ownership, it is difficult for shareholders to speak with one voice, and even if they did speak with one voice, they could often be ignored. Practically speaking, they can have little control without buying up a majority of shares through a takeover.[13]

The functionalist theory of corporate governance

Described in this way, it is hard to imagine why anyone with sense would buy corporate shares, handing their savings over to companies that offer them no control in return. Yet millions of people agreed to this deal— when Berle and Means wrote in 1932, about one in eight US adults owned shares, and AT&T alone had over a half-million shareholders. Why?

Financial and legal theorists concluded that Berle and Means must have got it wrong. If dispersed shareholdings left unaccountable managers in charge to run the company as they saw fit, then smart investors would bail out. And even foolish investors are not oblivious to their returns. If the stock market is efficient—or even paying attention at all—then the share price of companies run by indifferent managers would reflect this. A relatively low share price makes it costly to raise capital, which benefits competitors who have a higher share price. And if price falls low enough, a competitor or someone else is likely to buy enough shares of the company to take control and rehabilitate it for a quick profit—a takeover. Henry Manne, one of the seminal figures in contemporary law and economics, dubbed this process the "market for corporate control" in a remarkably influential 11-page article published in 1965. The notion of a market for corporate control implied that control of public corporations was always for sale in principle, and that this fact sets a limit on just how much management could ignore share price. "The lower the stock price, relative to what it could be with more efficient management, the more attractive the take-over becomes to those who believe that they can manage the company more efficiently. And the potential return from the successful takeover and revitalization of a poorly run company can be enormous."[14] Takeovers thus provided a get-rich-quick scheme for those able to identify undervalued companies—people later referred to as "raiders."

Manne's paper highlighted two ideas that became increasingly important in discussions around the corporation. The first is that the stock market is a good judge of managerial quality. Share price is an ongoing report card for management on this account, and management should be held accountable for it. The second is that institutions exist to keep corporate managers attentive to share price *even if ownership is widely dispersed*. Berle and Means had created an image of the managerial-ist corporation that had endured for decades. With ownership spread among thousands of powerless shareholders, these firms were allegedly controlled by managers with little financial stake in the company, able to ignore financial markets by relying on retained earnings. Yet from Manne onward, scholars began to re-think this position and to specify the mechanisms that oriented managers and the corporation toward share price, without having to rely on an owner/manager or a major outside stockholder such as a bank.

One early scholarly contribution set the tone by describing the corporation as a mere "legal fiction which serves as a nexus for contracting relationships."[15] The corporation did not have an inside or an outside—it was a nexus of contracts, a network. The contracting metaphor meant that the relationships were mutual and voluntary, and if dispersed shareholders had consented to this relationship millions of times over the course of decades, they must have had good reasons. As Berle and Means had argued, the separation of ownership and control introduced "agency costs" because managers' interests as agents were not perfectly aligned with those of their shareholder-principals. But this separation was not a license to steal; agency costs were simply another kind of cost that must be taken into account when considering what kind of organization was best on balance.

Moreover, just as Adam Smith described an invisible hand that led self-interested parties voluntarily to provide goods and services valued by buyers, so too did an invisible hand lead corporate managers to take actions that limited their own discretion and thus enhanced the value of shares to their buyers. Potential investors will pay more for shares in firms that have safeguards to monitor how the firm is managed and that bond managers to the firm's performance. Managers know this and spontaneously adopt such safeguards to get a better price for their equity. But why would they? Because "If the costs of reducing the dispersion of ownership are lower than the benefits to be obtained from reducing the agency costs, it will pay some individual or group of individuals to buy shares in the market to reduce the dispersion of ownership"—often leading to the managers' unemployment.[16] From this basic dynamic arises an entire system of institutions that address (but do not completely "solve") the control and incentive problems created by dispersed ownership.

This system of institutions is what we mean by corporate governance. As defined by economist Douglass North, "Institutions are the rules of the game in a society or, more formally, are the humanly devised constraints that shape human interaction."[17] According to governance theorists, the function of various institutions around the corporation was to orient company managers to shareholder value. Much as sociobiologists at the time interpreted various social institutions (e.g. the division of labor, family structures, altruism, war) in terms of their function in maximizing reproductive fitness, governance theorists interpreted corporate structures and practices, and the legal and other institutions that surrounded them, in terms of their function in maximizing financial fitness—that is, shareholder value. Following economic convention, these were referred to as "markets," no matter how unmarketlike they appeared in practice.

What were these markets? First, a labor market for corporate managers disciplines them in the pursuit of shareholder value. If markets for "human capital" operate like markets for financial capital, then managers know that poor performance now will be reflected in low wages down the road, and thus their expectations of higher future wages will induce them to better performance now. Top managers' performance is reflected in the current share price, and the pay and future prospects of those at lower levels in the organization are shaped by this measure as well, turning them into a Greek chorus that reinforces for top executives the importance of share price. Notably, these lower managers might also hope to get their bosses' jobs or even to leapfrog them to the top, creating healthy competition to be the boss of all bosses—a sort of internal market for corporate control that further sharpens attention to share price.[18]

Second, the board of directors acts as a referee in these contests, hiring, firing, and compensating top management and ratifying their important decisions. Managerialists, following Berle and Means, had argued that because managers controlled the proxy machinery, they effectively selected their own board of directors and often gave themselves a seat at the table. But most boards are composed primarily of outside directors, whose primary jobs are in other organizations. Their concern for maintaining their reputation in the outside world compels them to be vigilant and avoid the stigma that comes from being the target of an outside takeover driven by low share price.[19]

What about the fact that dispersed shareholders have no input into choosing board candidates, and that their votes are effectively meaningless? That simply reflects an efficient division of labor: directors are

good at directing, shareholders are good at shareholding, and it is rational for shareholders to be ignorant of board elections rather than to
invest the time and resources to become well-informed. The share price
reflects how well the company is being run, and if the board doesn't do
its job, the takeover market will protect shareholders from losing their
investment.[20]

Third, a basic premise of Berle and Means's analysis—that dispersed
ownership led to lower attention to profit—was false, or at least not
obviously true. If concentrated ownership leads to better monitoring,
then dispersed ownership can be an *effect* rather than a *cause*: if it pays
to have a monitor, then in equilibrium the companies that need monitoring (through concentrated ownership) will get it. Research suggested
that ownership concentration was higher in firms with more *variable*
profitability (that is, those likely to benefit from monitoring), while—
contrary to Berle and Means—more concentrated ownership did not
produce *higher* profitability.[21]

The upshot of this analysis was that managerial labor markets, boards
of directors, and the takeover market all compelled corporate managers
to pay close attention to their company's share price, even when ownership was highly dispersed. Moreover, devotion to share price drove
the other decisions that they made. Companies signal the quality of
their accounting to their investors by relying on auditors with sterling
reputations for rigor and honesty, and thus accounting firms have strong
incentives to maintain these reputations by providing thorough audits.
Companies, in turn, have incentives to use only reputable accountants.
Investment banks' reputations depend on thoroughly vetting the quality
of the securities they underwrite, and those that hope to do repeat business with investors will work with only high-quality clients and partners.
Financial analysts working at brokerages are rated by large investors
every year in widely read league tables, and thus they have incentives
to dig below the management propaganda to uncover and report on
the real condition and prospects of the companies they follow. In each
case, these intermediaries face reputational markets that induce them to
uphold honesty in the pursuit of shareholder value.[22]

Functionalist governance theorists discovered other markets as well, all of which were ultimately calibrated by the stock market. In the US, corporations are chartered by the fifty states, rather than by the Federal government, and thus states compete in a "market for corporate charters." But where managerialists saw a "race to the bottom," in which states offered lax corporate law in order to attract unaccountable managers, careful analysis showed that this competition was better seen as a "race to the top." Companies get higher valuations when they are incorporated in states with more exacting and well-specified corporate law, and Delaware gets the lion's share of incorporation because of its shareholder-friendly corporate law and its highly responsive judiciary and legislature. Because incorporation revenues account for about one-fifth of the state's budget and support a thriving indigenous population of lawyers, the state's officials stay in the vanguard of shareholder-oriented corporate law to avoid being out-competed by other states.[23] Thus, by 2005 60% of the 1,000 largest US corporations were incorporated in Delaware, the McDonald's of corporate law.

Similarly, stock markets compete for corporate listings on the same principle of investor friendliness. The New York Stock Exchange (NYSE) made its reputation in the late 1800s by enforcing rigorous standards for listed companies in order to attract British and other overseas investors. These investors had been scammed in the past by American promoters of railroad securities traded on other markets, and thus NYSE needed to create reassuring quality standards to lure them back. Nasdaq and the New York Stock Exchange compete for listings domestically and internationally, and because listing on them was taken as a sign of quality, overseas companies typically received an uptick in share price when they listed on these US markets. Stock markets were essentially in the business of manufacturing trust in order to attract outside investors.[24]

The globalization of stock markets has also led to a market for securities regulation. Companies listing shares in the US are thereby subject to American securities regulation, and similarly for London and other markets. In this way, regulators "compete" to attract companies to their jurisdiction, a process that—as with state corporate law—should bring about a race to the top, with the spoils going to the highest-quality jurisdiction. (US observers were accordingly troubled to find that foreign firms began seeking to de-list from the US market in the wake of Sarbanes–Oxley's strict requirements on corporate governance. Corporate "shoppers" were evidently finding the regulations in London or Hong Kong to be a better value for their shareholders, as the US had gotten *too* rigorous in its standards.)

Significance of the functionalist theory

The functionalist theory of corporate governance was a Copernican revolution in thinking about the corporation and its surrounding institutions. From Berle and Means onward, theorists had imagined a society organized around increasingly large and powerful corporations run by relatively autonomous managers. Explaining society, at least in the US, was tantamount to explaining the activities of a few hundred corporations and the people that ran them. But in the functionalist theory, institutions revolved around financial markets and their signals, not corporations. When managerialists looked at corporate boards of directors, they saw executives staffing the boards with inattentive cronies that would cheerfully overpay them. But functionalists saw competitive labor markets that compensated managers and directors according to the value they created. Sociologists saw state legislators acting under the influence of local business elites to pass corporate laws that favored their agendas. In contrast, the new theory portrayed states competing to provide shareholder-friendly laws because that would attract the custom of share price-oriented corporate managers. And while sceptics saw rampant conflicts of interest in accounting firms that provided tax consulting and IT services for their audit clients, investment banks that allocated IPO shares to the executives of client firms, and financial analysts that never issued a "Sell" recommendation, the reputational market provided a forceful counterweight.

This theory of corporate governance is remarkable in two regards. First, it relies quite heavily on deductions following from the efficient market hypothesis, an idea that had little currency until the late 1960s.

We have already discussed the appeal of the EMH as a privileged source of truth. Finding out that financial markets were efficient in this way was like finding out that magnets could be set up to unerringly point to true north. Entire realms of institutions could be linked backwards to this source, a great convenience for theorists. Conversely, if the EMH were false, then proponents of shareholder capitalism had some explaining to do.

Second, in retrospect it is clear that the theory was utterly at odds with the contemporary corporate world of the 1970s and early 1980s. Unwanted takeovers were extremely rare at that time. Managerial tenure was long and firings of CEOs uncommon. Managerial salaries below the very top tier were often set using bureaucratic procedures far removed from the market, and stock-based compensation at the top was a novelty. The 1970s was surely the high water mark of managerialism, when Berle and Means's description of empire-building managers was a virtual blueprint for conglomerateurs. The typical large company operated in several unrelated industries, like an overpriced mutual fund, with little constraint from boards or shareholders and nothing to fear from a legally constrained takeover market.[25] It required great theoretical imagination to look out on this situation and deduce that it was, financially speaking, the best of all possible worlds.

Corporate governance and shareholder capitalism

The functionalist theory of corporate governance provided the intellectual foundation for shareholder capitalism, a movement that took shape in the late 1980s and spread widely in the 1990s. Shareholder capitalism took its cues from this theory, as did policymakers. Changes in antitrust enforcement and state-level takeover laws in 1982 enabled a merger wave in which more than one in four Fortune 500 manufacturers faced a takeover bid, thus turning Manne's hypothetical market for corporate control into a reality. Increasingly activist institutional investors took on the cause of corporate governance reform, prompting changes in boardroom practices. Compensation for executives was increasingly tied to share price through devices such as stock option grants. And external managerial labor markets became more active, as companies increasingly sought outside CEOs rather than promoting from within. By the 1990s, few executives doubted that their companies existed to create share-holder value.

What kind of a theory was this? As a scientific theory, the functionalist approach to governance suffered from the same limitations of sociobi-ology, its contemporary cousin. Critics of sociobiology argued that it told "just-so" stories that were difficult to falsify, working backwards from what *is* to why it *must be*. Similarly, to look around at the sluggish conglomerates of the 1970s and to see the disciplined products of a Darwinian process played out in the capital markets seemed somewhat wilful. I discuss this in more detail in the next chapter.

As a normative theory, however, it had immediate policy relevance that became evident during the Reagan years. The prescriptions of Manne and other law and economics scholars came into play, and efforts to restrict takeovers by states, the federal government, or firms themselves, were to be resisted. The *Journal of Financial Economics* was filled with "event studies" documenting the share price consequences of various managerial policies (adopting a poison pill to defend against takeover, making particular types of acquisitions, recapitalizing to have more debt, being incorporated in a state that passed shareholder-hostile laws, and so on). Such studies provided an evidence-based guide to appropriate corporate strategies. Moreover, once the institutions of cor-porate governance in the US had been documented, the system became an exportable commodity, potentially useful for promoting economic growth in other countries. In by-passing the tortuous path through which America's capital market institutions had evolved, emerging mar-kets could quickly install best practices to encourage vibrant economic growth, funded by outside investors.

Finally, the functionalist theory provided a moral rationale for orient-ing companies to shareholder value rather than toward other "stakehold-ers." The case can be stated briefly. Let us suppose, following economist Milton Friedman, that companies maximize social welfare by maximiz-ing profits over time. Profit is simply the residual that is left after the revenue voluntarily paid by consumers has been used to pay off all of the other voluntary participants in a venture (suppliers, employees, debtholders); thus, it represents the "excess" value created by the company, a measure of the firm's enhancement of social welfare. According to the efficient market hypothesis, share price provides the best estimate of the future profit stream of the business. Therefore, companies maximize social welfare by maximizing share price, as long as they do not resort to lawbreaking, fraud, or market tricks that undermine their credibility. From this simple deduction, we have the purported moral rationale for shareholder capitalism. And from this, the missionary zeal of those seeking to spread shareholder capitalism around the world seems understandable.

While financial economists are prone to seeing the functionalist theory as a scientific theory, legal scholars typically regard it as a pragmatic theory for guiding policy. The case for shareholder value relies less on the importance of shareholders as a group than on the privileged epistemological status of share price. If share price reflects the distilled wisdom of crowds, then shareholders are, in effect, just placeholders. As one legal theorist put it, "if the statute did not provide for shareholders, we would have to invent them."[26] Moreover, the efficient market hypothesis may not be literally true (and there is a large and growing literature critical of the EMH), but it may be on balance the best available alternative: "it does not matter if markets are not perfectly efficient, unless some other social institution does better at evaluating the likely effect of corporate governance devices."[27] Delaware's most important jurist for several years, William Allen, stated that the shareholder value approach "is not premised on the conclusion that shareholders do 'own' the corporation in any ultimate sense, only on the view that it can be better for all of us if we act as if they do." The lawyer's brief for EMH and shareholder capitalism is like Blaise Pascal's case for God: act as if the EMH were true—and the deductions that follow from it—and society will benefit.

During the 1990s, as we shall see in the next chapter, the legal pragmatism of law and economics became the cynical pragmatism of the shareholder value-oriented managers, as tokens of devotion to share price and ritual use of the right accountants, investment banks, directors, and alliance partners became rampant.

Finance and governance as technology

If market efficiency is the best-documented claim in all of science, then we can see securities and the institutions of corporate governance as technologies for making use of this science. Economist Robert Shiller describes finance in this way, as a technology for managing risk. In his analogy, the science of economics builds on the new information technology as biology built on the microscope and astronomy built on the telescope. As the observational technology is refined, the ability to track regularities and deduce principles is enhanced. From this perspective, information and communication technologies (ICTs)—in particular, expansive access to data and the ability to process it through computers—have had a revolutionary effect on economics by allowing empirical tests of ideas that had been merely speculative models before. From pen-and-paper to the Internet, the empirical base of economics has expanded drastically. And finance allows practical applications of these ideas.[28]

Consider trading in company shares. In 1700 in England, new shareholders of a company were considered "members" and had to register their ownership with a written entry in the company's ledger. To signify their membership in the corporation, they would swear a public oath.[29] Today, day traders can buy and sell millions of shares in seconds via their mobile phones. ICTs thus enable unprecedented flows of capital around the world. Perhaps more importantly, ICTs and expansive access to information (e.g. consumer credit files, housing values, and so on) allow cost-effective credit ratings on small units, the creation of exotic synthetic securities, and quick price reactions to new information. This is why increasingly incomprehensible financial instruments are brought to market every day, to be bought and sold by highly sophisticated institutional investors seeking to fine-tune their exposure to risk.

The analogy to prior technologies is a useful device for thinking about financial innovation. Many financial innovations that are now widespread, such as the use of limited liability for company shares, were essentially stumbled into, as Shiller documents. And innovations often follow a peculiar path. Steam engines originated to pump water out of coal mines, and only much later were they seen as useful for powering textile factories, then locomotives, then ships. To find a receptive market, innovations often develop by analogy and family resemblance with what has gone before. In introducing systems of electric lighting powered by centralized generators, for instance, Thomas Edison purposely emulated the style and format of the established gas lighting systems to make electric light seem more familiar to potential consumers.[30] Similarly, the basic idea of creating asset-backed securities from mortgages was in place for some time before it was applied to auto loans and, later, credit card receivables, insurance payouts, and Bowie bonds.

Once the basic idea is accepted, financial entrepreneurs compete to establish new kinds of instruments for connecting potential buyers and sellers. Thus, if regular insurance payments can be turned into bonds, why not less-predictable payments—say, life insurance benefits for the terminally ill? Such contracts are called "viaticals" and spread during the early 1990s as investors bought the payoffs of insurance policies from AIDS sufferers and, later, the elderly. The practice of exchanging viaticals was initially considered ghoulish and fraught with malign incentives; for instance, by definition the investor's returns are higher the quicker the counterparty dies, while the counterparty has incentives to overstate how ill they are. But relatively quickly it became accepted, regulated, and—inevitably—securitized. As with mortgages, insurance contracts become more predictable in large numbers, when they are suitable for being re-sold as bonds. Insurance companies once again were often both the buyers and sellers of these instruments.[31]

But if innovations in finance are akin to technological innovations for managing risk, there are also important differences. Unlike other technologies, the ability of finance to work depends critically on both laws and perceptions—in short, on institutions. Institutions as we have defined them have relatively little importance for whether, say, a steam engine works. It is the laws of nature, not human laws, which matter. But financial markets are like orchids, requiring a very specialized institutional climate to flourish. Anti-usury laws that prohibit the paying of interest can make *any* kind of finance considerably more difficult. Laws restricting short-selling can make price changes asymmetric. Anti-takeover regulations in the US greatly raised the hurdles to changes in control during the 1970s. Moreover, perceptions and norms are essential to finance in ways that they are not for other technologies. Perceptions can hold Boeing shares aloft, but perception alone cannot hold Boeing jets aloft.

Because of this reliance on laws and perceptions, some of the regularities of the functionalist theory of corporate governance are bound to particular times and places. The philosopher David Hume described the logical limitations of inducing laws of nature from experience. For all we know, the laws of nature might change tomorrow, rendering our inferences based on past experience false. Much the same is true for corporate governance. Why are US corporations taken over? In the 1970s, for the most part, they were not, due to state-level laws limiting takeovers and to constraints on raising sufficient funds. Manne's "market for corporate control" was thwarted. In the 1980s, the answer was, in brief, that firms were taken over when their share price (more specifically, the ratio of their market value to their "book" or accounting value) was low, often because they had over-diversified. Manne's prediction had come true. But most companies adopted takeover defenses and most states adopted new anti-takeover laws later in the decade, and by then almost all conglomerates had been busted up, either voluntarily or through outside takeovers. Thus, in the 1990s, takeovers were overwhelmingly "friendly" deals among firms in the same industry. Banking, defense, pharmaceuticals, and many other industries consolidated during the 1990s in what was the largest merger wave in US history, but hostile "disciplinary" deals were relatively rare. In short, the "regularities" around the market for corporate control were not particularly regular.[32]

Similarly, the methods used to value the mortgages contained in mortgage-backed securities relied on statistical analyses of data from prior years. The likelihood of default, for instance, was inferred from what homeowners in similar situations had done in the past. But in the mid-2000s, the models lost their predictive power—people with good credit ratings started defaulting on their mortgages—which meant that bonds with high ratings were not nearly as safe as the raters (and those that relied on them) believed.[33]

Moreover, the science and institutions of finance co-evolved to a degree unknown in most other domains, often with the aid of financial economists themselves. Marx wrote in "Theses on Feuerbach" that "The philosophers have only interpreted the world, in various ways; the point is to change it," and financial economists and lawyers have taken up this call with a vengeance. Sympathetic economists in the Reagan administration greatly facilitated the creation of the 1980s takeover wave through changed antitrust rules that enabled more significant intra-industry mergers, through SEC enforcement friendly to takeovers, and through a steadfast refusal to regulate takeovers at the Federal level.[34] Professor Michael Jensen of Harvard Business School, co-author of several foundational articles on the finance-based theory of the corporation, was a highly vocal advocate for an unrestricted takeover market, which he argued was an essential tool for enabling economy-wide industrial restructuring.[35] During the legislative debate over Pennsylvania's restrictive anti-takeover law in 1989-1990, which was introduced largely to protect Pennsylvania-based Armstrong World Industries from a takeover bid by the Belzberg brothers, Jensen was a prominent signer of a petition from academics to the Governor and members of the state House urging them to reject the bill. He also served as the Belzbergs' nominee for the board, receiving compensation of 50,000 stock appreciation rights from the would-be raiders—a potential windfall if the takeover were successful.[36] Professor Daniel Fischel, corporate governance authority and former Dean of the University of Chicago Law School, earned millions by leading and, eventually, selling the Lexecon consulting firm, which provided litigation and other support for corporate and

legal clients such as Phillip Morris. And countless financial economists have set up extra-curricular fund management firms (Dimensional
Fund Advisors) and hedge funds (Long Term Capital Management),
with varying degrees of success (or catastrophic failure, in the case of
LTCM).

The economists' commitment to real-world practice suggests a further
limitation of the "science and technology" analogy of economics and
finance. When William Herschel discovered Uranus in 1781, he named
it the Georgian Star to honor King George III, but it is doubtful that
his actions had much influence on its orbit around the sun. But when
Russia was brought into the orbit of financial markets, first through
mass privatization and later through the chartering of mutual funds,
the Harvard-based advisors that guided the development of its securities
markets undoubtedly did influence its trajectory. In a remarkable exposé
published in *Institutional Investor* in 2006, David McClintick documents
how Harvard's advisors invested hundreds of thousands of dollars of
their own money in companies they were helping to privatize—allegedly
in violation of their and the university's contracts—and created opportunities for friends and lovers, one of whom received the first registration to
open a mutual fund from the Russian SEC and lucrative rights to manage
some government funds.[37]

Shiller notes that all new technologies have bugs at the start of their
development—early in the steam age, boiler explosions took many lives,
and airplanes crashed almost routinely at the advent of air travel—but
that these bugs get worked out and the technology is made more reliable
and safer over time. Similarly, financial bubbles and crashes may seem
dangerous, but we are still at a relatively early stage in the development
of financial technology. Presumably, the bugs will get worked out. Yet
the disanalogy between economics and physics is informative. We don't
imagine that physicists with money at stake had a hand in designing
Boyle's Law (that the volume and pressure of a gas are inversely related),
or that petitions from academics substantially influenced the law of
gravity. Economics, in short, is still a *social* science, and finance is a *social*
technology.

Conclusion

Advances in information and communication technologies and in economic theory have greatly expanded the domain of financial markets since 1980. The number of countries with stock exchanges has doubled, and the range of traded securities has expanded from traditional stocks and bonds to bundles of insurance contracts on the terminally ill and synthetic instruments that can only be valued using the latest information technology. As ICTs get cheaper and more powerful, the range of things that can be securitized—turned into securities tied to future cash flows—expands accordingly. We are in the midst of a financial revolution on a scale comparable to the Second Industrial Revolution at the end of the nineteenth century.

Although ICTs are essential for enabling low-cost valuation and trading of financial instruments, institutions are perhaps even more critical. Corporate governance—in particular, the set of institutions that grew up to orient corporations with dispersed ownership toward share price, without requiring direct intervention by bankers or large shareholders—is a *sine qua non* for market-based economies, and a potential American export. The functionalist theory of corporate governance was a Copernican revolution in thinking about the American corporation, describing an alternative account for the so-called managerialist corporation and highlighting devices that orient the corporation's elites toward shareholder value. It provided a practical and moral case for "shareholder value capitalism" that was remarkably influential in the 1990s, up through the burst of the market bubble in 2000. As this chapter has emphasized, and the next documents in more detail, the functionalist theory was more an "as-if" account than an apt description of the facts on the ground. But regardless of its status as a scientific theory, its influence on thinking about financial markets and their institutional surround is indisputable.

3

From Institution to Nexus: How the Corporation Got, Then Lost, its Soul

The corporation today is a paradox. On the one hand, it is impossible to ignore the rising power of multinational corporations in a globalized economy. Exxon Mobil's 2007 revenues of $373 billion matched the GDP of Saudi Arabia, the world's twenty-fourth largest economy. Wal-Mart has more employees than Slovenia has citizens. Blackwater Corporation has a larger reserve army than Australia. The individuals that run such corporations wield more influence over people's lives than many heads of state. In some respects, corporations transcend or even replace the governments that chartered them: states are stuck with more-or-less agreed land borders, but corporations are mobile, able to choose among physical and legal jurisdictions, and are thus effectively placeless and stateless. Moreover, corporations can fulfill many of the functions of states: they can have extensive social welfare benefit programs for employees, internal courts for disputes among their employee-citizens, foreign policies for dealing with nations where they do business, air forces for transporting executives, and offices of social responsibility to coordinate their good works. The distance between the imagined community of the nation and of many corporations is not so great. Indeed, some American multinationals look more like European welfare states than does the US government. The prophecy at the end of Berle and Means's 1932 book—that the corporation might one day supersede the state as the dominant form of social organization in the world—seems to have come true.

Yet as economic and legal theorists remind us, corporations are mere legal fictions, convenient devices that happen to have useful properties for raising financing. Anyone with a credit card and Internet access can create a corporation in moments (to incorporate in Liberia, visit www.liscr.com). A business firm is simply a nexus of contracts among free individuals—a dense spot in a web of connections among suppliers of labor, capital, materials, and buyers of their outputs. To describe a corporation as an actor that encompasses its "members," or to imagine that it has boundaries analogous to national borders, is to reify something that is simply a useful fiction. And to imagine that a network of contractual relations has either "power" or "social responsibilities" is to further the mistake. Thus, with a little sophistry, economic theorists reduce the corporation from a leviathan to a paper tiger.

The paradox of the contemporary corporation is that both of these portrayals are correct. Corporations are mere legal fictions with "no body to kick, no soul to damn," as Baron Thurlow put it. They are also social facts, given deference and responsibility in the law and in social practice. They may not *have* a body, but their very name comes from the Latin word for body, *corpus*. And corporations may not have a soul, but their participants—and sometimes the law—expect them to act as if they do.

The history of the Hershey Foods Corporation illustrates the strain between our views of the corporation as a social institution and as a financial entity. Milton Hershey founded his chocolate company at the turn of the twentieth century in Derry Church, which was quickly renamed Hershey, Pennsylvania. In addition to the usual institutions of a company town—recreational facilities, parks, churches—Hershey founded the Hershey Industrial School for orphans, and after the death of his wife, he endowed the school with stock in the company that ultimately evolved into a 77% controlling stake. Over the subsequent decades, Hershey grew to become the nation's largest candy-maker. The links between the company, the town, and the school grew dense, as their shared name indicates. The CEO of the company in the 1970s, for instance, had grown up in the orphanage, and half of the town's residents worked for Hershey.

In July 2002, the board of the Milton Hershey School Trust that oversees the School's endowment announced plans to sell its controlling stake in the company—in effect, putting the company up for sale. The economic rationale for the decision was indisputable: the most basic rule of portfolio management is to diversify, yet half of the Trust's assets were invested in the stock of a single company, leaving the School dependent on Hershey to a degree that was downright reckless. (Consider the implications of a food safety scare for Hershey's share price, and thus the School's endowment.) Moreover, potential buyers such as Nestle or Cadbury were certain to offer a substantial premium, giving the Trust an immediate windfall; indeed, the day the sale was announced, Hershey's stock price soared from $62.50 to $78.30, even before any bidder had appeared. Who could oppose selling some financial instruments in order to fund the education of underprivileged children more generously?

As it happens, virtually everyone in the community—employees, the union, residents, alumni of the school, and Pennsylvania politicians—was shocked at the trustees' actions and responded quickly to prevent the sale. Residents feared that the company's acquisition would result in closed plants and lost jobs for the town of Hershey. Mike Fisher, Pennsylvania's Republican attorney general (and candidate for governor), filed a motion in the Dauphin County Orphans' Court to prevent the sale due to the "irreparable harm" it would cause to local business and the social fabric of the town. (The Orphans' Court had jurisdiction over the Trust.) Nonetheless, Swiss-based Nestle and UK-based Cadbury offered to buy the company in late August, and Chicago-based Wrigley made an even larger bid a few weeks later, which seven of the trustees voted to accept. Fisher's effort to prevent the sale was successful, however, and the majority of the Trust's board was pressured to resign, to be replaced by a newly constituted board which vowed to retain its controlling interest in Hershey permanently. One study attributed a $2.7 billion loss in shareholder wealth to the forgone sale of the company.[1]

This was not the first time the state of Pennsylvania had intervened to prevent changes in control of local companies. In 1990 the state legislature overwhelmingly approved a so-called "other constituency" law stating that the board of directors of a Pennsylvania corporation "may, in considering the best interests of the corporation, consider to the extent they deem appropriate ... [t]he effects of any action upon any or all groups affected by such action, including shareholders, employees, suppliers, customers and creditors of the corporation, and upon communities in which offices or other establishments of the corporation are located," and moreover that the board "shall not be required, in considering the best interests of the corporation or the effects of any action, to regard any corporate interest or the interest of any particular group affected by such action as a dominant or controlling interest or factor." The law was passed during a hostile contest for Armstrong World Industries, a local company threatened with an unwanted takeover by Canadian raiders, with the intention of allowing the boards of Pennsylvania corporations to refuse such outside bids if they might harm their communities. The law responded explicitly to the widely held notion that corporations exist for the primary benefit of their shareholders: in Pennsylvania, they had other obligations (at least if the board agreed). But like most large US corporations, Hershey was incorporated in Delaware, not Pennsylvania—the "other constituency" law did not apply to Hershey. Yet the state—in the form of the Orphans' Court, no less—demonstrated that it could prevent a company's dominant owner from voluntarily selling out, even with the cooperation of the company's board. In its social context, Hershey was no more a "nexus of contracts" than a family, or a church.

In this chapter I describe the rise and fall of the corporation as a social institution over the course of the twentieth century. There have been three main eras of the American corporation during this time. The first was the era of *finance capitalism*, which arose out of the turn of the century merger wave, in which bankers maintained an ongoing influence on the management of the largest corporations. From the public's perspective, many of these new giants were little more than cartels created and controlled by Wall Street financiers. To combat this perception and avoid the potential political fallout stemming from the public's mistrust of the new "soulless corporations," the managers of many firms, like Milton Hershey, created programs of welfare capitalism to demonstrate their caring relations with their employees and communities. Other corporations, such as AT&T, engaged in public relations campaigns to portray themselves as benign entities, committed to serving the public at large.

The second was the era of *managerial capitalism*, lasting from the 1920s until the 1980s, in which financially independent corporations run by professional managers evolved into social institutions. The dispersion of corporate ownership after the initial period of finance capitalism—partly through conscious strategies on the part of their managers to broaden share ownership—allowed management, freed from direct shareholder oversight, to run their companies more along the lines of their PR. Prior efforts to give the corporation a soul were evidently successful, as policymakers and citizens began to expect corporations to live up to their self-portrayal as "soulful" social institutions. By the 1950s the soulful corporation came to dominance, and its reign coincided with rising wages and increased demands to enact social policies around equal employment opportunity, safe products, and environmental protection.

A third era of *shareholder capitalism* was ushered in by the takeover wave of the 1980s and the shift to post-industrialism, and it continues through today. In relatively short order, the social institution owned by dispersed widows and orphans was reduced to a mere contractual nexus, driven by signals on financial markets, and the widows and orphans increasingly relied on a handful of mutual fund companies to manage their shareholdings. As post-industrial corporations replaced large manufacturers as the central actors of American capitalism, the "social institution" view became difficult to sustain. The corporation has increasingly become the financially oriented nexus described by its theorists.

In this chapter I briefly describe the evolution of the corporate form prior to the twentieth century and then lay out the three eras of corporate capitalism during that century. Two predominant conceptions of the place of the corporation in society have vied for dominance over this period, one which sees the corporation as simply a legal device for financing business activity, and one which sees it as a social institution with broader obligations. The social institution view came to dominance with the rise of large-scale firms, particularly manufacturers, whose dispersed ownership gave their managers autonomy from shareholders. These corporations took on many of the functions performed by welfare states elsewhere in the world, providing stable incomes, health care coverage, and retirement security. But the bust-up takeovers of the 1980s and the advent of the shareholder value movement changed the dominant conception of the corporation, which increasingly came to look like a mere network guided by a share price-oriented system of corporate governance. The bubble of the 1990s, and the corporate scandals of the 2000s, revealed that there is large gap between the theory of shareholder capitalism as an arm's-length meritocracy, as described in the previous chapter, and how the system operates in practice.

The corporation in the law

Efforts to portray the corporation as a mere contractual device are swimming against a strong tide in history. Organizations, including corporations, have long been susceptible to "institutionalization"—being valued in themselves rather than simply as tools for accomplishing particular ends.[2] We seem naturally prone to perceiving collective actors as entities analogous to persons, with institutional personalities, and organizations have reinforced this tendency with their practices. The guilds of medieval and Renaissance times were initial predecessors of the business corporation in Europe and the US, and they were organized very much along the analogy of a body (*corps*). After years of apprenticeship, members joined a guild by swearing a religious oath of loyalty that signified a lifetime commitment, lasting until one's colleagues lowered one's body into the ground. The commitment worked both ways: masters (members) of the guild were typically entitled to guild-sponsored funerals, support for their widows, and aid in cases of sickness or disability. And the analogy of guilds with bodies was thorough:

> All bodies were composed of a variety of organs and members, which were hierarchically arranged and were placed under the command of the head. Each body was distinct from every other, with its own will, its own interests, its own internal order, and its own esprit de corps. Each body was made of a single internally differentiated but interconnected substance, and harm inflicted on any member was felt by the whole.

Moreover, guilds typically were treated by the law as a single (collective) person, and their members had no separate standing as individuals under the law.[3]

The organization of the first joint-stock companies in England built on some aspects of the guilds while adding features useful for finance. "Early companies, including the East India Company, were considered to be a kind of brotherhood. Shareholders were also members and as such had to take an oath upon entry into the company. They could be fined if absent from company meetings or if they engaged in improper conduct."[4] In the early years of the United States, creating a corporation required a separate act of the state legislature, and corporations were expected to serve a public purpose (such as building a bridge, road, or canal). Connecticut enacted a general incorporation statute in 1837, allowing the creation of corporations for any legitimate business purpose, and other states followed, making incorporation more common. Over time, corporations evolved the familiar features that distinguished them from their "members": limited liability, separate legal personality, and indefinite life. Corporations no longer *contained* their members; shareholders became anonymous, and employees could come and go at will. The most significant joint-stock corporations in the second half of the nineteenth century were the railroads, which were largely owned by foreign investors and were responsible for fleshing out many of the legal features of the modern corporation. Corporations came to be treated as artificial persons under the law, with individual rights under the US constitution. However, large-scale manufacturing corporations that brought hundreds of employees together under one roof remained rare until late in the century. It was their emergence, as palpable collectives situated in particular places, which prompted a re-thinking of the corporation as a social institution.[5]

The rise of the large US industrial enterprise at the turn of the century produced divergent responses: was it a collective entity with responsibilities, or a mere nexus? On the one hand, the populist backlash against the new giants prompted corporate managers to engage in campaigns to cultivate a positive public image, often emphasizing their enlightened employee relations. Henry Ford's institution of a $5 per day wage (more or less) in 1914 might count here. Yet there was a limit, enforced by the courts: in the famous 1919 *Dodge Bros. v. Ford Motor Co.* case, the Michigan Supreme Court ruled:

> A business corporation is organized and carried on primarily for the profit of the stockholders. The powers of the directors are to be employed for that end. The discretion of directors is to be exercised in the choice of means to attain that end and does not extend to a change in the end itself... it is not within the lawful powers of a board of directors to shape and conduct the affairs of a corporation for the merely incidental benefit of shareholders and for the primary purpose of benefiting others.

The corporation's overseers, in other words, still acted as contractually bound agents of the firm's profit-oriented owners, not as stewards responsible to a broader set of constituents.

Legal theorists have a sophisticated view of this tension and the process by which it gets resolved. Corporations are, of course, creatures of the law. In the US they are chartered by the fifty states, and thus what a corporation is, and to whom it is responsible, varies over time by jurisdiction. Moreover, jurisdiction itself is a choice: businesses can incorporate in any state they like, independent of the location of their operations (if any). A Texas-based company incorporated in Pennsylvania may have obligations to its community, while a neighboring company incorporated in Delaware may not. But the law is, in part, a residue of broader social processes. Fears of deindustrialization led to popular support of the Pennsylvania law making corporate boards responsible to "stakeholders," in spite of strong resistance by the financial community. Conversely, dependence of the state budget on out-of-state incorporation fees led Delaware to avoid such a stance. Thus, pragmatic legal thinkers do not seek to resolve what a corporation "really" is, but to apply a theory of the corporation that best serves society's interests, or that best predicts how judges might rule.[6] One theory is that shareholders own the corporation, and it should therefore be run for shareholder value—the view articulated in the *Dodge Bros. v. Ford* decision. As Delaware's top jurist noted, however, this view "is not premised on the conclusion that shareholders do 'own' the corporation in any ultimate sense, only on the view that it could be better for all of us if we act as if they do."[7] Thus, if it turns out that we would be better off imagining the corporation as a social institution, with obligations to its community, this can be arranged too—for instance, in Hershey, Pennsylvania.

If the corporation is a legal fiction, then the pragmatic question is what theory or genre of legal fiction works best under various circumstances. The historical question is what accounts for the prevalence of different views at different times and in different places. In particular, it is worth considering how the corporation came to be established as a social institution during the early decades of the twentieth century in the US, with the rise of large-scale industry, and how this view waned as the shareholder value view has come to predominate the post-industrial economy in the later decades of the century.

From legal fiction to social institution: how the corporation got its soul

The familiar US industrial corporation arose fairly abruptly around the turn of the twentieth century. Railroads had grown large prior to this time, of course, as had Rockefeller's Standard Oil, and there were a few substantial manufacturers such as Carnegie Steel—organized as a partnership dominated by Andrew Carnegie. But the large-scale, publicly traded manufacturer emerged over a relatively brief period through a series of Wall Street-financed mergers that turned dozens of local and regional producers into national oligopolies or monopolies. Edison's electric company was merged into General Electric, Carnegie's steel partnership was combined with suppliers and competitors into US Steel, and regional farm equipment manufacturers were rolled into International Harvester. In industry after industry, by 1903 the public corporation had become dominant in manufacturing. The governance of these firms reflected their origins: bankers, particularly those that had been responsible for their creation, continued to serve on the boards of dozens of corporations through the First World War. Banks, railroads, and industrial corporations were interconnected through ownership ties and shared corporate directors into identifiable "communities of interest"— the Rockefeller group, the Gould group, the Vanderbilt group, and of course the Morgan group.[8]

This was *finance capitalism*, a new kind of economic system in the US. Almost immediately it attracted a substantial political backlash among those that feared concentrated economic control and its political concomitants. Faceless monopolies were bad enough, but faceless monopolies controlled by a small handful of bankers in New York were worse still. Louis Brandeis published a series of articles on this question in *Harper's Weekly*, based on evidence uncovered in the 1912 Pujo Committee hearings in Congress. The articles (re-published in 1914 as *Other People's Money: And How the Bankers Use It*) documented a "money trust" in which a small handful of bankers—J. P. Morgan in particular—used their positions of economic power to "control the business of the country and 'divide the spoils.'" The vision of an economy controlled by financial oligarchs is a recurrent theme in American culture, but in this case the description was not far wrong. J. P. Morgan's associates, for instance, served on six dozen corporate boards, and executives of other banks also sat on the boards of hundreds of corporations. By most accounts, they were not without influence. Brandeis claimed that "When once a banker has entered the Board—whatever may have been the occasion—his grip proves tenacious and his influence usually supreme; for he controls the supply of new money." This situation was relatively temporary: firms became skilled at shepherding their retained earnings rather than relying on bank loans, and as business historian Alfred Chandler notes, the bankers had little industry knowledge and thus not much practical value to add to board meetings. Overt bank control thus declined as the scale of enterprise increased in subsequent decades.[9]

It was not just bank control of industry that alarmed the public, however, but the very size of the new corporations. Andrew Carnegie might serve as a public face for the steel company that bore his name, but many of the largest corporations were assembled through consolidating geographically fragmented industries into oligopolies. To the extent that General Electric or US Steel had founders, it was J. P. Morgan and his Wall Street colleagues who had stitched them together. These new entities were patently artificial, like the trusts that had been their predecessors, and equally untrustworthy due to their anticompetitive possibilities.

Corporate managers pursued two avenues to quell these concerns and to give their organizations a soul. The first avenue was *welfare capitalism*, a set of corporate practices that evolved from the turn of the century through the 1920s to provide an array of employee benefits on and off the job: pensions, paid vacations, health insurance, and housing assistance, among other things. Welfare capitalism was a distinctly American approach to dealing with the social problems associated with industrial society. The US had the smallest welfare state and lowest unionization rate of any industrialized nation at the turn of the century. Thus, in the US corporations managed the social risks that were seen as the responsibility of governments in Europe.[10] In some cases, welfare capitalism extended beyond financial benefits to include health and recreation programs, domestic education to teach middle-class virtues, and corporate social workers to help with problems at home. The intention was to inculcate a work ethic, to bind employees to their companies, and, of course, to forestall unionization and prevent government intervention. The result was to give the corporations that employed these tactics a personality and tangibility as an institution. In the case of Dayton's

National Cash Register, for instance, "NCR was never just a factory, rather [it was] a living organization. The company's real existence lay in the hearts and minds of its employees . . . a cohesion of values, myths, heroes and symbols." NCR was, in short, an imagined community, a miniature nation-state.[11]

In *Creating the Corporate Soul*, historian Roland Marchand documents campaigns by public relations professionals in the early part of the twentieth century to give massive new corporations such as US Steel, GM, International Harvester, and AT&T an aura of "institutionality." Advertisements in national magazines included renderings of picturesque factories to convey solidity and a connection to place; folksy notes from company founders or presidents; and touching images of the many individuals whose lives were improved by the company. Institutional advertising campaigns sought to portray corporations as benevolent entities driven by a higher social purpose then mere profit—in spite of the contrary view of the Michigan Supreme Court.

AT&T's thirty-year campaign was the most remarkable and, arguably, the most effective at giving the large corporation its soul in the eyes of the public. At the turn of the twentieth century, AT&T had a reputation as a ruthless monopolist relying on litigation and intimidation to crush its rivals. Poor service, arrogance, and predatory pricing had marked the company as a "bad trust," and the threat of antitrust action—or even public ownership—was always there. Independent locally based competitors portrayed AT&T as an unnatural monopoly headquartered back East, and the corporation had little public goodwill in reserve. Thus, in 1908 AT&T began an institutional advertising campaign to give itself a soul. The purpose of the advertisements was not to ring up more sales, but to convince the public of AT&T's institutional beneficence. According to this campaign, the phone company's size was not a threat, but a positive feature, promising "One Policy, One System, Universal Service." Images of brave linemen working through bad weather, and gracious operators connecting families from coast to coast, emphasized the human face of the corporation. Even the company's owners were not New York bankers but regular working people. Shareholders were portrayed in advertisements as a vast "investment democracy" comprising a demographic cross-section of America, with special emphasis on widows and orphans. AT&T was not a soulless monopoly, but "Ma Bell," bringing families together by phone and sending out dividend checks to the hundreds of thousands of ordinary working men (or their survivors) who owned its shares. AT&T had become a reliable and trusted member of the family. Not a bad accomplishment for a corporation representing "the largest aggregation of capital and resources that had ever been controlled by a single private company in the history of business."[12]

Efforts to create a personality and a soul for the corporation were evidently successful. After Standard Oil was split up in 1911, attempts to rein in corporations based on size and "soullessness" subsided, and the companies kept getting bigger. A second wave of mergers in the 1920s led to a great increase in the concentration of assets held by the largest tier of corporations. And by the 1920s control by financiers had waned, as the largest corporations sought to broaden their stock ownership along the lines of AT&T. The stock market boom of the 1920s vastly increased public participation in the market—the number of shareholders in the US quadrupled from 2.4 million to 10 million between 1924 and 1930—and thus by the end of the decade ownership had become widely dispersed in dozens of the largest corporations. As Berle and Means summarized these two trends, control of assets was *centripetal*, becoming ever more concentrated in a handful of companies, while ownership was *centrifugal*, becoming ever more dispersed. AT&T, for instance, had 454,000 employees in 1930 and 567,000 shareholders—none, as the company proudly pointed out, owning as much as 1% of the shares. The result of these two processes was that the bulk of the nation's industrial assets were controlled by professional managers with little ownership themselves and little accountability to the company's shareholders.[13]

This was the birth of *managerial capitalism*, the second era of the American corporation. In their 1932 book *The Modern Corporation and Private Property*, Berle and Means provided an astute assessment of the new "corporate system" and speculated on what the future would bring. A mere two hundred organizations had come to control half of the nation's non-financial corporate assets, and 44% of these firms were under management control—a proportion expected to grow into the future. The implications were profound:

> The economic power in the hands of the few persons who control a giant corporation is a tremendous force which can harm or benefit a multitude of individuals, affect whole districts, shift the currents of trade, bring ruin to one community and prosperity to another. The organizations which they control have passed far beyond the realm of private enterprise–they have become more nearly social institutions.[14]

And how would the few hundred men that controlled half of American industry use their power, if their shareholders were too dispersed to demand accountability? That was the critical question for the future. As Berle and Means concluded their analysis:

> The modern corporation may be regarded not simply as one form of social organization but potentially (if not yet actually) as the dominant institution of the modern world... The rise of the modern corporation has brought a concentration of economic power which can compete on equal terms with the modern state... The future may see the economic organism, now typified by the corporation, not only on an equal plane with the state, but possibly even superseding it as the dominant form of social organization."[15]

Managerialist dominance in the postwar period

Two decades after Berle and Means published their book, a consensus had begun to form among mid-century social theorists around the nature of this new economic organism. Gains by organized labor during the 1930s had promoted the spread of rationalized employment practices among large manufacturers, and the expansion of personnel offices and standardized benefits during the labor shortages of the Second World War had raised the bar for large-scale employers—which were increasingly prevalent. According to contemporary commentators, the new production and employment practices of large firms were not just different in degree, but in kind.

Thirty-five years after Brandeis outlined the characteristics of J. P. Morgan's finance capitalism in the pages of *Harper's*, Peter Drucker used the same forum to publish his analysis of the new managerial-industrial society. The stunning productivity of America's manufacturers during the War had demonstrated beyond doubt the superiority of the principles of mass production, from the fabrication of planes by the thousands to the D-Day invasion itself. The central institution of this new order was the managerialist enterprise: "the representative, the decisive, industrial unit is the large, mass-production plant, managed by professionals without ownership-stake, employing thousands of people, and organized on entirely different technological, social, and economic principles" than the small family-owned factories that had predominated in the early period of industrialization. Drucker asserted that the principles of mass production had spread broadly, from manufacturing to agriculture to clerical work, and even to scientific and medical research. Society had been reorganized along the lines of the automotive assembly line. And the corporations that embodied these principles also left their stamp on the psyches of that interacted with them, as workers, customers, and neighbors. Through its pervasive influence on daily economic activity, the industrial corporation "determines the individual's view of his society," including perceptions of prosperity and social mobility, even for those that did not work there. "The big enterprise is the true symbol of our social order . . . *In the industrial enterprise the structure which actually underlies all our society can be seen*" (emphasis added).[16]

Finance had become largely irrelevant to this new system:

> The mass-production revolution has completed the destruction of the power of the land-owning aristocracy of the *ancien regime* which began two hundred years ago. But it has also dethroned the ruling groups of bourgeois society: the merchant, the banker, the capitalist. Symbolic of this change is the slow but steady decay of the great merchant oligarchies:

73

the "City" in London, "Wall Street" in New York," "State Street" in Boston. Where only twenty years ago the bright graduate of the Harvard Business School aimed at a job with a New York Stock Exchange house, he now seeks employment with a steel, oil, or automobile company.[17]

Shareholders had completed the descent into irrelevance described by Berle and Means:

> In non-socialist countries today the owner—that is, the shareholder—has largely abandoned control. A growing number of our large enterprises are run on the model which Owen D. Young proposed twenty years ago, when he was head of the General Electric Company: the stockholders are confined to a maximum return equivalent to a risk premium. The remaining profit stays in the enterprise, is paid out in higher wages, or is passed on to the consumer in the form of lower prices."[18]

If it was not run primarily for the profit of its shareholders, then what did this new organism want, and how did it accomplish its ends? Economist Carl Kaysen asserted in 1957 that the soul of the corporation, so much in doubt at the turn of the century, had been found by its managers: "No longer the agent of proprietorship seeking to maximize return on investment, management sees itself as responsible to stockholders, employees, customers, the general public, and, perhaps most important, the firm itself as an institution." The cynically motivated good works of the early corporations had evolved into *noblesse oblige* on the part of the contemporary corporation: "Its responsibilities to the general public are widespread: leadership in local charitable enterprises, concern with factory architecture and landscaping, provision of support for higher education, and even research in pure science, to name a few." And the employment practices used by welfare capitalists to evade unionization had become standard in both unionized and non-unionized firms: "The whole labor force of the modern corporation is, insofar as possible, turned into a corps of lifetime employees, with great emphasis on stability of employment." Through its enveloping labor practices, "membership in the modern corporation becomes the single strongest social force shaping its career members."[19] Corporations had become the new guilds, creating lifetime attachments to their members through devices that extended from health care to retirement pensions that rewarded those that spent a career with the company. The Organization Man had been born.

Now that they were established as the central institutions of American society, corporations came under increased systematic scrutiny from social scientists of various kinds. A specific sub-discipline arose to study them—organization theory—with its own central texts. The idea of a theory of organizations was something new. As Peter Drucker pointed out in "The New Society of Organizations," the word "organization" in this sense was unknown to the *Concise Oxford Dictionary* as late as 1950, yet by the end of that decade organizations were seen as the building blocks of modern industrial society. In their 1958 book that announced the new discipline of organization theory, James March and Herbert Simon stated that the organization was "a sociological unit comparable in significance to the individual organism in biology," ubiquitous and enveloping in modern life, yet something about which surprisingly little was known systematically.[20] If members of organizations expected to spend their lives there, moving up the hierarchy (or not), then it was appropriate to understand why organizations had the structures that they did, and with what effect on members. Economic theories of the firm provided little insight here—firms were essentially a black box—so theorists worked with the materials available: the managerialist industrial firm. Remarkably, financial considerations had become so distant that the word "profit" did not appear in the index; the theory was presumed to apply to all types of organizations, whether large corporations, non-profits, or universities. Organizational members (and presumably firms) did not maximize, they "satisficed"—seeking alternatives that were above threshold, rather than the best possible.

Economists in the early 1960s began to theorize these new "satisficing" entities. If firms did not maximize profits for their shareholders, then it was necessary to understand how the motivations of those that ran them translated into corporate policies. The simplest answer was that firms sought growth: bigger firms paid better and provided greater prestige, and the more levels of hierarchy there were, the more opportunities there were for advancement. High-level executives rarely switched employers in the 1960s, and salaries were much more correlated with firm size than profit, particularly for those at the top. As a result, executives had strong incentives to pursue organizational growth to best serve their own self-interest. Profits could not be ignored completely, of course: if a company's share price were low enough, and the company were small enough, it might be taken over by outside raiders, so management had to pay at least some attention to share price. But according to Robin Marris, an early theorist of takeovers, "the giants who produce the bulk of the output would remain relatively immune" from takeover in any world imaginable to economists of the mid-1960s, giving further incentives to get big.[21] Big firms did not face takeovers, and they rarely failed. The best working assumption, then, was that managerial motivations were aligned with making the organization grow large—even at the expense of profitability.

What had happened to social class in all of this? Sociologist Ralf Dahrendorf argued that the separation of ownership and control described by Berle and Means had meant the end of capitalism as we knew it, and referred to the new corporate-industrial system as "post-capitalist." The US was still an industrial society, defined by "mechanized commodity production in factories and enterprises." But capitalism required the "union of private ownership and factual control." By this definition, the US was no longer a true capitalist system: the managers were now in charge, not the owners. To be sure, the class conflicts endemic to capitalism had not disappeared; they had simply been transferred to conflicts within the enterprise itself. Executives were the new upper class, and workers the new proletariat. With ownership of the means of production rendered moot, conflicts now revolved around the exercise of authority at work. Position within a bureaucracy defined one's social class in post-capitalist industrial society, not the ownership of property. The social organization of production within firms had become the primary basis of class struggle. Moreover, this struggle did not transfer outside of the enterprise: one's position in a corporate hierarchy had as little to do with broader political interests as the sports team one rooted for. The managerial class was therefore not a ruling class in any political sense—at least according to Dahrendorf.[22]

Not everyone agreed with this assessment, of course. In his 1956 book *The Power Elite*, C. Wright Mills argued that a new ruling class had emerged out of the confluence of political, economic, and military elites stemming from mobilization for the Second World War. Mills described how the large national corporation had expanded during and after the War to insinuate itself into the formerly isolated power structures of the smaller cities, creating for the first time a national power elite centered around a few dozen corporations. Owners and executives of these corporations—the "corporate rich"—were more-or-less intermingled as a class, through devices such as intermarriage and shared directorships on corporate boards. The financial world had been banished to irrelevance: "Not 'Wall Street financiers' or bankers, but large owners and executives in their self-financing corporations hold the keys of economic power." These "self-financing corporations" may have severed their ties to high finance, but they were not disconnected from political power. The connections among top executives in the corporate, military, and political worlds created a set of overlapping cliques among elite decision-makers, many of whom moved among these worlds and thus knit them closer together. "As an elite, it is not organized, although its members often seem to know one another, seem quite naturally to work together, and share many organizations in common. There is nothing conspiratorial about it, although its decisions are often publicly unknown and its mode of operation manipulative rather than explicit." But it was, unmistakably, a ruling class, with top corporate executives at the center.[23]

Conglomerate growth and decline

And yet the corporate elite did not have complete control over the rules of its own game, as the corporate quest for growth collided with antitrust policy in the 1950s and 1960s. One of the outcomes of the Second World

77

War was a greater concentration of corporate assets among the largest firms. This generated concern in Congress about the anticompetitive implications of having three or four oligopolists dominating most substantial industries, and thus led to the Celler–Kefauver ("anti-merger") Act of 1950. Celler–Kefauver amended the Clayton Act of 1914 to prevent anticompetitive mergers in which firms bought competitors or important suppliers. This obviously limited pathways to corporate growth, to the frustration of those that ran the firms. If acquiring competitors or suppliers was out of the question, then firms that wanted to grow via acquisition—the quickest way to get big—had to turn to targets outside their industry. New financial tools, and the development of the multi-divisional organizational structure, created a means to buy and manage these targets much as investors bought equities for their portfolio. The result was a merger boom during the 1960s that created a new kind of company: the diversified conglomerate. ITT, originally known as "International Telephone & Telegraph," completed hundreds of acquisitions in dozens of industries during the reign of CEO Harold Geneen in the 1960s, including Sheraton Hotels, various auto parts manufacturers, the makers of Wonder Bread, a chain of vocational schools, insurance companies, and Avis Rent-a-Car. At the end of a decade of acquisitions ITT had grown to be the fifth largest corporate employer in the US. By the 1970s, the notion of treating the corporation as a diversified portfolio of businesses had become widely accepted among managers and the consultants that advised them, and the trend toward diversification continued through the end of the decade to encompass most large manufacturers.[24]

In a society organized around large corporations, in which the middle class aspired to a career moving up the ladder of a Fortune 500 firm, policymakers began to treat corporations not simply as economic entities but as levers of public policy. The largest employers—AT&T, General Motors, Ford, General Electric, Sears—had been in the vanguard of progressive employment practices for decades, and their practices were widely emulated by other firms (while being decried as "industrial feudalism" by some critics). Internal promotion ladders, employer-sponsored pensions, and health insurance coverage came to be standard practice among corporate employers. Thus, the management methods and structures of a relative handful of firms had leverage over a wide swath of business practice.[25] In the early 1970s the Nixon Administration presided over a series of policy changes that held corporations accountable in areas from workplace safety to employment discrimination to environmental impact. The Environmental Protection Agency (EPA) was created in 1970 to protect the natural environment, for instance, by regulating toxic outputs in manufacturing and auto emissions. The Occupational Safety and Health Administration (OSHA) was established in 1971 to protect employees from dangers on the job. The Equal Employment Opportunity Commission gained litigation authority in 1972 and promptly set up task forces to investigate discriminatory employment practices at four of the six largest US employers—GM, Ford, GE, and Sears—which led to the creation of affirmative action programs at corporate employers. If "membership in the modern corporation [was] the single strongest social force shaping its career members," as Kaysen had claimed, then there was a public interest in assuring that they did it fairly.[26]

In spite of its reputation for enforcing a stifling conformity, a career in a bureaucracy had much to recommend it. As Richard Sennett points out, the corporation could be a cultivator of virtue, teaching self-discipline and delayed gratification for its long-term members. A corporate career allowed a stable life narrative, long-term social relations, and a site to develop one's talents. The corporation provided a form of identity and a connection to past and future, like a community. As long as it kept growing, the company provided more rungs to climb on the ladder. And at the end of one's career, one could look forward to retiring with a company pension and health care coverage.[27]

Yet just at the point when the corporate system had achieved its dominance, and it appeared that a handful of ever-expanding conglomerates would end up controlling the bulk of the American economy—under the watchful guidance of Federal policy—the system began to fall apart. In retrospect, the oil crisis of 1973 signalled the end of the long postwar economic boom in the US, and with it the growth that had underwritten the promises of the corporate system. Firms continued to grow through acquisitions in diverse industries, but organic growth was stunted. Moreover, the core of the American economy had always been its large-scale integrated manufacturers, perhaps best represented by the big three Detroit automakers. But American manufacturing was in long-term relative decline, not least in employment. Much of this was attributable to competitive pressures: oligopoly at a national level did not guarantee global competitiveness, and American automakers, as the most prominent examples, began a long slide in market share.

Perhaps a more fundamental trend than growth in international trade was growth in productivity, which implied by simple mathematics that more work could be done with less labor. Manufacturing was bound to follow agriculture in having bountiful outputs produced from minimal labor inputs. Daniel Bell identified the emerging situation as "post-industrialism," in which the majority of the workforce is engaged in services of various sorts rather than agriculture and manufacturing. This had important implications for workers' attachments to their employers and colleagues. American-style mass production had been marked by large-scale workplaces: Ford's Rouge Plant housed 75,000 Ford employees in a single vast, integrated facility, and many workers spent their entire careers there. By the early 1970s, however, most Americans worked in services. Although service industries can be organized through large-scale employers (e.g. chain stores), the norm for services was relatively small-scale establishments. Wal-Mart, for instance, employed 1.42 million Americans in 2008 and operated 4,141 stores in the US, implying a maximum of fewer than 350 employees per workplace. Further, the tenures of employees were much lower on average in services—according to the January 2004 Current Population Survey, the median employee in retail was 38 years old and had been with their employer for 3 years, compared to 44 and 8 for transportation manufacturing. Hierarchies with growing employment can provide employment security and advancement, but there is a limit on how high one can rise in a chain store, on how long one was likely to stay there.

The challenges to manufacturers were particularly acute for conglomerates. Their rationale had always been a bit suspect: why did one need a costly corporate office to oversee the business units that were doing the real work? How does a bakery benefit from sharing a corporate parent with a rental car company, or a car parts maker? Hierarchical levels above the "portfolio" of divisions were, in some sense, pure overhead. Thus, the shares of conglomerates typically traded at a discount relative to what a group of separate free-standing firms operating in the same industries would get. According to the stock market, the whole was worth less than the sum of the parts, with the obvious implication that their shareholders would be better off if the conglomerates were split into free-standing companies operating in their own industries. Fortunately for their managers, Robin Marris had been right: given their size, large conglomerates faced little threat of takeover, at least in the 1970s. But this situation would not last for long.

Reagan's takeover wave and the end of managerialism

A central goal of the Reagan Administration in the early 1980s was economic revitalization, drawing on a new set of theories about how that might be achieved. One of the most important elements was the "market for corporate control," a phrase coined by Henry Manne in his influential 1965 article, discussed briefly in the previous chapter. Manne was one of the leading lights of the "law and economics" movement, a group of scholars centered on the University of Chicago that sought to analyze law and regulation using the tools of economics. From an economic point of view, the idea of managerialism was intolerable: firms that failed to maximize profits, by using their resources to pay employees more than necessary or charging customers less than they could, distorted the operations of markets and allocated resources inefficiently. Moreover, not everybody believed that unfettered managerial dominance was as widespread as it seemed. Following Marris, Manne had argued that poor management was reflected in a company's share price, and that if the price were low enough there were incentives for outsiders to buy the company and rehabilitate it, to be rewarded through the increased value of the firm.

Manne made the critical point that control of a company was an asset that could be bought by outsiders—that managerial control was contestable, even if ownership was dispersed. This was often an attractive option for outsiders, as taking over poorly run firms "is one of the most important 'get-rich-quick' opportunities in our economy today."[28] Mergers and takeovers benefit shareholders as well, because they usually gain a premium over the company's market price. Takeovers may even rescue poorly run firms from declining into bankruptcy. But because those best able to recognize and address under-performance were competitors in the same industry, antitrust concerns often prevented value-enhancing mergers. Thus, Manne implied that mergers in the same industry were not always anticompetitive, and that antitrust should be reformed to allow welfare-enhancing takeovers. As a corollary, efforts to make takeovers more difficult, such as the Williams Act (passed three years later) and state corporate laws like Pennsylvania's, should be given critical scrutiny in light of the efficiency-enhancing benefits of an active market for corporate control: "Only the take-over scheme provides some assurance of competitive efficiency among corporate managers and thereby affords strong protection to the interests of vast numbers of small, non-controlling shareholders."[29]

Subsequent academic economists went further still in their critique of managerialism. Among the most influential was a 1976 article by Michael Jensen and William Meckling, which revived the view of the corporation as a nexus-of-contracts, but made the financial market orientation more central. The critique had two main parts. First, it didn't seem reasonable to believe that shareholders would routinely invest in underperforming firms when there were better alternatives. "How does it happen that millions of individuals are willing to turn over a significant fraction of their wealth to organizations run by managers who have so little interest in their welfare? ... Why, if non-manager-owned shares have such a serious deficiency, have they not long since been driven out by fixed claims?"[30] Berle and Means seemed to imagine that, as ownership grew dispersed, hapless shareholders came to find themselves disempowered, with management in control. But investors are fairly sophisticated about where they put their money—or else they do not hang onto their capital for very long—and therefore the people that run corporations need to make a compelling case to sceptical investors that they are going to get their money back, and more. Thus, managers seeking outside investment typically include a set of safeguards to demonstrate their commitment to shareholders, and are rewarded with a higher valuation, which gives them an advantage over their competitors. Those that fail to show sufficient devotion to shareholders are likely to be taken over, per Manne, and to pay a higher cost of capital. Through this invisible hand, corporations spontaneously come to be structured to serve shareholder interests.

A second point was about the ontological status of the corporation. Those that viewed the corporation as a social institution were deluding themselves.

> Contractual relations are the essence of the firm. . . . most organizations are simply legal fictions which serve as a nexus for a set of contracting relationships among individuals . . . Viewed in this way, it makes little or no sense to try to distinguish those things that are "inside" the firm (or any other organization) from those things that are "outside" of it. There is in a very real sense only a multitude of complex relationships (i.e. contracts) between the legal fiction (the firm) and the owners of labor, material and capital inputs and the consumers of output . . . We seldom fall into the trap of characterizing the wheat or stock market as an individual, but we often make this error by thinking about organizations as if they were persons with motivations and intentions.[31]

Manne had made clear the benefits of an unrestricted takeover market, arguing that the divine right of management could and often should be challenged from the outside. Jensen and Meckling had undermined the idea that there was any essential unity or integrity to the corporation, that there was an "inside" or an "outside." In combination, these arguments provided a rationale for the 1980s takeover wave, which essentially ended the reign of the conglomerate. If there was no compelling financial reason for keeping conglomerates together, then why not bypass their managers and break them back up?

The strategy of making acquisitions in unrelated industries had spread from being an aberration among a few peculiar firms to the dominant approach among large American manufacturers during the 1970s. By 1980, the median Fortune 500 firm operated in three distinct industry categories, and many were in dozens. Beatrice, originally a packaged-foods manufacturer culpable for La Choy Chinese foods and several other brands, came to include within its corporate boundaries Airstream travel trailers, Culligan plumbing equipment, Harman Kardon stereo equipment, Samsonite luggage, and many others. It was far from alone in its rococo approach to industrial diversification, as business schools and consulting firms spread the portfolio method of strategy broadly throughout the corporate sector. But such firms were chronically under-valued by the stock market, worth more as a set of parts than as a whole. All that was needed was a catalyst to bring about a wholesale re-shuffling of the industrial deck.[32]

The Reagan Administration provided such a catalyst. In 1982, the Justice Department's Antitrust Division issued a new set of merger guidelines that greatly reduced the effective barriers to intra-industry mergers. Since firms in the same industry are typically the most enthusiastic acquirers, this created a set of potential buyers for the parts of conglomerates. During the same year, the Supreme Court ruled in the *Edgar v. MITE* decision that the Illinois law regulating tender offers for domestic (i.e. Illinois-incorporated) corporations was unconstitutional under the Commerce Clause, and thus struck down similar state anti-takeover laws across the country. And the Administration had staffed the Justice Department, the Securities and Exchange Commission, the Office of Management and Budget, and the Council of Economic Advisors with those sympathetic to the views of Manne and other law-and-economics theorists. Thus, the regulatory climate was ripe for Manne's dream of an active market for corporate control to come true. And with the aid of innovations for financing takeovers, it did, in the form of the largest takeover wave in US history up to that point.

The 1980s merger movement is aptly characterized as a bust-up takeover wave. Between 1980 and 1990, 28% of the Fortune 500 largest manufacturers received tender offers, that is, offers by outsiders to buy control directly from shareholders—most of them hostile, and most successful. By the end of the decade, through bust-up takeovers and mergers, one-third of the largest corporations in the US had disappeared as independent entities. Conglomerates were particularly hard-hit. Given the so-called "conglomerate discount," an entrepreneur with access to bridge financing could make a killing by making a premium-priced tender offer for a diversified firm and immediately selling off its component parts to buyers in related industries. One financial firm's valuation model, used to calculate the degree to which a conglomerate was undervalued by the stock market, was whimsically titled "chop shop": like cars that are stolen and dismantled for parts, conglomerates could also be disassembled for profit.[33]

At the time, the bust-up takeover wave was something of a shock to corporate America. When one-third of the largest companies disappear in a brief period, it is clear that a moment of reckoning has arrived. There were several consequences of the takeover wave. First, companies became far more industrially focused. Figure 3.1 shows the average level of industrial diversification of the largest American manufacturers from 1980 to 2005. Firms became substantially more focused during the 1980s, and the trend continued through the subsequent decade and a half. By 1995, the median large manufacturer operated in a single broad industry category—not three, as in the early 1980s—and there has been no large-scale return to conglomeration, even as the threat of unwanted takeover subsided. The manufacturing conglomerate has been almost completely de-legitimated in the US, hanging on only in a few idiosyncratic cases (notably GE and United Technologies).[34]

Second, it became holy writ among management that the ultimate purpose of the corporation was "to create shareholder value." The phrase recurred in the mission statements of hundreds of American

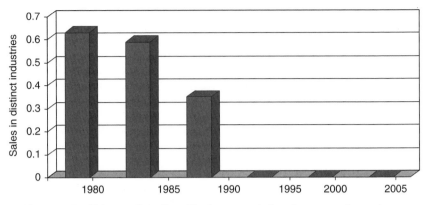

Figure 3.1 Declining median diversification across industries among the 500 largest
(Fortune 500) US manufacturers, 1980–2005 (see n. 34)

corporations: "We exist to create value for our share owners on a long-term basis by building a business that enhances The Coca-Cola Company's trademarks;" "Sara Lee Corporation's mission is to build leadership brands in consumer packaged goods markets around the world. Our primary purpose is to create long-term stockholder value." This, in turn, became the stated rationale for restructurings aimed at achieving corporate focus. When Ford spun off its large finance unit in 1997, the company's CEO explained it in terms of shareholder value: "We believe the market value of the The Associates is neither fully nor consistently reflected in Ford's stock price. Because the market views Ford as an automotive company, it has not fully recognized or rewarded us for our diversification in nonautomotive financial services businesses." Similarly, when Sara Lee announced plans to divest most of its manufacturing facilities to focus more on brand management, like Nike, its CEO stated: "Wall Street can wipe you out. They are the rule-setters. They do have their fads, but to a large extent there is an evolution in how they judge companies, and they have decided to give premiums to companies that harbor the most profits for the least assets. I can't argue with that."[35]

Perhaps the most compelling reason for executives' new-found religious devotion to shareholder value was the massive shift in compensation practices that occurred during the 1980s and 1990s. It was not just how much CEOs were paid that changed, but in what currency: stock options and other share-price-based compensation became like milk for growing children, where too much was never enough. Stock options are warrants to buy shares at a set price—in principle, the price of the stock on the day they were granted (although subsequent experience shows that many boards illicitly backdated the options to the point that the stock had achieved its lowest recent level). As a form of compensation, options were touted by corporate governance critics as a means to more effectively align the interests of managers and shareholders: the value of the options depends on how much the share price increases from the time of the grant, giving the options-holders reason to ensure that the share price goes up. During the 1990s, the average value of options grants to corporate CEOs increased by ten times, tying their pecuniary interests ever more tightly to share price. Few doubt that the ubiquitous use of stock options had the effect of focusing executive attention on the company's share price above all else. This was not entirely benign, of course: Federal Reserve Chairman Alan Greenspan argued that large grants "perversely created incentives to artificially inflate reported earnings in order to keep stock prices high and rising ... The incentives they created overcame the good judgment of too many corporate managers."[36] We return to this theme later in the chapter.

Finally, the prevalence of bust-up takeovers undermined the notion that organizational boundaries were somehow sovereign. Instead, it became clear that the boundaries were a provisional device. There was no essential unity or integrity to a particular corporation. It was, evidently, simply a nexus-of-contracts, just as the financial economists had stated. What had sounded like a radical provocation in the 1970s—that stock markets provided the best measure of a corporation, and that the boundaries were ephemeral—became the common sense of corporate America by the 1990s.

"Shareholder value" and the employment relation

The bust-up takeover wave, and the pervasive spread of executive compensation tied to share price, drove home the message that corporations existed to create shareholder value—or at least that they had better act as if they did. The result was a wholesale re-shuffling of the industrial deck. Consider some examples. Westinghouse Electric Company was founded in 1886 in Pittsburgh to build electric generating equipment and for decades was the major competitor of the General Electric Company, formed in 1891. Over the course of the twentieth century its businesses grew to include household appliances, radios, broadcasting equipment, locomotives, nuclear power facilities, office furniture, and financial services, among others, and by the early 1980s it employed nearly 150,000 workers. It was a stalwart of the Pittsburgh business community for decades, and in 1942 endowed a national science prize that generations of high school students competed to win. As with other conglomerates, however, its depressed stock valuation weighed on the company in the 1980s, and in 1993 the company recruited Michael Jordan, a former McKinsey consultant and Pepsi executive, to lead a turnaround. This included the divestment of various business units, the 1995 acquisition of CBS, and the 1996 acquisition of Infinity Broadcasting. By 1997 Westinghouse was primarily a media company, a transition that was ratified by disposing of its remaining industrial businesses, changing its name to CBS, and moving its corporate headquarters to New York City, at which point it employed 29,000 people. Two years later CBS was acquired by media giant Viacom; seven years after that it was spun off again as CBS.[37]

ITT, the prototype conglomerate once thought powerful enough to help topple the democratically elected government of Chile in 1973, went through multiple rounds of restructuring in the 1980s and split the remaining businesses into five separate companies in 1994. Its residual stub—primarily in the hotel and casino business—was ultimately acquired in 1997 by Starwood Lodging. And AT&T—the largest private employer in the US in the early 1980s, with 850,000 workers—was broken up into a long-distance company and seven Baby Bells in 1984; acquired and divested computer equipment-maker NCR in 1991 and 1996; became the nation's largest cable television provider by buying two cable companies in 1999 and 2000 (which it then sold off in 2002 to re-focus on its core competence); acquired a cellular phone company in 1994 that it spun off in 2001; and after a long slide in sales and employment (to below 50,000), ended up being acquired itself by SBC, one of its former Baby Bells, in 2005—which promptly changed its name to AT&T. Location, industry, identity, and employment, which had been relatively fixed during the corporate-industrial era, had become labile in the shareholder-value, post-industrial period.

The changing relation between firms and workers was reflected in the composition of the largest corporate employers. Table 3.1 shows the ten largest employers in the US in 1960, 1980, 2000, and 2007, the latest year for which data were available at the time of this writing.[38] Whereas seven of the top ten were manufacturers or oil firms in 1960, and six were in 1980, none was by 2007. (IBM and GE both derived most of their revenues from services by the late 1990s.) Employment became less concentrated among large firms over this period. The top ten firms in 1960 collectively employed the equivalent of 5% of the US nonfarm labor force in 1960, which declined slightly to 4.6% in 1980 and to below 3% in 2000. This also overstates the level of employment concentration, as the

Table 3.1. *Ten largest US-based corporate employers, 1960–2007*

1960	1980	2000	2007
GM	AT&T	Wal-Mart	Wal-Mart
AT&T	GM	GM	UPS
Ford	Ford	McDonald's	McDonald's
GE	GE	UPS	IBM
US Steel	Sears	Ford	Citigroup
Sears	IBM	Sears	Target
A&P	ITT	IBM	Sears Hldgs
Exxon	Kmart	GE	GE
Bethlehem Stl	Mobil	Kroger	Kroger
ITT	GTE	JC Penney	SBC/AT&T

largest firms outside the retail, restaurant, and telecom sectors employed many or most of their workers outside the US. Thus, of the dozen largest corporate employers of Americans in 2007, nine were in retail or food service: Wal-Mart, UPS, McDonald's, Target, Kroger, AT&T, Sears Holdings, Home Depot, Verizon, Walgreen, Lowe's, and Safeway. Put slightly more dramatically, Wal-Mart employed more Americans than the twelve largest manufacturers combined.[39]

Moreover, the duration of the bond between firms and employees was very different among these firms. According to the January 2004 Current Population Survey, the median employee in transportation equipment manufacturing (GM, Ford) had been with their employer for eight years; those in primary metals (US Steel) had median tenures of seven years; electrical equipment and appliance manufacturing employees (GE) had ten years' tenure; and workers in petroleum manufacturing (Exxon), eleven years. Large manufacturers, in short, maintained very long-term attachments with their typical employees. In contrast, the median employee in the food services industry (McDonald's) had been with their employer for 1.5 years, while those in retail (Wal-Mart, Sears, Target, Home Depot) logged three years on average. Service providers—with the notable exception of state and local governments—maintain substantially shorter tenures among their employees, and dramatically so in the case of retail and restaurants. They also provided lower wages, stingier benefits, and shorter career ladders—although of course this is much less true for some firms (e.g. IBM) than others (Wal-Mart).

In short, the largest employers in 1980 provided the prospect of long-term employment, health care coverage, and adequate retirement pensions—the hallmarks of the managerialist industrial firm. The largest employers in 2007 offered a polyester uniform that would last longer than the job itself. Moreover, even the vanguard employers of the post-war era began an aggressive program to renounce their former welfare-capitalist ways. "Neutron Jack" Welch, the widely admired CEO of GE, made it clear that employment at his company was not a lifelong commitment when he cut 100,000 jobs between 1981 and 1985. In a 2001 discussion with Harvard Business School students, he explained the new social contract that he had helped usher in: "If there's one thing you'll learn—and dot-coms have learned it in the last year—is no one can guarantee lifetime employment… You can give lifetime *employability* by training people, by making them adaptable, making them mobile to go other places to do other things. But you can't guarantee lifetime employment."[40] Not if you exist to create shareholder value, which GE emphatically did under Welch. Recall that Welch's predecessor Owen Young regarded shareholders as fixed claimants, with any "excess" profits returning to the firm itself and its employees and customers. Welch clearly regarded the shareholder as king—the residual claimant, entitled to a pot of earnings that increased by 15% every year.

The concept that the corporation exists to create shareholder value, and that it is nothing but a nexus of contracts, had clear implications for employees: they were all temps, whether they realized it or not. The economists Armen Alchian and Harold Demsetz stated it bluntly in a highly influential 1972 article that may have stood as the clearest academic rationale for the new employment relation. There is nothing magical about the relationship between a firm and an employee that distinguishes it from a customer's relation to a grocer, they argued: "I have no contract to continue to purchase from the grocer and neither the employer nor the employee is bound by any contractual obligations to continue their relationship. Long-term contracts between employer and employee are not the essence of the organization we call a firm."[41] Workers were free agents all along, even if they didn't recognize it. After the bust-ups of the 1980s, the idea that the corporation was nothing but a nexus, and that it had no special connection with its employees, became increasingly true. Firms became adept at retaining contractors rather than hiring permanent employees; outsourcing tasks outside their "core competence;" and engaging in more-or-less temporary alliances rather than vertical integration. The conglomerate had rendered dubious the idea that the corporation had an organic unity: parts came and went through acquisitions and divestitures, and to find a "core" or "essence" to an ITT was a fool's errand. The network organization took the next logical step: the corporation was not attached to particular parts, or even to particular members. It was, "in a very real sense," simply a nexus of contracts that existed to create shareholder value.

If employees could not expect to spend a career at GE, or any other company, then firms should no longer be held responsible for their well-being after they left. Thus, IBM froze the level of benefits offered through its defined benefit pension plan in 2006 so that additional years of service would not result in additional retirement payouts. GM and Sears quickly followed suit, and GM capped its retiree health care coverage so that increases would be borne by the retirees and their families, not the company. These were all part of a general trend to phase out corporate obligations to retirees and to move workers to portable personal accounts such as 401(k)s, which did not bind them to a particular firm. American companies would no longer be in the business of providing long-term benefits to employees, as they had done for half a century or more. As Boston College's Alicia Munnell put it, "Our employer-based social-welfare system is collapsing." Meanwhile, the former welfare capitalist firms had found themselves burdened by obligations that were assumed by governments in other advanced industrial nations, putting them at a competitive disadvantage. GM's CEO noted that the company's health-care and retirement plans were designed in the 1950s, when GM ruled the world's auto market. But "We're now subject to global competition. We're running against people who do not have these costs, because they are funded by the government."[42] When the heads of America's largest manufacturers speak longingly of socialism, we are clearly in a different world. The irony, of course, is that the firms themselves had created this system in part to forestall the "socialistic" government programs that now benefited their global competitors.

The practices previously described as corporate feudalism—long-term attachments between employees and firms, promotion ladders, social welfare benefits, and *noblesse oblige* on the part of corporate management—are now the stuff of nostalgia. The late 1990s saw a brief period of enthusiasm for the free-agent contract worker, liberated from the shackles of corporate servitude by their 401(k).[43] But this enthusiasm died down considerably with the burst of the "new economy" stock market bubble in 2000. Within a few months, the job title "Independent consultant" had become a synonym for "unemployed," and corporate co-dependence had regained its appeal. The transition from feudalism to market capitalism had been accompanied by decades of wrenching social upheaval, and it was not unreasonable to expect the same for the end of corporate feudalism, particularly given the limited social welfare institutions in the US—a theme we take up in Chapter 6. In contrast to Europe, investor-citizens in an ownership society could no longer rely on a social safety net from their employer or their government. They were free agents whether they liked it or not.

Shareholder value and corporate form

The new consensus around shareholder value made clear what the purpose of the corporation was, and this consensus had a decisive hand in shaping the transition of the American manufacturing economy. Financial considerations—market valuation—would drive choices about the boundaries and strategy of the firm. Firms should focus on doing one thing well, and that one thing was often determined by the stock market. Thus, if the stock market undervalues a combined car-and-finance company, then the solution is to split them into separate parts. Corporate executives were quite explicit about this: when ITT announced a plan to split into three separate companies in 1997 (following its prior five-way split a few years earlier), its CEO stated "We just think that having these three companies acting and operating and being evaluated in their own business environments will provide investors, analysts and those who deploy debt a simpler, more clear way to evaluate us." Had the split occurred, the remaining entity known as the ITT Corporation would have been primarily in the business of publishing phone directories in Europe.

By the same token, many valuation-driven changes led firms to shed physical assets, such as manufacturing facilities, in favor of "intellectual capital" (broadly construed). When Sara Lee "de-verticalized" in the late 1990s by selling off its manufacturing base to please Wall Street, the rationale was clear. "Slaughtering hogs and running knitting machines are businesses of yesterday," as the CEO put it, while shareholder-oriented corporations are in the business of ideas—in this case, designing and advertising bras and hot dogs to be manufactured and distributed by outside vendors. The new corporate model was that of the ironically titled "original equipment manufacturer" (OEM), in which the tasks of making and delivering physical goods are done by contractors. A Hewlett-Packard vice president explained why the company no longer needed to make its own PCs and instead contracted with generic "board stuffers," who assembled and distributed computers for HP and several of its rivals: "We own all of the intellectual property; we farm out all of the direct labor. We don't need to screw the motherboard into the metal box and attach the ribbon cable." Said another executive: "The consumer doesn't care if all the computers [bearing different brands] were made on the same production line. The only thing that matters is who will stand behind it." OEMs were, in effect, service businesses. They need never touch the physical products bearing their names. With the rise of offshore contract manufacturing, hundreds of American companies had reached the same conclusion.[44]

If the post-industrial corporation was a mere nexus, enmeshing various forms of intellectual capital (such as the trademarked slogan "Gentlemen prefer Hanes" for Sara Lee), how was it to be evaluated? The folk wisdom among corporate executives was that the stock market yields a higher valuation for intangible assets than tangible ones—advertising tag lines are more valuable than production lines. But it was also evident that companies were valued for their social capital, particularly when their intellectual capital was hard to parse. Biotechnology companies routinely took years to come up with a product, and years more to get it through the process of testing and evaluation by the government before it could come to market. How much is a revenue-free biotech firm like ImClone worth?

As a nexus of contracts, the corporation is also a network of affiliations, and this provides clues to a potency that is otherwise hard to assess. Thus, a sign that ImClone was likely to produce a blockbuster product was the fact that John Mendelsohn, the head of the prestigious

M. D. Anderson Cancer Center, served on its board. Another was that discriminating investors, such as pharmaceutical company Bristol Myers Squibb, had invested in it. The nodes in a corporation's nexus—its law firm, accounting firm, investment bank, alliance partners, investors, directors, top executives, major customers, and so on—implicitly provide their imprimatur for the firm. And while it is a cliché that one is known by the company one keeps, this cliché can have financial consequences: "At the height of his wealth and success, the financier Baron de Rothschild was petitioned for a loan by an acquaintance. Reputedly, the great man replied, 'I won't give you a loan myself; but I will walk arm-in-arm with you across the floor of the Stock Exchange, and you soon shall have willing lenders to spare.' "[45] Being seen in the company of Wilson Sonsini, Kleiner Perkins, Goldman Sachs, or Stanford University can boost your stock, and these ties are particularly important for new companies seeking to go public. Thus, savvy entrepreneurs may put more time into configuring the right constellation of affiliates to impress external evaluators than they do running the business itself. For a weightless post-industrial firm driven by stock market valuation, the network *is* the business. Pragmatically, if the right affiliations bring a higher valuation, then the entrepreneur has done her job, and the problem is solved.

There is a certain Potemkin Village aspect to this valuation-by-networks model.[46] Yet to the extent that corporations are attuned to the stock market, their leaders are prone to fine-tuning the appearance yielded by their networks. Corporate boards, for instance, routinely select members for their affiliations, as adding a former cabinet officer or CEO who serves on several other boards brings luster to any group. Research shows that companies seek to recruit such "star" directors when they face high levels of investor scrutiny, as indicated by receiving anti-management shareholder proposals, having a large financial analyst following, or being owned primarily by institutional investors rather than individuals. Well-connected directors have no discernible impact on profitability—directors rarely have the kind of direct managerial control necessary to influence operating performance—but they do significantly increase the esteem in which the company is held by outside analysts and executives, as measured by *Fortune Magazine*'s annual survey.[47] Thus, calculated choices of affiliates do seem to work in placating the investment community.

American cronyism[48]

By the late 1990s, the question of the purpose of the corporation had evidently been resolved once and for all in the United States. Corporations existed to create shareholder value. Moreover, the problem of managerialism—that non-owning professional managers might behave in ways contrary to shareholder value creation—had also been resolved, as the typical CEO derived the vast majority of his or her compensation from stock options and other forms of share ownership. But providing the right motivation was not sufficient to remove the corporation from its broader social context. "Create shareholder value" turned out to be insufficient guidance for running a company.

In the American system, share price is like a global positioning system for those managing corporations. Yet share price provides a peculiar measure of value because it is based on expectations about the future, rooted in present-day information. Prior performance is rewarded only in as far as it provides information about what future performance will be. Moreover, market value depends in large part on what other participants think market value *should* be. Managing for shareholder value therefore contains an essential perceptual component of anticipating how the market will react to the announcement of news about the company. It is a form of rhetoric where the audience to be persuaded is not a particular individual (say, a bank loan officer) but the market.

This does not mean that rampant dissembling is a sustainable approach to management, or that deception goes unpunished: outside monitors have incentives to uncover falsehoods and can make money by betting against firms that commit them. But research on corporate governance suggests that many managers systematically behave as if impression management were a core part of their task. For example, share buybacks—that is, a company's repurchase of its own shares, which reduces the number outstanding and signals that management believes its shares to be underpriced—are typically greeted by increases in share price. Yet savvy corporate managers in the 1990s found that it was possible to increase value merely by announcing a buyback program without subsequently following through. Descriptions of executive compensation plans crafted to convey allegiance to shareholder value boosted share prices more than the same plans described in more generic terms. And releases of so-called pro forma earnings announcements, giving more positive impressions than certified earnings figures, became rampant in the late 1990s. Corporate managers took seriously the rhetorical injunction to know one's audience. The most visible members of this audience are large institutional investors, the financial media, and financial analysts working at brokerage houses.[49]

The blueprint for the American system of corporate governance revolves around arm's-length relationships that prevent personal ties from influencing the operations of the various markets that comprise the system. Yet inevitably, social ties are widespread and influential. Studies of corporate boards find that shared directors—individuals serving on two or more boards—have been pervasive among American firms since the early part of the twentieth century, when Louis Brandeis warned about the undue influence of J. P. Morgan and other New York bankers. Among the 1,000 largest US companies in 2001, the average company that shared a director could reach every other company in under four steps. Conseco, considered one of the worst-governed companies, could reach Colgate Palmolive, one of the best, through this path: Conseco director David Harkins served on the Fisher Scientific board with Michael Dingman, who served on the Ford board with Robert Rubin, who served on the Citigroup board with Reuben Mark, then-CEO of Colgate Palmolive. An airborne flu virus that infected the Enron board in January 2001 could have made its way to 650 Fortune 1000 companies by May through monthly board meetings.

The significance of the small "diameter" of this network was foreshadowed by C. Wright Mills in *The Power Elite.* Mills argued that those in powerful positions often seem to know each other or to have acquaintances in common through their connections to the same organizations, and that they turned to each other for guidance on shared problems. As a result, responses to issues of corporate governance, or practices that are perceived to create shareholder value, spread rapidly among companies through shared directors. Dozens of studies in recent years document that shared directors act as conduits for the spread of practices, information, and norms, which accounts for some of the surprising conformity among corporate managers in their approaches to corporate governance. The adoption of takeover defenses, the creation of investor relations offices, and the adoption of compensation practices all have been shown to spread through a contagion process among boards via shared directors. Shared directors also created a means for collective political action; for instance, the legislatures of states with densely-connected corporate elites were more likely to adopt anti-takeover legislation in the 1980s than were legislatures in disconnected states.[50]

Moreover, to the extent that there is a "culture of the boardroom," it is evidently one that protects its own, as Mills might have anticipated. Thus, when Dr. Mendelsohn of the M. D. Anderson Cancer Center came under fire for serving on the boards of two companies implicated in investor fraud—Enron and ImClone—he found understanding and forgiveness among his director colleagues. Charles Miller, Chairman of the University of Texas Systems Board of Regents, which oversees the Center, had himself served on a dozen corporate and non-profit boards. As he put it: "We could all see, 'There but for the grace of God go I.'" The president of Rice University echoed: "All of us at one time or another have been up to our elbows in alligators." Unlike the Amish, corporate directors evidently do not practice shunning.[51]

Directors' understandings of how best to create shareholder value were not an immaculate conception. Jack Grubman, the former star telecommunications analyst at Citigroup's Salomon Smith Barney unit, attended board meetings to advise the directors of a half-dozen telecom firms that he followed and touted to clients, including WorldCom (subsequently the largest bankrupt in American history), Global Crossing (also bankrupt), McLeodUSA (ditto), and others. The easy relationship between Grubman and the telecom sector he policed worked both ways.

Salomon preferentially allocated shares of firms about to make an initial public offering (IPO) to the personal accounts of telecom executives such as Bernie Ebbers, acquisitive CEO of WorldCom. IPO shares typically shoot up in value on the first day of trading and generally provide an immediate payoff—what one investment banker called "free money." Ebbers made $11 million from his IPO shares. Ebbers's firm in turn sent tens of millions of dollars in fees to Salomon for investment banking services (although Salomon insisted there was no quid pro quo). Moreover, the value of an IPO firm depends in part on its affiliations, as we have seen: an announcement of a contract or alliance with WorldCom during the late 1990s, for instance, would generally enhance the expected profitability of a telecom firm about to do an IPO, and thus the value of its shares. The incentives created through the web of connections among directors, executives, analysts, and investment bankers would seem to favor the Potemkin Village approach to "creating shareholder value."[52] In the next chapter, I describe more fully the conflicts of interest created by the new financial conglomerates.

Far from being a system of impersonal transactions based purely on merit, then, the American system of corporate governance turns out to be thick with social connections among the most important decision makers. Corporate directors and the executives they oversee, financial analysts, investment bankers, and state legislators responsible for creating corporate law, are connected by more or less dense ties that belie the schematic portrayal of an anonymous meritocracy policed by independent analysts, auditors, and legislators. But while the financial incentives for promulgating corporate Potemkin Villages may produce speculative bubbles, as we saw during the late 1990s, such excesses will ultimately give way.

Conclusion

The transition to post-industrialism, coupled with the dominance of the shareholder value ideology, has meant the twilight of the corporation as a social entity in the US. It could have been otherwise. So-called corporate feudalism lives on elsewhere in the world, and even some private companies in the US, such as SAS Institute, continue to provide the kind of "company town" welfare capitalist benefits that characterized some early twentieth-century US corporations.[53] But for large-scale employers, it is hard to imagine this system coming back. Notions of corporate social responsibility are built on an attachment to a particular place. But shareholder value-oriented multinationals are, in the memorable phrasing of Martin Wolf, "rootless cosmopolitans" with only vestigial ties to nationality or employment.[54] Hershey may still reside in Pennsylvania, but its competitors in the consumer packaged goods industry, like Sara Lee, are effectively placeless.

The subsequent history of Hershey reveals that even companies explicitly seeking to balance commitments to shareholders and community may have a difficult time. In October 2007, five years after the Milton Hershey School Trust had launched its abortive attempt to sell the company, the reconstituted board of the Trust released an unusual public statement saying, in part, "the Trust is not satisfied with the Company's results. The Company has been underperforming both the market and its own stated expectations" and the Trust had accordingly lost "more than $1 billion in market value during this period of unsatisfactory performance." This came on the heels of an announcement the CEO would be stepping down; the Trust, in the meantime, had opened (unsuccessful) discussions with Cadbury about the renewed possibility of a merger—subject to the constraint that the Trust would retain voting control of the company. A month later, the Trust fired six Hershey directors, and two more resigned, leaving just the incoming CEO and a representative of the Trust. By mid-2008 Hershey faced new competition as its former suitor Wrigley merged with its arch-rival Mars. Analysts urged the company to consider a sale to maintain its global competitiveness, but the Chairman of the Trust repeatedly vowed that Hershey would remain independent, evidently regardless of the economic consequences: "Simply put: We will not sell the Hershey Co." By mid-2008, Hershey's shares had slid back to where they were six years before, and the Trust was seemingly no closer to a workable strategy to diversify its holdings on behalf of the orphans.[55]

Corporations in the US have been transformed by information and communication technologies and the shift to a shareholder value orientation. But the finance industry has seen an even greater shift, as the basic model of financial intermediation has undergone a fundamental transformation. In the next chapter, we examine how the growth of financial markets has changed the nature of financial intermediation and its most important institutions, as banks rooted in particular places have been replaced by placeless financial markets.

4

From Banks to Markets: How Securitization Ended the "Wonderful Life"

Banking in the US has seen a fundamental shift since the 1980s, as the traditional banking function has been increasingly supplanted by market-based intermediation. The result has been a large-scale restructuring of the financial services industry and a blurring of the boundaries around what we think of as *finance*. The long-standing distinction between commercial banking—taking in deposits and making loans—and investment banking—underwriting and dealing in securities—has effectively dissolved through deregulation and the expansive use of securitization. Moreover, the range of players participating in the "financial services industry" has become vast, from traditional industrial conglomerates like GE, to free-standing financial specialists dealing in home mortgages like Countrywide (prior to its 2008 acquisition by Bank of America), to murky utility players like hedge funds. "Wall Street" is now everywhere, as gas station proprietors speculate in oil futures to hedge their business against shocks in the Middle East, American homeowners find their mortgages owned by Norwegian villagers, and Midwestern toll roads end up being owned by Australian pension funds. And traditional notions of risk and power have been wildly reshuffled thanks to the financial revolution, rendering our old maps of the financial system deceptive and our regulatory system comically mismatched to the entities it is supposed to oversee.[1]

The credit crisis that began in 2007 illustrates the new conundrum of market-based finance. In a one-week period around Halloween 2007, the CEOs of one of the biggest commercial banks and one of the biggest investment banks in the world both lost their jobs due to multi-billion dollar losses on collateralized debt obligations (CDOs). CDOs are bonds ultimately backed by bundles of loans such as subprime mortgages (that is, mortgages held by relatively risky borrowers). As housing prices across the US began to reverse their upward surge from earlier in the decade, many mortgage holders found themselves owing more on their house than it was worth, and a wave of defaults began, resulting in rapid declines in the value of the bonds backed by their payments. At Citigroup, Charles Prince—handpicked successor to Sandy Weill, Citigroup's architect—resigned when it was discovered that the bank had to write down $11 billion in CDOs on its books. And at Merrill Lynch, Stanley O'Neal, widely credited with a profitable strategic re-orientation at "mother Merrill," also lost the support of his board due to unexpected multi-billion dollar losses after Merrill had succeeded in becoming the largest issuer of CDOs on Wall Street. Among the many remarkable aspects of these events was that CDOs barely existed twenty years ago, yet they were now credited with job losses of top executives at several of the world's largest financial firms, including banks, broker-ages, and insurance companies. And their reverberations beyond Wall Street were even more profound, as investors around the world were surprised to learn that bundles of American mortgages—considered a stodgy investment, nearly as safe as Treasury bills—were far riskier than they thought.[2] Meanwhile, millions of homeowners across the US were threatened with foreclosure, decimating neighborhoods from Detroit to southern California.

As the mortgage crisis broadened to become a full-scale global financial crisis, the extent to which "financial services" had been transformed was revealed. From the financial regulations of the Great Depression to the 1990s, finance had been divided among a number of separate industries including commercial banking, investment banking, consumer and mortgage banking, and insurance. By the early years of the twenty-first century, "financial services" had become a vast meta-industry encompassing a surprising range of competitors. The list of companies that had failed, or been taken over under duress due to the financial crisis, included AIG, Washington Mutual, IndyMac, Wachovia, Fannie Mae, Freddie Mac, Countrywide, New Century, and many more.[3] Most stunningly, every major free-standing investment bank had disappeared. The Fed arranged for JP Morgan to acquire Bear Stearns in March 2008. Lehman Brothers filed the largest bankruptcy in US history in September 2008, while at the same time Merrill Lynch was agreeing to be acquired by Bank of America. Within a week, Goldman Sachs and Morgan Stanley announced plans to convert themselves to bank holding companies, thereby effectively ending the era of free-standing investment banks in the US.

The fallout from the financial crisis spread well beyond financial services to include home builders, auto dealers, and the broader consumer economy, which had counted on consumers cashing out their rising home values to fund their shopping sprees. Contraction in the credit market led to abrupt drops in consumption, tipping dozens of retailers into bankruptcy and sending the American auto industry to the brink of oblivion. The financial revolution had managed to turn the most plain-vanilla product—the home mortgage—into an exotic financial instrument whose risks were beyond the ken of even Wall Street's best minds, and whose fluctuations could place the entire economy at risk.

The transformation of banking may not have been evident from the outside prior to the financial crisis. There were still companies called "banks," but they were largely shells—in effect, portals for financial markets. They still maintained branches with marble-columned fronts and august names, but these were like buildings in historic districts in which the façade is retained but the structure within is thoroughly transformed. Activities traditionally separated by law—investment banking, commercial banking, insurance—had been combined, while activities traditionally combined—originating loans and holding them on the balance sheet—had been divided.

The traditional separation of industry and finance had also been thoroughly breached. The *Wall Street Journal* reported that by 2000, "Almost 40% of the earnings of the companies in the Standard & Poor's

500-stock index in 2000 came from lending, trading, venture investments and other financial activity," one-third of which was attributable
to non-financial firms like Enron and GE.[4] *Fortune Magazine*'s ranking
of the ten largest diversified financial corporations in 2006 illustrated
the diversity of "finance": it included GE (which derived one-third of
its profits from commercial and consumer finance); American Express;
Countrywide (since acquired by Bank of America); Marsh & McLennan
(parent of an insurance company, a benefits consultancy, a private inves-
tigator, and a mutual fund); insurance giant Aon; student loan provider
Sallie Mae; commercial finance firm CIT Group; real estate services
provider CB Richard Ellis; conglomerate Leucadia; and New Century
Financial, the now-bankrupt mortgage issuer.

  And after two decades of consolidation, the traditional money-center
commercial banks were bigger than ever. A company called Bank of
America, the largest bank by deposits in 1982, was again the largest in
2007. Yet the 2007 version of "Bank of America" was the successor to
Charlotte-based North Carolina National Bank, which over the course
of a two decade-long acquisition program swallowed up First Repub-
licBank of Dallas, C&S/Sovran of Virginia, Boatmens' Bankshares of St.
Louis, Barnett Banks of Florida, San Francisco-based Bank of America,
and Boston's FleetBoston, along with dozens of smaller acquisitions.
The result was, in effect, the first genuinely national bank in US history, gathering nearly 10% of the nation's bank deposits through its
roughly 6,000 branches. JP Morgan Chase followed from the mergers
of many of the largest New York banks, including Chase Manhattan (# 3
in 1982), Manufacturers Hanover (# 4), JP Morgan (# 5), and Chemical Bank (# 7), as well as First Chicago (# 10) and National Bank of
Detroit (# 24). The latter two had merged in 1995 and were acquired by
Ohio's Bank One (# 37) in 1998, which was itself acquired by JP Morgan
Chase in 2001. Citibank, unlike its two main competitors, had largely
avoided intra-industry consolidation within the US and instead ended
up creating a vast conglomerate spanning commercial banking, global
retail banking, brokerage, and investment banking. By mid-2008, these
three banks each had assets of over $1.2 trillion, vastly outstripping their

remaining competitors in size.[5] The Big Three had also been given the task of buying up many of their stricken competitors: JP Morgan Chase ended up acquiring the remaining assets of investment bank Bear Stearns and Washington Mutual (formerly the largest savings and loan in the US), among others, while Bank of America acquired investment house Merrill Lynch and Countrywide, previously the nation's largest mortgage lender.

Paradoxically, while "Wall Street" had become more powerful than ever, and the biggest banks operated at an unprecedented scale, it was also clear that particular institutions and individuals were not in control. Even the CEOs of the biggest banks in the world could be fired if they failed to create shareholder value—or failed to understand the risks held in their portfolios. When Louis Brandeis described the dominant "money trust" at the center of early twentieth-century finance capitalism, he could name three New York banks and the individuals who ran them: George F. Baker at First National, James Stillman at National City, and J. P. Morgan and his company. But it would be impossible to do that now, as new players and industries rise and fall with remarkable speed. In spite of the apparent stability at the apex of American banking, the power structure and most important players in finance have shifted in the past twenty-five years, and no entity or "bank trust" has a chokehold on capital, from the hedge fund district of Greenwich, Connecticut, to the new global banking capital of Charlotte, North Carolina, to the abandoned mortgage banks of southern California. Over a decade ago, former SEC Chairman Richard Breeden noted that in other industrialized countries "investment decision-making is concentrated in the hands of just a few dozen gatekeepers at banks and investment firms," whereas the US has "literally hundreds of gatekeepers in our increasingly decentralized capital markets."[6] Borrowers that are denied loans by a bank can turn to GE, or a hedge fund, or an Australian pension fund.

In this chapter I argue that the basic function of financial intermediation changed fundamentally due to securitization—turning loans and other obligations into securities. Mortgages, commercial loans, receivables, insurance payouts, and lawsuit settlements could all be turned into securities relatively cheaply; financial firms had a strong incentive to maintain the flow of new issuances of these securities; and institutional investors around the world created a demand for them. A result was that debt securities far outstripped the stock market in value.[7] Thus, finance became both larger in scale and more decentralized than ever before. A consequence of decentralization and the reorganization of the financial services industry was that many activities were beyond the scope of their traditional regulators, leaving governmental bodies largely outgunned in their efforts to exercise control. Some entities such as Citigroup came to be regulated by multiple entities (potentially including state banking regulators, the Federal Reserve, the SEC, and the New York Stock Exchange), while others faced only minimal regulation. By 2005, most subprime mortgages were issued by companies facing no federal regulation, such as free-standing mortgage firms that operated through independent brokers.[8] And hedge funds, once a boutique industry catering to wealthy individuals, grew to massive scale in a few years, in part through their artful avoidance of oversight as they expanded their investor market to include pension funds and other institutional investors. The funds are almost inevitably described by journalists as "lightly regulated," and they typically elect to organize their legal shell outside the US in the Cayman Islands.

The risks in the new financial system are unpredictable, as the financial crisis demonstrated. Firms in bankruptcy were traditionally among the riskiest possible borrowers. Yet such firms can access the capital markets at attractive interest rates by securitizing their receivables (that is, issuing bonds backed by the expected payments borrowers will receive from those purchasing their products): the value of receivables is premised on the creditworthiness of the purchaser, not the borrower, so the risk of default may be quite low. Conversely, mortgage-backed securities had historically been among the safest investments: homeowners normally place the highest priority on paying their mortgage, and traditional issuers such as Fannie Mae had relatively strong safeguards in place to qualify their loans. Yet through the expansive use of securitization and clever methods of dividing mortgage pools into different slices with different risk profiles, CDOs became wildly risky, with many of them losing most of their value as the wave of defaults took hold.[9]

In the rest of this chapter I will survey the new world of banking and how it has been reshaped through securitization. I first describe traditional commercial banking, the challenge from securities markets, and the diverse restructuring paths taken by the main players. I then describe two of the major beneficiaries of the growth of financial markets: investment banks and mutual funds. Both grew enormously during the past two decades through the increased participation in financial markets by buyers (particularly household retirement investments) and issuers (through the upsurge in securitization, among other things). Alternative financial firms also arose to challenge the traditional banking and investment functions, including asset finance firms that lent to companies, mortgage firms that take up the space formerly occupied by banks and S&Ls, and hedge funds that both work with and challenge traditional investment banks and mutual funds. I close with a description of the evolution of Citigroup and some of the conflicts of interest raised by breached industry boundaries. In Chapter 6 I build on this discussion to analyze in more detail the mortgage crisis and its impact on households and the broader economy.

Banking: It's a wonderful life

The basic function of banking is to channel funds from savers to users. Savers might be households or companies with cash on hand, and banks pay a fee to take in their savings as deposits (which are liabilities on the banks' balance sheets). Users might be businesses or potential homeowners that need a loan to buy property or make investments in their business, for which they pay the bank a higher fee. (For the banks, these loans are assets.) Banks profit on the difference between the interest they pay to gather deposits and the interest they charge borrowers. This is the simple model explained by Jimmy Stewart as George Bailey in the bank run scene in *It's a Wonderful Life*. Panicky depositors had lined up at the local Bailey Building & Loan hoping to empty their accounts before everyone else did, while George tries to persuade them to leave their deposits in place:

> No, but you... you... you're thinking of this place all wrong. As if I had the money back in a safe. The money's not here. Your money's in Joe's house... right next to yours. And in the Kennedy house, and Mrs. Macklin's house, and a hundred others. Why, you're lending them the money to build, and then, they're going to pay it back to you as best they can. Now what are you going to do? Foreclose on them?

By explaining that depositors were funding the mortgages of their friends and neighbors, George was able to stanch the run and save the town from the predations of the heartless big banker, Mr. Potter.

For most of the twentieth century, banks in the US had been geographically and industrially fragmented by law. The McFadden Act of 1927 prohibited banks from operating branches outside their headquarters state, and it required nationally chartered banks to follow the branching laws of their home states. Thus, until the 1980s, commercial banks were generally prohibited from opening branches in more than one state, and states had idiosyncratic local regulations. Indeed, some (like Iowa) prohibited banks from operating more than a single branch. The result was a remarkably localized industry with multiple layers of regulation. Although banks might bear grand names such as "Bank of America," their ability to gather deposits beyond a geographically constrained area was severely limited. (They could, of course, also issue securities and thus limit their local dependence.) More distinctively, and in contrast to banks in the rest of the world, American commercial banks were prohibited from owning stocks and dealing in securities. Bankers found ways to evade this restriction through subsidiaries and other affiliates in the early part of the twentieth century, and this intermingling was regarded by many as the source of much of the financial meltdown that precipitated the Great Depression. Thus, after the Glass–Steagall Act of 1933, commercial banks and investment banks could not be affiliated through the same holding company, leading to the division of the fabled

House of Morgan into JP Morgan (parent of Morgan Guaranty Trust, a commercial bank) and Morgan Stanley (an investment bank) in 1935.[10]

The separation of commercial and investment banking strictly limited the financial services that commercial banks could provide to their corporate clients. And by the fourth decade of the century, the biggest corporations were largely self-financing, relying on retained earnings rather than bank loans as their primary source of funds. In spite of this, commercial banks maintained a central position in the corporate economy, particularly the so-called "money center" banks that catered to large corporate clients. To a remarkable extent, these banks were localized in Manhattan. Table 4.1 lists the twenty biggest banks in 1982 by assets.

The dominance of New York reflected a number of factors. First, New York City was by far the most popular headquarters location for major corporations, with three times as many New York Stock Exchange-listed companies housed there as in Chicago. Multinationals were especially concentrated in New York, and those headquartered elsewhere often maintained a New York office for their financial functions (e.g. General Motors). Second, New York also had Wall Street, allowing two-stop (if not one-stop) shopping for corporate finance. Finally, New York state laws were favorable for corporate banking. Corporate clients are not limited to their local banks for large-scale debt financing, and thus New York City ended up as an industrial district for both commercial and investment banking oriented toward the largest firms.

Yet geographic restrictions meant that locally based commercial banks could thrive virtually anywhere there were businesses, and the number of banks in a city was highly correlated with the number of other kinds of companies headquartered there. Indeed, for decades commercial banks served as social and political hubs for their local industrial economies. One sign of this was the composition of their boards of directors. The roster of bank directors served as a virtual Who's Who of local business elites. In the mid-1980s, for instance, the board of Bank of Boston was staffed by top executives of Computervision, Dennison Manufacturing, General Cinema, Gillette, Prime Computer, Raytheon,

Table 4.1. *Twenty largest bank holding companies by assets, 1982*

Rank	Name	Headquarters	Assets ($bn)
1	Bank of America	San Francisco	121
2	Citicorp	New York	119
3	Chase Manhattan	New York	78
4	Manufacturers Hanover	New York	59
5	JP Morgan	New York	53
6	Continental Illinois	Chicago	46
7	Chemical New York	New York	45
8	First Interstate	Los Angeles	37
9	Bankers Trust	New York	34
10	First Chicago	Chicago	33
11	Security Pacific	Los Angeles	33
12	Wells Fargo	San Francisco	23
13	Crocker National	San Francisco	22
14	Marine Midland	Buffalo	19
15	Mellon	Pittsburgh	18
16	Interfirst	Dallas	17
17	First National Boston	Boston	17
18	Irving Bank	New York	16
19	Northwest Bancorporation	Minneapolis	15
20	First Bank System	Minneapolis	15

Source: *Moody's Bank and Finance Manual*, 1982.

and Wyman Gordon—all Fortune 500 companies headquartered in Massachusetts. Pittsburgh's Mellon Bank similarly boasted executives of Air Products, Allegheny International, Alcoa, Joy Manufacturing, PPG Industries, Quaker State Oil, Sperry, and US Steel, also local companies. The same was true in Chicago, Cleveland, Atlanta, Dallas, and most other major cities: each had one or two major commercial banks that served as connecting points for the local business elite. And at the apex of this network of interconnected directors were the New York banks, whose boards were both very big (about twice the size of other corporate boards) and staffed with elites from major multinationals.[11]

The rationale for these large star-studded boards had two parts. First, banks needed to signal their status to corporate clients. A well-connected board was an effective way to convey a bank's credibility, giving it the implicit endorsement of the firms led by its outside directors. Second, the board could provide broad intelligence about the economy to help guide the bank's decision-making. CEOs of Fortune 500 companies might not be especially useful in vetting particular loans, but they did have forward-looking information about industries in different locales—including overseas. One has to imagine that the quality of the post-meeting gossip at a Chase Manhattan board meeting was extraordinary.

Bank boards also served a latent function as a meeting place for the corporate elite. Monthly meetings of the heads of the most significant local businesses and nonprofits provided a convenient device for, say, fundraising for the local art museum, or drumming up support for an Olympics bid. Indeed, for decades banks served as staging areas for philanthropy: local worthies routinely left it to bank trust departments to guide their giving, and such giving tended to stay local, often directed toward the charities favored by the board. Moreover, bank boards could serve a political function as well, allowing elites to come to understandings outside the public eye. Sociologist Mark Mizruchi found that, indeed, firms whose CEOs served on the same bank boards also tended to support the same political candidates through their PAC contributions. Local bank boards, in short, were like Facebook for the corporate elite.[12]

Disintermediation and the challenge from markets

The limitations of the "wonderful life" model of banking became apparent by the 1970s. Blue chip corporate borrowers could fund their short-term needs by issuing commercial paper at relatively low interest rates, thus bypassing the banks. And in an inflationary economic environment, legal caps on the interest rates that banks could pay to depositors made savings accounts an unattractive option. One response by the banks was rapid overseas expansion during the 1970s. By world standards,

American banks were surprisingly provincial prior to the 1960s: fewer than ten had branches outside the US in 1960, and most of these were operated by Citibank (an early and voracious globalizer). But by the 1970s, most large banks had begun to open overseas branches, and by the middle of the decade half of the largest banks' profits came from business outside the US—more than three-quarters in the case of Chase Manhattan. The foreign assets of American banks increased 100-fold from 1960 to 1980, at which point over 150 US banks operated foreign branches. By the early 1980s banks—American money center banks in particular—had become the largest source of external fund flows to developing countries, according to the World Bank.[13]

The globalization of American banking rapidly switched into reverse in late 1982, when Mexico suspended payment on its bank debt and triggered a wave of defaults among developing countries. The largest banks—particularly Citibank—were the hardest hit, and some were at risk of insolvency. As John Reed put it some years later, when he took the Chairman's job at Citi in 1984, the bank had $4.7 billion in capital and $16 billion in exposure in heavily indebted countries, a situation that took eight years to recover from.[14] Dozens of American banks exited from international markets, and by the early years of the twenty-first century, the big three were responsible for nearly all the overseas business of US-based banks. (In the meantime, "low-income countries" were re-christened as "emerging markets," and market-based investment replaced bank loans as the primary source of capital inflows.)

But the domestic market posed its own challenges, as the basic model of taking in deposits and lending them out again at a higher interest rate was being undermined on both sides. On the asset side, credit-worthy borrowers found that they could go directly to markets or to other alternatives that offered debt at lower interest rates than banks. The largest corporate borrowers did this first, through the issuance of commercial paper, but the bar for "creditworthy" became progressively lower as better information technology made available more extensive data about prospective borrowers. Banks run on information, and one of the advantages enjoyed by banks was access to thick information about prospective clients. But with electronic credit scoring, and the prospect of combining loans and reselling them, the cost advantage of banks was reduced. By the mid-1990s, the value of outstanding commercial paper roughly equaled the value of commercial and industrial loans held by all banks. Eventually this logic trickled down to the household level. George Bailey from *It's a Wonderful Life* might want to look his customers in the eye and stop by their house before making a loan, but a FICO score is just about as effective, and a whole lot cheaper, allowing borrowers to access lenders from virtually anywhere in the world. Standardized methods made it easier to do lending on a wholesale level rather than a retail level. Thus, Reed predicted that ultimately banking would be reduced to "a little bit of application code in a smart network," a prophecy that proved more or less true by the time of the mortgage bubble earlier in this decade.[15] The results were dramatic: banks' share of the nation's credit declined from 40% in 1982 to 19% two decades later.[16] Business lending had not entirely disappeared—barber shops, after all, are still going to go to banks, and lines of credit are still essential for most corporations—but the banking function was much transformed.

On the liability side of the equation, corporate and household savers found that they could get much better returns outside the traditional banking system. Money market mutual funds allowed households to invest indirectly in commercial paper with relatively high returns and relatively low risk. And once they had dabbled in money markets, the doors were opened to alternative market-based savings vehicles, such as equity mutual funds. The Federal Reserve's triennial Survey of Consumer Finances reported that the proportion of households with savings accounts declined from 77% in 1977 to 44% in 1989. At that point, households held 30% of their financial assets in banks. By 2004, this had declined to 17%. On the other hand, the proportion of households that invested in mutual funds increased from under 6% in 1980 to nearly half by 2000, and the proportion of household financial assets in stocks, bonds, mutual funds, and retirement accounts increased from 50% in 1989 to 69% in 2004. Banks found themselves chronically starved for deposits, as households had taken to heart the notion that markets are safe and lucrative relative to banks. By 2006, the ratio of deposits to assets on hand at banks was at the lowest level since the Great Depression.[17]

In short, the basic franchise of commercial banking—taking in deposits and making loans—was being fundamentally undermined on both sides by market-based financing. As Dick Kovacevich, CEO of Wells Fargo, put it in the 1990s, "The banking industry is dead, and we ought to just bury it."[18]

One of the consequences of the retreat from traditional corporate lending has been a change in corporate governance for the banks. Bank boards had been large and well-connected for decades, providing fodder for conspiracy theorists from Brandeis and his "money trust" onward. Chase Manhattan's board of directors included the CEOs of over a dozen multinationals in 1982, and between them the twenty-three directors of JP Morgan served on over four dozen corporate boards. (Alan Greenspan, for instance, served on the boards of Alcoa, Automatic Data Processing, General Foods, and Mobil in addition to that of JP Morgan in 1982.) Similar numbers held for all the major money center banks. But as banks reduced their domestic corporate lending, they shrunk their boards and limited their recruitment of well-connected CEOs. By 2007, the board of JP Morgan Chase—the last one standing after mergers among a half-dozen money center banks—was down to twelve directors, including a mere three outside CEOs. Bank of America's board boasted seven retirees among its seventeen members and bore few of the hallmarks of a major power broker.[19]

Some banks initially responded to the decline in their lending franchise by morphing into investment banks. JP Morgan and Bankers Trust, for instance, gained permission from the Federal Reserve to underwrite certain kinds of bonds in the late 1980s, and by the mid-1990s they were significant corporate bond underwriters. (Later in the decade investment banks in turn were allowed to issue loans in addition to underwriting.) Others pursued an alternative approach, recasting themselves as broad "financial service providers" and offering a range of client services. But many of those that wanted to stay in traditional banking embraced securitization broadly, first with home mortgages, then with car loans, credit card receivables, and eventually corporate loans. Securitization provided an alternative business model for banks: rather than making loans and holding them on their balance sheet, banks could originate loans and then re-sell them, to be turned into securities and marketed to institutional investors. This became particularly prevalent for loans made to finance corporate buyouts, as more than half the loans made for buyouts in 2006 (the peak of the recent boom) were bundled together and re-sold as "collateralized loan obligations" (CLOs)—an instrument that Michael Milken hailed as one of the most important innovations of the past quarter-century.[20] Thanks in part to securitization, the bond market (valued at $27 trillion in late 2007) had become far larger than the stock market, and perhaps of greater economic significance. Securitization had in effect provided a lifeline for banks, premised on a new hybrid business model that straddled commercial and investment banking.

But securitization also provided another way to avoid banks, by dividing up the value chain of banking into separate free-standing providers. If borrowers can be vetted by computers using readily available credit files, and if loans are going to be quickly re-sold rather than held on the balance sheet, then why use banks? In the mortgage market, the large majority of home buyers went to brokers rather than bankers for loans by the 2000s, and these brokers in turn often dealt with free-standing mortgage firms rather than banks. Originating loans, servicing them (that is, collecting payments from borrowers), securitizing them, and buying them—functions traditionally bundled together in a single bank in the "wonderful life" model—could be unbundled and performed by separate specialist firms. The same model provided an implicit threat to the basic business of banking, a tension that has yet to be fully resolved.

Deregulation and consolidation

The pressures on the banking industry continued to mount over the course of the 1980s. The large banks that had lent heavily to developing countries survived, but some were still limping at the end of the decade. Continental Illinois, the nation's sixth-largest bank in 1982, had failed in 1984; First Republic (the biggest bank in Texas) failed four years later, as did Bank of New England three years after that. The latter two banks had been sunk by their undiversified loan portfolios concentrated in local real estate, which illustrated the risk of geographically segmented banking. Economists and bankers had long objected to the geographic restrictions on banking. Interest rates on loans might vary wildly by place, with loans of similar risks being priced differently in Iowa compared to California. Moreover, local concentration of banking also concentrated the risks for loans held in the bank's portfolio, leaving them susceptible to failure, as with First Republic and Bank of New England. It was simply not obvious why the US could get by with eight big accounting firms (or six, or four) and a half-dozen major investment banks (or two, or none), but needed over 12,000 locally based commercial banks in 1990. There were counter-pressures against consolidation, of course: local bankers had reason to fear national-scale competitors, and they were often influential with local politicians and state regulators (who stood to be out of a job if banking lost its local flavor).[21] But by the early 1990s, it appeared that the pressures on banking to consolidate were too great to resist.

The regulations maintaining geographic segmentation began to crumble in the 1980s, as "multibank holding companies" (MBHCs) were allowed to own different banks operating in more than one state. The Riegle–Neal "Interstate Banking and Branching Efficiency Act" of 1994 repealed the McFadden Act's prohibition on interstate bank-ing, and a subsequent wave of interstate bank mergers created first super-regional and—with NCNB/Bank of America—national networks of retail branches for banks. Bank of America had become much like McDonald's, offering a familiar format nationwide.

An unexpected outcome of the banking merger movement was that New York lost its place as the undisputed banking capital, while North Carolina became a global banking center. Table 4.2 shows the distrib-ution of the twenty largest banks in 2007 and the surprising shift in geography from twenty-five years earlier.

Table 4.2. *Twenty largest banks by consolidated assets, 2007*

Rank	Name	Headquarters	Assets ($bn)
1	Bank of America	Charlotte, NC	1,290
2	JP Morgan Chase	New York	1,244
3	Citibank	New York	1,233
4	Wachovia	Charlotte, NC	557
5	Wells Fargo	San Francisco	445
6	US Bank	Minneapolis	226
7	HSBC US	Wilmington, DE	182
8	Suntrust	Atlanta	172
9	National City	Cleveland	142
10	Regions Bank	Birmingham, AL	134
11	Citizens Financial	Providence, RI	133
12	State Street	Boston	131
13	BB&T	Winston-Salem, NC	126
14	PNC	Pittsburgh	120
15	Bank of NY/Mellon	New York	113
16	Capital One	Mclean, MA	96
17	Keybank	Cleveland	93
18	LaSalle	Chicago	73
19	Comerica	Dallas	60
20	Bank of the West	San Francisco	59

Source: Federal Reserve "Large Commercial Banks," September 2007.

New York still had commercial banks, but it was no longer the dominant industrial district. Chicago had none in the top ten, California had only one, while # 1 and # 4 were both headquartered in Charlotte, North Carolina. Christopher Marquis of the Harvard Business School finds that this unexpected distribution reflected the history of bank regulations in the American states: some states (notably North Carolina and Ohio) had effectively provided a training ground for acquisitive banks, so that when the regulations against interstate banking were removed and the consolidation movement began in earnest, banks from those states had a head start. On the other hand, after a wave of bank mergers and acquisitions, most big cities were left without a major local commercial bank. Using a size cutoff of $20 billion in assets, this list included Los Angeles, Houston, Philadelphia, Phoenix, San Antonio, San Diego, and San Jose. In other words, seven of the ten largest cities in the US lacked a financial institution that could serve as an anchor for the local economy.

Following the reduction of geographic restrictions in the mid-1990s, the industrial boundaries separating different forms of banking were also lifted. Glass–Steagall was finally, and inevitably, repealed in 1999 in the wake of the Citicorp–Travelers merger the year before.[22] Almost immediately, the biggest commercial banks grew to become the biggest investment banks, and the universal banking format prevalent in the rest of the industrialized world quickly came to dominance in the US. By 2007, Citigroup and JP Morgan Chase were # 1 and # 3 in global debt underwriting, as well as major forces in equities underwriting. Conversely, investment banks now did loans, generally as part of a broader package of client services.

The industry structure of commercial banking was thoroughly transformed by the mergers of the 1990s and 2000s. By 2005, there were about 7,500 FDIC-insured commercial banks left in the US—just over half what there had been twenty years earlier—but with almost twice as many branches in total. Yet industry consolidation had taken a peculiar form: while the three top national banks were clearly dominant, there was also a flurry of bank foundings at the community level, leaving the industry with an hourglass structure analogous to beer brewing, in which a small number of national giants are complemented by a large population of local microbrewers. The ten largest banks held nearly 40% of all domestic deposits and 51% of the industry's assets, but small banks proliferated at the community level—both at the expense of the middle of the market.[23] Even at the top, the three big banks followed somewhat different strategies. Citigroup emerged as a financial supermarket, with a dominant position in global retail banking (where it operated over 60% of all US-owned overseas branches). Bank of America, in contrast, focused on domestic retail banking, and nearly reached the legal limit of holding 10% of the nation's deposit base. And JP Morgan Chase resembled a more traditional European universal bank with a substantial corporate focus.[24]

The traditional rationale behind keeping American banks relatively small and local was a fear of concentrated economic power. The last time the US had a private bank with national scope was in the years after the War of 1812, with the Second Bank of the United States. When President Andrew Jackson sought to kill the bank by vetoing the bill renewing its charter in 1832, he wrote to Congress: "There is danger that a president and directors [of the bank] would ... be able to elect themselves from year to year, and without responsibility or control manage the whole concerns of the bank during the existence of its charter. It is easy to conceive that great evils to our country and its institutions will flow from such a concentration of power in the hands of a few men irresponsible to the people." He was particularly concerned about foreign influences: "If we must have a bank with private stockholders, every consideration of sound policy and every impulse of American feeling admonishes that it should be *purely American*" so as to avoid foreign influences and potential conflicts of interest.[25] Jackson would presumably have been concerned that Citigroup's largest shareholder was Saudi Prince Alwaleed bin Talal, who owned a 4.3% stake—or that, in the wake of the mortgage crisis that led to its CEO's ouster, Citi received a $7.5 billion capital infusion from the Abu Dhabi government's investment arm for a potential 4.9% ownership position.

The theory behind bank deregulation, on the other hand, was that geographic and industrial diversification, and the large-scale use of financial markets, would spread risk broadly and thus insulate banks from local crises, making the financial system safer. While conglomeration was poison for American manufacturers, it was evidently a good thing when it came to financial services. And to the extent that securitization was intended to spread risk, it clearly succeeded in the case of mortgage-backed securities: investors around the world, and firms in a dozen industries, all managed to suffer the consequences of the mortgage crisis.

Perhaps the most obvious immediate consequence of allowing diverse financial businesses under one roof was the diverse conflicts of interest created. Commercial banks that only do loans must offer their wares on a take-it-or-leave-it basis. But banks that also do securities under-writing, merger advisory, and other services can request a quid pro quo. A straightforward instance of this is "loan tying," in which banks require those seeking loans—which offer relatively meager returns for the bank—to purchase other services. This kind of arrangement has been illegal since the 1970s. But in 2004 the *Wall Street Journal* reported a survey finding that

> 96% of the corporate-finance executives at large companies who responded said they had been pressured by lenders to buy underwriting, merger advice and other services from a bank in exchange for loans. Nearly two-thirds of the surveyed chief financial officers and treasurers at large companies—those with revenue of $1 billion or more—said a bank had denied credit or raised loan prices because the finance executives didn't buy other services. Almost half said such pressure had risen in the past year.

The article went on to note that the three biggest banks between them arranged more than half of the most common credit lines for companies, leaving little doubt about which banks were doing the pressuring.[26]

As we saw in the previous chapter, the Internet and telecom stock bubble of the late 1990s was driven in part by similar conflicts of interest. Although financial theory imagines investors being equal before the efficient market hypothesis, it is also clear that some are more equal than others—particularly when they run companies that do business with the biggest commercial banks, like WorldCom's Bernie Ebbers. And as we shall see later in this chapter and in Chapter 6, the mortgage bubble provides an informative context to understand the new face of deregulated banking and its pathologies.

Investment banks

The greatest beneficiary of the shift in financial intermediation from banks to markets, at least initially, was the investment banking industry. Investment banks and brokerages perform a number of functions that connect investors to markets. They underwrite securities that companies and other issuers want to sell to the public, such as stocks and bonds (and collateralized debt obligations). They advise clients on strategy, and particularly mergers and acquisitions. They typically provide investment advice for wealthy individuals and institutions. And they frequently own brokerages that buy and sell securities on the market for clients, including individuals, institutions, and hedge funds. Until the industry collapsed in late 2008, the "big four" leading American investment banks included Goldman Sachs, Morgan Stanley, Merrill Lynch, and Lehman Brothers—joined after the repeal of Glass–Steagall by Citigroup (parent of the former Salomon Brothers and Smith Barney) and JP Morgan Chase.[27]

Like American commercial banking, the American investment banking industry had a peculiar history by global standards. In particular, two distinctions importantly shaped the banks' evolution: they were segregated from commercial banks, and they were typically organized as partnerships. Outside the US, it is common for the investment banking function to be performed by units of commercial banks. But American investment banks grew up separated from commercial banks, particularly after Glass–Steagall, and they evolved their own strategies as free-standing entities. They were the industrial equivalent of the Galapagos Islands, with a distinctive ecosystem and norms of competition. Banker Tony Golding points out another important implication of this industrial segregation, namely, that free-standing investment banks formed an influential constituency for financial markets that was absent from most other nations.[28] Investment bankers are among the largest donors to political campaigns, for instance, and alumni of Goldman Sachs often end up in important economic policy positions—chairmen of Goldman served as Treasury Secretaries under both Clinton and Bush.[29] This may help explain the far more expansive use of financial markets in the US compared to other industrialized nations.

The fact that investment banks were typically organized as partnerships meant that bankers had incentives to take the long view, as the value of the bank (and therefore of partnership in the firm) depended on its reputation. The centrality of a bank's reputation to its business helped to resolve a paradox in the industry. Investment banks get much of their revenue from completing particular transactions, and in any given deal they may be able to collect their fees and walk away—not necessarily the best incentive for honest dealing. What was to prevent bankers from underwriting poor-quality securities, or recommending bad acquisitions? Banks had many opportunities to take unfair short-term advantage of their clients—both the companies they advised and those that bought their products. Yet for decades investment banking was described as a "relationship business" rather than a transactional business, and banks often maintained very long-term connections with their clients. Ford, for example, used Goldman Sachs as its primary bank for decades, and Goldman partners have served on Ford's board of directors.

The reason bankers were scrupulous in upholding the reputation of their firm, and maintained long-term relationships even in the face of countervailing incentives, was stated by a Morgan partner almost a century ago: "To banking the confidence of the community is the breath from which it draws life." According to another, bank partners "have generally drifted onto these various railroad and industrial boards because we had first undertaken to place a large block of the corporation's securities with our clients, and we felt a sense of responsibility to those clients which we fulfilled by keeping an eye upon the corporation in which they had invested. We felt that that was a strong factor in enabling us to market these securities, and while the responsibility was a very onerous one, nevertheless, we shouldered it." A textbook on investment banking in 1929 described the "investment banker, intimately connected as he is with the affairs of the corporation for which he has sold bonds, since the continued meeting of the obligations on these bonds is essential to the maintenance of the investment banker's prestige ... [investors] place so much stress, in purchasing securities, on the character and reputation of the house of issue."[30] A bond dealer's word was his bond, in other words, and a bank's reputation was a valuable asset that should not be squandered for short-term gain. Moreover, because investment banks were organized as partnerships, partners had much of their net worth tied up in the value of the bank, which in turn depended on its reputation. As "reputational intermediaries," banks (like accounting firms) were as valuable as their word, which was vouchsafed by a partnership structure.

Notably, Goldman was the last of the major investment banks to abandon the traditional partnership model when it went public in 1999. Merrill Lynch listed on the New York Stock Exchange in 1971, Morgan Stanley had gone public in 1986, and Lehman Brothers listed in 1994. An implication of the decline of the partnership model was that compensation for bankers became much more closely tied to transactions and short-term results. Where the old partnership model tied bankers to the long-term health of the firm and gave them a strong interest in its "character and reputation," bankers now are much more oriented to this year's bonus. The "onerous responsibility" of looking after the affairs of companies whose securities they have underwritten (or the homeowners whose mortgages they have securitized) is evidently a thing of the past.[31]

Innovation

Banks' dependence on discrete deals makes them incubators for innovation, seemingly generating new products daily to compete with traditional corporate stocks and bonds. Securities can be created out of nearly any kind of actual or potential stream of cash. Home mortgages are perhaps the prototype: mortgage-backed securities are bonds backed by the mortgage payments of homeowners. The value of the home and the credit history of the homeowner, along with some information about the neighborhood and historical data on mortgage payments, provide a reasonable basis for valuing a particular mortgage, and it is a simple matter to combine a few thousand of them into a single bond issue. Student loans, auto loans, and credit card receivables are natural follow-ons, as are commercial mortgages and commercial loans. Bonds backed by royalties from entertainment products (e.g. Bowie bonds, or bonds backed by syndication of popular television shows) are slightly more exotic, as are bonds backed by bundles of veteran's pensions, or life insurance payouts of the terminally ill, or collections on tax liens—but all of them have been tried. It is a safe bet that if there is an income stream, someone on Wall Street has contemplated a way to turn it into a financial instrument.

Collateralized debt obligations, the proximal source of the credit crisis of 2007, are an example. CDOs combined slices of different mortgage-backed securities with different risk profiles into pooled instruments, rendering them two (or more) steps from the original mortgages upon which they were based. In principle, the new products could be fine-tuned to meet the needs of investors (and the requirements of the debt-rating agencies charged with evaluating their risk), but as it happened they became far more difficult to value than was expected. In spite of this, the worldwide pools of investment capital created a market for them, and CDO issuance increased from $52 billion in 1999 to $388 billion in 2006.[32] The presumption in the market was that buyers of CDOs were sophisti-cated institutions capable of taking care of themselves when purchasing these exotic instruments. Because banks get paid by the transaction and have high fixed costs in the securitization business, they have incentives to keep creating new securities such as CDOs even when creditworthy borrowers have become scarce—as happened in the subprime mortgage meltdown. *The Economist* quotes James Mason as saying "Once you get into it, it's a bit like heroin," and Alan Greenspan compared high-yield CDOs to cocaine. The combination of a need for new deals and compensation tied to short-term results, with products whose risks were borne by someone else, made for a volatile blend.[33]

The drive for deals also gets investment bankers involved in the corpo-rate strategy business. One of the most lucrative practices in investment banking is merger and acquisition advisory, and thus bankers routinely pitch deals to potential corporate clients. In some cases, banks have been responsible for massive changes in industry structures. UBS bankers were heavily involved with HealthSouth's strategy in the years leading up to the accounting scandal that led to the ouster of its flamboyant founder, Richard Scrushy, and they frequently attended corporate board meetings over several years. Citibank analyst Jack Grubman attended board meetings for over a half-dozen of the competing telecom firms he followed, advising them on mergers and other aspects of strategy. And many industry consolidations were driven at least in part by the bankers advising on the deals. Although investment bankers did not transform industries on quite the same scale they had in the 1890s, it is fair to say that in telecoms and the Internet, banks had a decisive influence in creating the asset price bubble that emerged in the late 1990s.[34]

The 1990s stock market bubble

The Internet/telecom bubble and its burst were outsized on any number of dimensions, from the speed of its rise and fall to the value created and lost. Over 2,400 companies first sold shares to the public in the US between 1996 and 1999, creating thousands of paper millionaires overnight.[35] (For comparison purposes, the New York Stock Exchange listed fewer than 2,000 US-based companies in 1995.) And economist Robert Shiller estimated that the dollar value lost on the market between 2000 and 2002 in the US was "roughly equivalent to the destruction of all the houses in the country."[36] There are any number of explanations for the bubble and its collapse, but there is reasonably widespread agreement that conflicts of interest at investment banks played a major part in inflating the bubble.

The process of underwriting initial public offerings (IPOs) gives a window into how this happened. New companies typically experienced a large run-up in price on the first day of trading—often doubling from the beginning to the end of the first trading day. Thus, access to shares was, in the words of one investment banker, "free money." If the only business of an investment bank were underwriting, then the run-up of IPO share prices would be of only modest interest. But because banks often do many kinds of business with many kinds of clients—including brokerage and wealth management, lending, and proprietary trading— conflicts of interest were rampant, creating seemingly irresistible pressures to expand the supply of "free money."

Two practices that came to light in the wake of the market bust were "spinning" and "laddering." Given that IPO shares typically go up substantially during the first day of trading, the best situation for an investor is to be able to buy shares at the initial offering price and quickly re-sell ("spin") them. (Insiders, such as the firm's managers and venture capitalists, typically must hang on to their shares for a specified period after going public and thus cannot benefit directly from the first-day pop.) Shares that are purchased at the initial offering price, but still eligible for trading, are therefore particularly prized, and their allocation was highly fraught. Banks commonly set aside so-called "friends and family" shares to be preferentially allocated to acquaintances of the company's founders. But the definition of "friends and family" was fairly elastic, extending to include vendors and customers of the IPO company and, ultimately, unrelated executives who were clients of the bank. Friends-and-family shares became a currency to be allocated to the personal accounts of executives at client firms, to influence those executives to use the banks' services or to allocate contracts to the IPO firms.[37]

The value of this currency depends, of course, on the ability to generate the first-day price pop and subsequent momentum. Banks had several tools at their disposal to ensure this. "Laddering" is a practice in which investors are allocated shares at the opening price in return for promises to buy more shares later in the day to keep the price momentum going. Investment banks were occasionally accused of encouraging laddering among some institutional clients. But of greater significance was the role of so-called "sell-side" analysts in inflating the estimated value of telecom and Internet shares. The job of a securities analyst is to assess the value of a company's business and make informed predictions about its future. Buy-side analysts are those that produce internal research to inform their own firms' trading (e.g. at mutual funds or other institutional investors). Sell-side analysts, on the other hand, are those that work for brokerages and other firms that buy and sell securities on behalf of clients; thus, their reports are generally made public and are used to influence the trading of their clients. Brokerages draw on analyst reports when advising their clients on trades and broader investment strategies. In theory, analysts are informational intermediaries that combine features of restaurant reviewers and investigative journalists, digging through a company's filings and press releases, attending conferences, meeting with management, and making site visits to render informed judgments about the company's prospects. In practice, however, analysts often fall short, and in the case of sell-side analysts, their position is inherently compromised by potential conflicts of interest.

The task of an analyst has some peculiar features. First, to the extent that financial markets are informationally efficient, then analysts are irrelevant: the future prospects of a stock are already taken into account in its price, and therefore a monkey throwing darts at the financial pages would do as well as an analyst at picking winners and losers. (This is the "random walk" hypothesis.) At the very least, by the time a retail investor received an analyst's report, the price would have already been set by the smart money. Anyone expecting to beat the market by relying on sell-side analysts is, therefore, not smart money. Second, many analysts work for firms that do business with the companies about which they report. Their incentives to render harsh judgments on actual or potential clients of their employer are, to say the least, mixed. As a result, it is extremely rare for analysts to place a "sell" recommendation on a stock: most analysts rate the companies they analyze as "Hold," "Buy," or "Strong buy," while analysts with genuinely negative opinions about a company are more likely to simply drop coverage rather than recommend selling. Securities analysts follow the rule that, if you can't say anything nice, don't say anything at all.[38]

The penchant for relentlessly positive reporting by analysts reached new heights during the late 1990s bubble, when it seemed that even the most ill-conceived business could go public to a chorus of "buy" recommendations. Investors, particularly retail investors, are at a huge disadvantage when buying shares in new and unfamiliar companies such as the many dot-com IPOs. They were thus particularly prone to relying on intermediaries like analysts for recommendations. Unfortunately, analysts at investment banks had evolved into essentially shills for the banking side of their employers. The basic conflict arises from the fact that analysts don't bring in revenue—brokers and bankers do. Yet the bankers that underwrite companies and bring new issues public need the analysts' clout to get and keep clients who would otherwise be unknown to investors. Analysts—particularly "star" analysts that regularly appeared in the increasingly pervasive financial media, such as Henry Blodgett at Merrill Lynch, Mary Meeker at Morgan Stanley, and Jack Grubman at Salomon—had the ability to whip up investor interest in "the next Netscape" (or Amazon.com, or Google). And it was evident that the banks' own clients were those most prone to being future stars. In order to insure that clients had a large and enthusiastic analyst following, several banks, including Lehman Brothers, UBS, and Paine Webber, tied analyst compensation to the investment banking fees they helped generate. At Piper Jaffray and other firms, analysts went on sales calls with bankers, where they previewed the "Strong Buy" recommendations they would offer when the client went public. JP Morgan offered "extended warranties" to some clients, assuring them of ongoing coverage by their analysts. Morgan Stanley and others went as far as to hire outside analysts at other firms to cover its banking clients, creating a more compelling illusion of objectivity. It wasn't always easy to overlook a company's defects, but analysts managed somehow: Merrill's Blodgett conceded that his Internet research group had never issued a "Sell" recommendation, even on companies referred to in internal e-mails as "dogs" and "crap." The smart money knew enough to ignore such analysts because of their conflicting interests, but retail investors were clearly at a disadvantage in parsing the analysts' reports. A Lehman analyst stated it frankly to an institutional investor: "Ratings and price targets are fairly meaningless anyway... but, yes, the 'little guy' who isn't smart about the nuances may get misled, such is the nature of my business."[39]

It would be unfair, of course, to imply that sell-side analysts were relentlessly upbeat—sometimes they used their coverage as a stick to beat prodigal clients that failed to play by investment banking's implicit rules. Small firms are particularly vulnerable to the demands of banks—biotech startups often have only a single analyst, working for the bank that initially brought them public. Thus, Piper Jaffray's biotech analyst dropped coverage of Antigenics Inc.—previously rated a "strong buy" for two years after Piper Jaffray took it public—when the firm announced that it would be using a competitor for a subsequent offering. Antigenics executives charged that Piper went even further, persuading major investors to drop or reduce buy orders for their new offering in order to "teach clients a lesson."[40] (On the other hand, clients might also overstate the degree to which analysts work against them. The famously litigious founder of Overstock.com claimed that analysts, reporters, and short-sellers were part of a conspiracy led by a "Sith lord" to drive down his company's stock, belying the impression that analysts are all Pollyannas.)[41]

The analyst dreamworld eventually came face to face with reality in the form of New York Attorney General Eliot Spitzer, who pursued several of the biggest names on Wall Street for their conflicted practices. In April 2003, ten Wall Street firms paid $1.4 billion to settle charges by a group of national and state regulators around analyst conflicts. Grubman and Blodgett were banned from the securities industry for life, and banks agreed to a series of structural changes that prevented analysts from going on sales calls with bankers, required separate supervisory structures for analysts and bankers, and mandated disclosure of potential conflicts in analyst reports. The agreement also addressed charges that Citigroup and Credit Suisse First Boston used "spinning" of IPO shares to executives to encourage business from their firms. Thus, at least one corner of the conflicts of interest in financial conglomerates had been temporarily addressed.[42]

The end of an era

The peculiar history of the American investment banking industry took a more dramatic turn in September 2008. Over the course of a remarkable week, Lehman Brothers was allowed to fail, creating the largest bankruptcy in American history and triggering panic in the financial markets about the viability of its three remaining competitors. Merrill Lynch quickly agreed to be acquired by Bank of America, following the previous lead of Bear Stearns, while Goldman Sachs and Morgan Stanley both received approval from the Federal Reserve to convert themselves from investment banks into bank holding companies. This conversion subjected them to much tighter regulatory scrutiny from multiple agencies and greatly dampened their ability to take risky but lucrative bets. On the other hand, it allowed them to gather capital from depositors and, most crucially at the time, to gain access to the Fed's massive bailout funds. The distinctive American-style investment banking industry had effectively disappeared, a victim of its own success.

Mutual funds

If investment banks were the greatest beneficiaries of the rise of securitization and the mania for going public, then mutual funds were the most obvious beneficiaries of the shift of household savings from banks to markets. To simplify slightly, Americans used to hold their savings in bank accounts; they now put their medium- to long-term savings into mutual funds. The Federal Reserve's triennial Survey of Consumer Finances documents the magnitude of this shift: in 1983, 20% of households had some money invested in the stock market, while by 2001 this had risen to 52%. In 1983, "Most families that own stock did not appear to be active investors. For example, of the one-fifth in the sample who reported owning stock, only 40 percent reported owning shares in more than one company. An even smaller percentage of stockowners reported having a brokerage account (35 percent) or trading stock in 1982 (27 percent)."[43] But by 2001, perhaps as many as half of households owned shares of diversified mutual funds, either directly or through retirement accounts. That is, rather than only owning stock in their employer or the local utility company, they were invested broadly in "the market." Moreover, while households held 30% of their financial assets in banks in 1989, this declined to 17% in 2004, while the proportion invested in financial markets increased from 50% to 69% over the same period.

Through retail investment and 401(k) plans, much of the growth in stock ownership has been channeled through mutual funds. The number of mutual funds in the US increased from 564 in 1980 to over 8,000 in 2005, while their assets under management increased from $134 billion to more than $8 trillion. The 1990s in particular was a period of remarkable growth. Steve Fraser reports that "More was invested in institutional funds between 1991 and 1994 than in all the years since 1939." The vast growth in household investment in the market provided the raw material for a stock market boom in the 1990s and boosted mutual funds to become the predominant owners of corporate America. The assets of the mutual fund industry grew 1000% from 1990 to 2005, and the three biggest fund families (Fidelity, Vanguard, and the American Funds) each topped over $1 trillion in assets. And because compensation at mutual funds flows largely from assets under management rather than from performance, the biggest funds were richly rewarded for their asset-gathering.[44]

The growth in investments in mutual funds was not an obvious development. In 1980, few households (under 6%) availed themselves of mutual funds—their fees were high for small investors, and they tended to be the domain of well-off households that also owned company shares directly. But several factors increased their attractiveness. Banks were constrained in the interest they could pay on savings accounts, and by the early 1980s the mandatory cap was several percentage points less than inflation—in other words, the value of money held in a savings account actually declined over time relative to inflation. Money market accounts faced no such cap, nor did mutual funds, which were risky but undoubtedly preferable to losing money by "saving." Mutual funds also declined in cost for small investors, providing a relatively easy channel for investment.[45]

Finally, and perhaps most importantly, the IRS clarified the tax treatment of the 401(k) retirement plan, effective in 1982, which induced a large number of corporate employers to shift from so-called "defined benefit" plans (which paid employees a set amount upon retirement from the company) to "defined contribution" plans (in which employees contribute pre-tax earnings to a fund, often matched by their employer). Typically 401(k) plans offer employees a choice of investment options, including perhaps a half-dozen mutual funds. An attraction of the plans for employers is that it takes them out of the business of pension management—once they have made their contribution, they are no longer responsible for the investment risks. For employees, the plans are relatively portable, allowing people to change jobs and bring their pension savings with them. Thus, the number of 401(k) plans increased dramatically during the 1980s and 1990s, and the number of partic- ipants more than tripled from 7.5 million in 1984 to over 23 million in 1993. As described in the last chapter, if they can help it, relatively few companies continue to indulge in traditional pension plans that tie employees to firms. Mutual fund companies, on the other hand, found a great opportunity for asset gathering and grew huge as a result.

Although the number of mutual funds has grown tremendously in the past two decades, the biggest fund families continue to hold the largest market share. The five biggest fund complexes control nearly 40% of the industry's assets, a proportion that has stayed relatively con- stant since the early 1990s. The best-known funds from the early days— Fidelity, Vanguard, American Funds, T. Rowe Price, Janus, Putnam— had several advantages in maintaining their position. Mutual funds are able to use a percentage of their assets under management for mar- keting purposes, which helps explain why advertisements for them are pervasive in the financial media. And their size gave them early entrée into the 401(k) business, which (through monthly contributions) pro- vided a drip-feed of new assets. Fidelity in particular grew to become the largest 401(k) provider in the US. A result is that the funds have become predominant owners of corporate America. Mutual funds as a group own almost 30% of corporate shares in the US, compared with 8% in 1990. And their ownership is relatively concentrated, reversing the situation described by Berle and Means in the 1930s. Fidelity is the single largest shareholder of about one in ten US corporations on any given day, a position of concentrated ownership by a financial institution unheard-of since the days of finance capitalism in the early twentieth century.[46]

Scandals

The early 2000s saw a series of scandals strike the mutual fund industry that ensnared several of the largest players. Most prominent was the late trading scandal. Mutual funds value their assets at the market price at 4:00 p.m. in New York, when the US markets close. But information does not stop at 4:00 Eastern Standard Time, and some equities (particularly those outside the US) continue to trade after that time, leaving a potential gap between the 4:00 price on the books and the actual value of the equities. The arbitrage opportunities in "late trading" (i.e. buying and selling shares after the market close at the 4:00 price) were apparent to many traders. The cost of late trading is borne by the funds' other shareholders, and mutual funds typically ban trades ordered after the market close. But some allowed preferred clients to do late trading in exchange for other favors. The scandal implicated several of the largest fund families—Alliance, Invesco, Janus, and Putnam— as well as several financial firms, including Merrill Lynch and Bank of America. Indeed, Eric Zitzewitz of Stanford found statistical evidence of late trading in thirty-nine of the sixty-six fund families he investigated, suggesting that the practice was rather widespread. It appeared to be particularly prevalent among more diversified financial firms with more potential conflicts of interest. Notably, both Fidelity and Vanguard, the largest funds, escaped accusations of late trading, perhaps because they were independent and had no similar conflicts.[47]

The late trading scandal brought to light other troublesome aspects of mutual funds. Although they had become perhaps the predominant savings vehicle for American families, the average person knew surprisingly little about how the industry operated. Thus, while corporate boards of directors faced increasingly intense scrutiny as institutional investors became more active in issues of corporate governance, mutual fund boards continued their peculiar traditions. One norm in the industry is that the fund trustees (the equivalent of directors) commonly oversee dozens or even hundreds of funds. In 2004, Vanguard's independent trustees served on the boards of roughly 120 separate funds, while Fidelity's trustees oversaw nearly 300 funds with a vast range of investment styles and objectives. Marvin Mann, former Chairman of Lexmark, served as lead independent trustee on the boards of 292 Fidelity funds. Close oversight of particular funds may not have been necessary but, practically speaking, it was impossible.[48]

Another idiosyncrasy of the mutual fund industry is Rule 12b1, adopted in 1980, which allowed the investment managers running funds to use up to 1% of their assets under management per year on marketing expenses. These indirect expenses mean that current shareholders may be paying commissions to securities firms and financial advisors to solicit additional investors, a hidden cost with no obvious benefit to them. Finally, mutual funds are among the largest traders in the market, and, although their size should give them great clout in negotiating commissions for trading, it is common practice to pay higher amounts ("soft dollars") in exchange for other services from brokers. Because the soft dollars are paid at the expense of shareholders, rather than out of the investment manager's own capital, they provide another way for fund managers to profit at shareholder expense.[49]

Mutual fund shareholders responded to the late trading scandal in part by shifting their investments from the stigmatized funds to "clean" funds such as Fidelity and Vanguard. Neither of these firms was part of a larger financial conglomerate, and thus they were perhaps less tempted by conflicts. But their enormous size created its own dilemmas, namely, how does a fund maintain market-beating performance when it is, to a great degree, the market? As primarily an index fund, Vanguard faces little conflict here: its performance exactly matches its benchmark, and thus its strategy for success is to keep expenses low and keep gathering assets. But Fidelity is actively managed, and its investments are closely watched. With $1.3 trillion in assets under management, Fidelity ends up being a very large shareholder in spite of itself: during 2005, Fidelity held 5% or more of the shares of over 450 NYSE-traded corporations. (Notably, although Fidelity routinely accumulates large stakes, it also manages to trade out of these fairly quickly: on average, its 5% holdings last for less than three years.)[50]

Fidelity responded to this dilemma by moving into related lines of business that built on its assets. In particular, after its successful foray into pension management, the firm built a vast human resource and benefits management business, with the intention of growing this business to be half its revenues. The firm's CEO was quoted as stating in 2003 that "What mutual funds were to the first 50 years of Fidelity, benefits outsourcing will be to the next 50 years." Thousands of corporations now use Fidelity for pension and benefits outsourcing, and the coming retirement of baby boomers opens up new opportunities for the firm. Yet this business creates just the sorts of conflict that free-standing mutual funds were thought to avoid: by 2005, at least one in five of Fidelity's portfolio firms was also a client who could presumably choose to go elsewhere.[51]

The original finance capitalism brought about a populist backlash against concentrated financial power, with J. P. Morgan and the firm he led embodying the notion of financial oligarchy. Today, few could name the CEO of Fidelity, even though Fidelity-managed funds hold the largest concentration of corporate voting rights in American history, and the founding family continues to own nearly 50% of the privately held company. If anything, critics such as John Bogle (founder of rival Vanguard) wonder why Fidelity and its cohorts do not exercise more of their power for corporate reform, given the corporate scandals earlier in the decade. One answer, not unexpectedly, is conflicts of interest. An analysis of proxy voting by Fidelity and roughly two dozen other large mutual fund families revealed that proxy voting on issues of corporate governance is closely related to how much business the parent company does with corporate managers: there was a nearly perfect correlation between the number of pension clients a fund had and its propensity to vote with management (that is, against shareholder-initiated reforms). Fidelity, with by far the most corporate pension clients, was also by far the most management-friendly in its voting patterns. Ironically, rather than becoming another JP Morgan, with a web of agents out controlling corporate America, Fidelity appears to be just as conflicted as the other latter-day financial conglomerates.[52]

Life insurance: just another financial service?

Although the insurance industry has been less implicated in scandals than banking and mutual funds, insurance companies were not immune to the broad shift in the economy toward financialization. Life insurers in particular succeeded in turning their product into just another financial service during the 1980s, and reaped the consequences in subsequent decades. The notion of life insurance (which is, in fact, "death insurance") has a history of controversy, as documented by sociologist Viviana Zelizer and others. Life insurance is essentially a bet, with the payoff contingent on the death of the insured. On the face of it, this creates obvious hazards by giving the beneficiary incentives to encourage the early demise of the insured, and the industry worked hard to build its legitimacy and limit the prospects for betting on mortality. State regulators dealt with this problem by requiring those seeking life insurance to have an "insurable interest," that is, a stake in the survival in the insured. In other words, one could not buy insurance on one's unwitting neighbors (or their house) and then leave rags and gasoline around their yard.

During the 1980s, however, growth-minded life insurers found a potential niche among corporate employers. Firms had long been able to insure so-called "key men," executives who were crucial to the operations of the business. Insurance companies persuaded dozens of state insurance regulators to lower the bar for an "insurable interest" to potentially include *any* employee. The market for these contracts was not individuals seeking to provide for their survivors, but companies that could use the insurance as a tax shelter and an alternative income source. Corporate-owned life insurance (COLI), known informally in the industry as "janitor's insurance" or "dead peasant's insurance," was marketed widely to corporate clients, including Nestle USA (18,000 workers covered), Procter & Gamble (15,000), and Pitney-Bowes (23,000). The biggest buyer of all was undoubtedly Wal-Mart, which took out policies on 350,000 of its workers during the 1990s. The *Wall Street Journal* noted that "These policies yield tax-free income as their investment value rises, just like conventional whole life policies. Companies also borrow against the policies to raise cash." Until 1996, the companies could take tax deductions on interest for loans backed by COLI. Death benefits from the policies can be used for any purposes, including executive compensation. The president of the Association for Advanced Life Underwriting, Albert Schiff, stated that "These future death benefits become an attractive off-balance sheet asset" for companies.[53]

Consumers responded to the shift in the life insurance industry, but not in ways that the industry would have preferred. An early sign was the market for so-called viaticals, which emerged in the late 1980s. The AIDS epidemic left thousands of relatively young men and women with huge medical bills and an expectation of an early death in the 1980s. Many of them had life insurance policies purchased when they were still healthy, and thus entrepreneurs found that they could make a market by matching AIDS patients with investors willing to pay cash to be named as the beneficiaries of their life insurance policies. Patients (here known as "viators") benefited by getting access to cash needed for their medical and living expenses, and investors benefited by owning an investment whose payoff was (presumably) uncorrelated with the market. The ghoulish practice highlighted the tension at the heart of life insurance—the faster the time to death, the higher the returns to investors. This created peculiar incentives on both sides: insureds had reason to overstate their illness, as the price they received was higher the closer they were to the "payoff." But with well-capitalized insurance companies, the major uncertainty was not whether investors would get paid, but when.[54]

The concept of buying payoffs from viators spread to other terminally ill persons, changing its name along the way to the more-neutral "life settlement," and in 2004 viaticals were finally (and inevitably) securitized. Much the same had happened to other categories of insurance settlement, e.g. J. G. Wentworth runs television ads seeking to pay cash upfront to purchase the rights to insurance settlements that pay out over time, then bundling these together into bonds. Veterans also face come-ons from companies offering to pay lump sums in return for their veteran's pensions—at least in states where it is not illegal.

The notion of life settlements eventually shifted from the ghoulish to the mainstream, to the consternation of the insurance industry. One of the economic premises of the industry is that individual policyholders frequently let their insurance lapse when they reach old age and their children have reached adulthood, thereby relieving the insurance company of its obligation. But the example of viaticals for the terminally ill showed the prospect of using insurance payouts as investable assets, and created a new sub-industry in speculator-initiated life insurance, or "spin-life," aimed at financially savvy elders. Spin-life policies entail investors making loans to the elderly to induce them to take out high-payout life insurance policies, to be retained or sold to other investors. The payoffs are highly lucrative, and investors in them range from hedge funds and investment banks to Warren Buffett. Eighty-year-old Marvin Margolis received $2 million in return for taking out a $7 million policy, telling the *New York Times*, "This is a wonderful opportunity to use my body as an asset." Human capital had come to take on an even more expansive meaning.[55]

The banking value chain and alternative financial institutions

Perhaps the most visible consequence of banking deregulation and the rise of securitization has been the creation of financial conglomerates such as Citigroup, which span investment banking, commercial banking, and other financial services. But an equally significant consequence has been the division of the "value chain" of banking into free-standing components, and their recombination into alternative competitors to banks. As with globalization, manufacturers had a head start here. The Nike organizational model, in which Nike designs and markets sneakers but manufacturing is primarily done by a network of contractors and their sub-contractors, has pervaded manufacturing in the form of the "OEM model": so-called "original equipment manufacturers" typically contract with other firms to do the production and distribution of their goods while focusing on the higher value-added tasks of product design and marketing, in industries ranging from PCs and cellphones to dog food. (The tainted pet food scandal in early 2007 revealed that an Ontario-based manufacturer produced chow for more than 100 competing brands, including Colgate-Palmolive's Science Diet, Procter & Gamble's IAMS, and Wal-Mart's Ol' Roy—many of which contained an industrial chemical traced to a cost-cutting Chinese supplier.)[56] The OEM model makes plain that many parts of a manufacturer's value chain can thrive as free-standing companies. While a customer sees "Dell" or "Toyota" or "Ol' Roy Dog Food," behind the finished product might stand dozens of vendors in a production network.

Much the same process has happened in banking. The most basic functions of a bank—taking in deposits, which are kept on the book as liabilities, and using these deposits to make loans, which are kept on the books as assets—have traditionally been integrated into a single organization, but are now readily divided and re-combined into new formats. This has happened most dramatically in the home mortgage market, but also works for business lending (where asset finance firms compete with banks to provide loans and leases) and more diverse businesses (where hedge funds have proliferated into a range of alternative forms).

Mortgage banking

From their origin in the 1830s until the 1970s, savings and loan associations (also known as "thrifts" in the US and "building societies" in the UK) were a prominent source of mortgage financing for American homeowners. As their name indicates, their primary functions were to take in household savings and to make loans for mortgages and new home construction. As described previously for banks, the interest rate cap on savings accounts became a substantial constraint on gathering deposits during the 1970s and hobbled the industry. Deregulation in the early 1980s lifted this cap and expanded the types of businesses S&Ls could do beyond home mortgages, putting them into more direct competition with banks. By the late 1980s, S&Ls that had wandered into diverse lines of business found themselves failing—indeed, roughly

1,000 S&Ls failed in the late 1980s and early 1990s, creating a substantial gap in the banking market for those providing home mortgages.

By this point, a large fraction of mortgages originated by banks and other lenders were being sold to third parties, securitized (pooled with other mortgages and turned into bonds), and re-sold on the secondary mortgage market, thereby freeing up capital for the lenders to make additional loans. The major players early on were government-sponsored enterprises Fannie Mae (formerly the Federal National Mortgage Association) and Freddie Mac (the Federal Home Loan Mortgage Corporation). Fannie Mae was established in 1938 to facilitate home financing by buying mortgages from lenders, and in 1981 it began to issue mortgage-backed securities, creating what would ultimately become a multi-trillion dollar market. As befit its quasi-public status, Fannie Mae had strict standards for "conformable" mortgages and would only finance certain kinds of dwellings within certain price ranges. Thus, "jumbo" mortgages above a certain size were off-limits to Fannie Mae, as were mortgages for non-standard dwellings (such as some condominiums). Moreover, borrowers with problematic credit histories were also declined. Coupled with an implicit government guarantee, this made Fannie Mae's bonds safe, while unintentionally shaping the kinds of homes that would be built.[57] But it also left large areas of under-served markets that would be pursued more aggressively by alternative lenders.

Because mortgage-backed securities allow lenders to sell their loans to third parties, they made it possible for entities that were not banks or thrifts to get into the mortgage business. If one is not going to hold a thirty-year mortgage on the books, then one need not take in deposits to fund the loan, which thereby freed mortgage lenders from the need to operate branches. Free-standing mortgage lenders thus stepped into the breach created by the S&L crisis by focusing on functions around securitization: making loans and bundling them into securities to be sold to institutional investors. Rather than operating branches with marble lobbies to impress depositors and borrowers, like banks or S&Ls, mortgage lenders could be more-or-less virtual enterprises. Originating loans is more usefully done at a homebuyer's dwelling anyway, and thus "loan officers" need not even operate out of an office.

A surprising array of competitors to banks arose to offer home mortgages. Firms entering the mortgage market included GMAC (General Motors Acceptance Corporation, the financing arm of General Motors that traditionally made auto loans), GE, and H&R Block, the retail tax-preparation company. The attraction of the market was clear: home buyers almost always made their mortgage payments on time, and they had collateral that almost always rose in value to back their loan. The mortgage market was as close to a sure thing as one could imagine.

The financing arms of industrial conglomerates were not the only ones to see the opportunities in the mortgage market. Free-standing mortgage companies quickly grew to become a huge industry. Under the guidance of its extravagantly compensated CEO, Angelo Mozilo, Countrywide expanded from a modest two-person shop in Anaheim to the nation's largest mortgage lender in 2006, at which point it was making one in five home loans in the US. Although part of this growth was financed by gathering deposits—unlike most mortgage firms, Countrywide also operated a bank (later converted to a thrift)—it is hard to imagine the firm achieving this scale without the magic of securitization. Countrywide combined several banking functions: in addition to financing mortgage loans, it also serviced loans for other mortgage lenders (that is, it received and processed mortgage payments from homeowners). Although most mortgages were re-sold, Countrywide still held "residuals" on many, subjecting it to first losses from defaults, which put it in a precarious position. Thus, Countrywide required a $20 billion capital infusion from Bank of America in mid-2007, and ultimately agreed at the end of that year to sell itself to Bank of America.[58]

With several hundred branches in operation, Countrywide represented one model of a reconfigured value chain for banking. New Century Financial, a southern California rival founded in 1996 (and shuttered in 2007), represented an alternative model. Rather than building an internal sales force operating out of branch offices, New Century worked primarily with independent mortgage brokers, allowing extremely rapid growth. And because it did not take deposits but relied on Wall Street for credit, New Century and its ilk faced no federal regulators. (Mortgage brokers, typically free-standing businesses and individuals that work with multiple vendors to arrange mortgages for home buyers, are licensed by the states where they operate, but also face no federal supervision.) Because New Century offered quick turnaround on loans and was notoriously relaxed about documentation from borrowers, it quickly became a favorite of brokers, who got paid a commission upon completion of a deal and thus prized speed. Through its aggressive tactics and a move into the subprime segment, New Century's loan originations grew from $6.3 billion in 2001 to $59.8 billion in 2006, making it the second-largest subprime lender, and a valued client of Morgan Stanley and other Wall Street firms—that is, right up until its implosion in early 2007, when its funding was cut off and it declared bankruptcy. Unlike Federally-regulated banks, the California mortgage firms evidently lacked an adequate cash cushion. Moreover, by 2005 most subprime mortgages were made by finance companies with no Federal supervision such as New Century; three years later, over 200 of them had been closed.[59]

Thanks to free-standing mortgage firms like Countrywide and New Century, an ecosystem of different businesses rapidly evolved to serve the market for home mortgages that had been vacated by the S&Ls, and to profit from a newly vibrant market for mortgage refinancing. According to the Federal Reserve's Survey of Consumer Finances, about half of those owning mortgages in 2001 refinanced them in the subsequent three years, and of these about one-third took on more debt than they owed on the original mortgage. Higher nominal home values meant that refinances could take out additional cash to supplement their income, as long as there were mortgage companies willing to lend. By the end of 2006 there was $6.5 trillion in securitized mortgage debt outstanding, due in large part to refinancing. (The effects of the mortgage boom and bust on homeowners are taken up in Chapter 6.)

Rampant refinancing spawned an employment boom for mortgage brokers. Mortgage brokers were virtually non-existent in 1980, when loan officers at banks and thrifts dominated the origination of mortgages on new homes. By 2005, however, brokers originated seven in ten mortgages, and the industry had grown vast, with roughly 50,000 mortgage brokerages employing upwards of 400,000 brokers—more jobs than the entire American textile industry. Mortgage brokerages proved to be one of the great entrepreneurial opportunities in the late 1990s and early 2000s. The cost of entry was low—a state license, a cellphone, a computer, and a fax machine were usually sufficient, while a formal office was unnecessary, since contracts could be signed in the buyer's home. Moreover, there were few economies of scale, as the tedious paperwork and dozens of signatures had to be collected by hand. Brokers got paid on a piece rate according to the size of the transaction, and thus the opportunities for enrichment were limited only by the energy of the broker and the magnitude of the local housing market. It was, in short, a get-rich-quick scheme that produced a flowering of local entrepreneurship. Best of all, changes in interest rates, housing values, or in the nature of one's previous mortgage encouraged frequent refinancing and therefore more transactions.[60]

Refinancing seemed to change the nature of homeowners' connections with their residences and their communities. Like stockbrokers, mortgage brokers benefited from frequent transactions. As a result, brokers had incentives to encourage owners to see their house less as a deep connection to a particular place and more as a semi-liquid asset with attractive tax properties. A house was simply a category of investment that always rose in value and thus could safely be used for leverage to finance other investments. One broker rented time on Chicago radio station WLS to broadcast an informative call-in show extolling the virtues of refinancing, telling listeners "You are either a homeowner or an investor." It was clear enough which one was the smart choice, and which the sucker's bet. (Although mortgage brokerage appeared to be a bright spot in the job market, many of the routine tasks involved in originating mortgages appeared to be ripe for offshoring—a fate averted by the collapse of the housing market in 2007.)[61]

The demand among investors around the world for bonds backed by American mortgages appeared to be insatiable in the early 2000s. Although the low-end tasks of mortgage origination and servicing had spawned new industries, like mortgage finance and brokerage, key players on Wall Street found ways to turn plain-vanilla mortgage-backed securities into more exotic financial instruments, tailored to the demands of investors seeking higher returns and willing to take on higher risks. In mortgage bonds, the value of the underlying mortgages that are pooled together is determined by a handful of relatively simple factors, such as the imputed value of the collateral, the credit scores of those taking out the mortgage, and the chances that mortgage buyers will pay off early (e.g. through refinancing). Of course, some elements of a pool of mortgages are riskier than others, and thus they can be divided into slices with different risk profiles and different returns. By combining risky slices from multiple mortgage pools, bankers created new instruments called "Collateralized Debt Obligations" or CDOs. In principle, aggregation makes them safer—that's the theory underlying mortgage bonds and other asset-backed securities in the first place. In the case of CDOs, however, valuing the bonds became almost unfathomably complex. Keep in mind that even the simplest mortgage-backed securities did not appear until the early 1980s because there was not sufficient computing power to value them. As the *Wall Street Journal* put it,

> Mortgages today are dispersed among banks as well as more than 11,000 investment pools, each of which may have hundreds, if not thousands, of investors. Many of these pools have been further repackaged into specialized funds [such as CDOs] ... Indeed, coming up with a value for a CDO entails analyzing more than 100 separate securities, each of which contains several thousand individual loans—a feat that, if done on any scale, can require millions of dollars in computing power alone.[62]

But CDOs managed to attract buyers from around the world, from Chinese sovereign wealth funds to Norwegian villagers.

The mortgage meltdown of 2007-2008, which we will discuss more fully in Chapter 6, has already far outstripped the losses associated with the S&L crisis and precipitated a broad financial crisis that has laid bare both the extent and the dangers of securitization. Early estimates put the losses to financial firms and investors at $400 billion. Expectations are that trillions of dollars in real estate wealth will disappear, along with perhaps 2 million homes lost to foreclosure—although the true figures are anybody's guess. The broader effects have yet to be seen at the time of this writing: nearly one-quarter of the jobs created between 2003 and 2006 were in housing-related industries, and entire neighborhoods are being decimated by losses in local tax revenues and the grim sight of homes in foreclosure. And if the so-called wealth effect, in which consumption is driven by increases in the value of one's assets, works the same way on the way down, then there are more surprises in store as the housing bust drags down the broader consumer economy. Through the mortgage market, Wall Street came to Main Street like a tornado in a trailer park.

Asset finance

Commercial banks found a number of new competitors in their core business of corporate lending as well, in the form of asset finance. In contrast to banks, asset financers commonly make loans backed by customers' assets and equipment rather than based on cash flow, where they may be better able than the banks to value such assets. They can also provide value-added services that banks cannot. The prototype in this industry is GE Capital, the financing arm of General Electric. The firm started out in the 1930s providing credit to purchasers of GE appliances, much as GMAC provided loans to auto purchasers, but by the 1990s GE Capital had grown to be the largest lender and leaser in the US, and by 2002 its assets outpaced those of all but the three largest commercial banks. GE Capital leased products from airplanes and railcars to satellites, and provided commercial loans as well as, of course, residential mortgages. It had a number of advantages over banks, including access to vast market intelligence via the highly diverse businesses of GE and their clients. It also had the ability to advise clients on more than just finance.

Through a diverse range of consumer and corporate businesses, including insurance, credit cards, truck leasing, mortgages, and reinsurance, GE Capital grew to be a central pillar of the shadow banking system.[63]

CIT Group, another alternative lender, operated in several markets similar to those of GE Capital. Although it was founded a century ago and grew primarily through auto financing, it expanded into broader consumer and commercial financing and factoring (i.e. buying receivables). Acquisitions in the 1990s built CIT Group into the second-largest equipment finance and leasing firm (after GE Capital), and it was briefly acquired (in 2001) and divested (in 2002) by Tyco International, the troubled New Hampshire/Bermuda-based conglomerate. Like GE Capital, CIT Group had been essentially a non-bank bank, making loans to businesses and providing credit to consumers, but without gathering deposits, relying instead on commercial paper, bonds, and asset-backed securities for most of its funding. As with many troubled financial firms, in November 2008 CIT Group followed Morgan Stanley and Goldman Sachs in applying to convert to a commercial bank holding company, which would allow it to gather deposits and access the Federal bank rescue fund.

Hedge funds

A final component of the shadow banking system is hedge funds. The term "hedge fund" covers an extremely broad class of entities that have grown from the fringe of financial services to become central players. (The funds originally gained their names because their investments were hedged, such as through short-selling, implying that their potential losses were limited.) By law, hedge funds typically are open only to a limited number of individual or institutional investors with a high net worth (over $5 million in assets), and they usually have high minimum investments—often $1 million. They commonly organize offshore as limited partnerships and are almost inevitably described as "lightly regulated," escaping much of the regulatory scrutiny of mutual funds and other investment companies. In spite of their shadowy disclosure practices and their very high management fees (typically 2% of assets under management and 20% of annual returns), the assets under management by hedge funds grew from $40 billion in 1995 to $1.1 trillion in 2005, according to one estimate. (Because of their sketchy disclosure requirements—US funds face essentially no oversight from the SEC—accurate estimates are hard to come by.)[64]

Much of the growth in hedge funds is due to the fact that, while mutual funds are largely stuck with investing in stocks and bonds, hedge funds can engage in strategies that make money even if the stock market is down, including short-selling and trading in complex derivatives. This was particularly an advantage during the 2000s, when the stock market stayed relatively flat for several years—a phenomenon seemingly common in the period after a market boom. The limited opportunities in the stock market contrasted with the large pools of investment capital looking for outlets, which combined to make hedge funds an attractive alternative for institutional investors and helped create booming growth in the industry—as far as we know.

Hedge funds have a peculiar relationship with Wall Street. Given their frequent trades, they provide a stream of fees to investment banks that handle their transactions. They are also major customers of commercial banks when they take on debt to support their leveraged strategies. But they are competitors to both institutions as well. Some funds do long-term loans, like commercial banks. Others make long-term equity investments, like venture capitalists. And some provide funding to buy-out firms, like investment banks, or do buyouts themselves. They are thus among Wall Street's best customers and fiercest competitors. And because their strategies are murky, they are subject to potentially severe conflicts of interest: unlike banks, a hedge fund could in principle lend a company money on the one hand, and short its stock on the other. Hedge funds, in short, are perhaps the shadowiest part of the shadow banking system that has evolved in the past twenty-five years.[65]

Citi and the future of financial institutions

The actions of one company over the past decade–through the repeal of Glass–Steagall, the technology-driven stock market bubble of the late 1990s, and the housing bubble of the 2000s–aptly illustrate the prospects and perils of the new financial conglomerates. Citibank has been one of the largest American banks, and by far the most internationally expansive, for decades; according to *Forbes Magazine*, it was the largest corporation in the world in 2007. The nearly 200-year-old New York institution brought together First National and National City of New York in 1955, two of the three members of the "money trust" identified by Brandeis in 1914. And with its 1998 merger with Travelers, an insurance and investment banking conglomerate, it became the most diversified financial corporation in US history. It had by far the most foreign branches of any US-based bank (by late 2008 almost 70% of all foreign branches were operated by Citi), was the world's largest underwriter of debt, had a vast brokerage network, vied for being the largest credit card issuer, and operated in nearly every sub-segment of the financial industry. This diversity was both a strength and a weakness: on the one hand, it provided one-stop-shopping for financial services, from individual consumers to global corporations. On the other hand, the potential conflicts of interest created could be overwhelming.

Citi's exalted status was by no means foreordained. In the early 1990s, the bank struggled due to bad real estate loans and the Latin American debt crisis. As the most ardent globalizer, Citibank was especially exposed to the debt of low-income countries, and as late as 1991 it was deemed "technically insolvent" and "struggling to survive" by Congressman John Dingell.[66] Over the course of the 1990s, it emphasized a global consumer business and corporate lending overseas, while diminishing its domestic corporate lending. The 1998 merger with Travelers was the biggest merger in history at that time, with a value of $70 billion. The resulting company was of a scale not previously seen in American finance. In contrast to many of its money-center competitors, which acquired regional banks to create national branch networks, Citi had focused on the "financial supermarket" model. The merger brought together under one roof a commercial bank (Citi), a property and casualty insurance underwriter (Travelers), an investment bank (Salomon), and a retail brokerage (Smith Barney). On the face of it, the merger seemed to violate almost every regulation of the financial services industry since the 1930s. But the Glass–Steagall Act was finally repealed the following year, and the Travelers insurance business was spun off and later merged with St. Paul.[67]

There were dozens of potential conflicts of interest created by having so many businesses under one umbrella, and Citi had been accused of many of them. Conflicts arise when investment banks do private banking for wealthy clients, a business in which Citi was among the top three in the world. Spinning—allocating IPO shares to the personal accounts of executives from client firms—was evidently a common practice at Citi during the bubble. Salomon, Citi's investment banking unit, was particularly prominent in telecoms thanks to its star analyst Jack Grubman, and it underwrote a number of high-visibility telecom offerings. This turned out to be a great opportunity for those telecom executives in a position to choose their firm's underwriters, as many of them saw IPO shares allocated to their personal accounts with Citi. Bernie Ebbers, CEO of the voraciously acquisitive WorldCom, made $11 million from twenty-one IPOs in which he received friends-and-family shares from Salomon, his firm's primary banker. More dramatically, Citi also made personal loans to key decision makers. Ebbers received an astonishing $552 million in loans from Citi, which he used to fund a number of his side businesses (including yacht building and cattle ranching and, most prominently, a half-million acres of timberland that Citi had been pitching to another buyer).[68]

Sell-side analysts at investment banks are notoriously prone to conflicts of interest, but Salomon Smith Barney's Jack Grubman took it up to a new level. While an analyst's formal role is to research companies and provide dispassionate guidance to brokerage clients, Grubman was far more intimately involved with the telecom firms he followed. He attended the board meetings of a half-dozen firms he covered, many of whom were also banking clients, and regularly visited Ebbers—even attending his wedding in 1999. Notably, Grubman remained bullish on WorldCom until shortly before it entered bankruptcy. To the extent that Citi's retail clients relied on Grubman's advice, their accounts at the firm were far smaller at the end.[69]

Grubman's relation to AT&T was more fraught. He had worked for the company in the early 1980s, but as an analyst he had placed low ratings on AT&T from 1995 onward, and thus Salomon was one of two big Wall Street firms denied top underwriting spots when the company spun off its Lucent unit in 1996. AT&T's CEO Michael Armstrong served on the Citi board and its Weill-run predecessors since the early 1990s, and Sandy Weill joined the AT&T board in 1998. Armstrong reputedly complained to Weill about Grubman's negative coverage of the firm, and, given their frequent contact at board meetings, it was undoubtedly an uncomfortable situation. Weill thus encouraged Grubman to take a "fresh look" at AT&T. On November 5, 1999, Grubman wrote Weill a memo about his coverage of AT&T, and also noted that he was seeking to get his twins into the prestigious 92nd Street Y preschool, asking Weill to use his connections to help get them in (and helpfully attaching a list of the Y's board members). Weill approach Joan Tisch, a board member of the Y and wife of Loew's co-chairman, about the Grubman twins' application and indicated that he could arrange a donation from Citi, which led to a $1 million gift from Citigroup to the Y. The twins were admitted; Grubman raised his AT&T rating to a "Strong Buy" in November 1999; and Salomon was subsequently selected as a lead underwriter for the huge AT&T Wireless offering, receiving $44.8 million in fees—after which Grubman lowered his rating again.[70]

In April 2003, Citi and several other banks reached a $1.4 billion settlement on conflicted analysts and IPO spinning. Grubman was banned from the securities industry for life. Charles Prince, at the time CEO of Citi's investment banking unit and later CEO of Citigroup overall, publicly apologized for the firms' actions: "We deeply regret that our past research, IPO and distribution practices raised concerns about the integrity of our company and we want to take this opportunity to publicly apologize to our clients, shareholders and employees." But this was hardly the end of Citi's conflicts.[71]

A long-standing rationale for keeping investment banking separate from commercial banking was that firms in both businesses would have conflicting incentives that put their clients at risk. WorldCom shareholders in 2002 sued Citi and JP Morgan Chase because the two firms had both underwritten the firm's bonds and made loans to it, among other things. Citi eventually settled with WorldCom investors in 2004 for a record $2.65 billion.[72] (Citi also paid $1.66 billion in 2008 to settle claims with the remaining stub of Enron that it had knowingly aided the company's executives in disguising the firm's true financial condition.) It was also argued that "universal banks" that do commercial and investment banking have too much power with respect to clients and compel them to buy services. Loan tying—making loans explicitly contingent on other business, such as investment banking or merger advisory services—has been illegal since the 1970s, but corporate financial executives claim it is pervasive in the industry. Since the big three banks (Citi, JP Morgan Chase, and Bank of America) arranged more than half of the most common corporate credit lines, and Citi was the largest in investment banking, it was fairly clear whom the executives had in mind. In their defense, some bankers say it's the clients who demand low-profit loans in exchange for their other business.[73] But outsiders saw Citi as the one holding the cards.

And although size was supposed to provide safety in financial institutions, the mortgage meltdown revealed that even the biggest firms were not necessarily safe. Citi's CEO Charles Prince resigned in November 2007 when it was discovered that Citi had lost at least $11 billion due to exposure to subprime mortgages. (The ultimate figure for the quarter was $18 billion.) Along with several other major Wall Street firms, Citi was forced to seek an infusion of capital, which in a brief period has left American banks largely owned by so-called "sovereign wealth funds" owned by foreign governments. In November 2007 Citi received a $7.5 billion investment from the Abu Dhabi Investment Authority, with the potential to convert to a 4.9% ownership stake, and another $6.9 billion from a Singapore government fund in January 2008. These investors joined Citi's long-time shareholder Prince Alwaleed of Saudi Arabia, who owns 4.3% of the firm. During the same period, Morgan Stanley sold a 9.9% stake in itself to a Chinese government fund, while Merrill Lynch sold just under 10% of itself to Temasek Holdings, a Singaporean sovereign fund, as well as a smaller stake in preferred shares to a Korean government fund. After a year of catastophic losses in 2008 and multiple bailouts, Citi finally bowed to the inevitable in January 2009 and announced plans to split itself up, thus ending the era of the "financial supermarket".[74]

In the decade after the repeal of Glass–Steagall, it began to appear that a deregulated Wall Street had achieved unprecedented power, and that banking was now dominated by a small handful of financial conglomerates. Yet in a brief period during the credit crisis, Wall Street came to be increasingly owned by government-backed investment funds in the Middle East and Asia. Both of Andrew Jackson's nightmares—concentrated control of banking, and foreign ownership—had come true, one after another. The troubled case of Citigroup gives us a window into the ways that changes in finance and an uneven regulatory system can create malign incentives in the financial services industry. As "wonderful life" banking has given way to the "originate, securitize, and distribute" model of banking, we are seeing the broader effects of these malign incentives on business and society.

In October 2008 the Treasury Department marked a new turn in the history of the American banking system by announcing a plan to buy preferred shares in dozens of US banks, including the nine largest—whether the banks wanted it or not. The government put $25 billion apiece into Bank of America, Citigroup, JP Morgan Chase, and Wells Fargo (now the fourth-largest traditional commercial bank after its slated acquisition of Wachovia), and $10 billion each in Goldman Sachs and Morgan Stanley. At the time of this writing, the implications of this unprecedented move had yet to be worked out. Early reactions included shocked statements from US senators that the Bush Administration was turning the United States into a socialist country—perhaps even France! Where the administration of the newly elected President Barack Obama would guide this American experiment in "socialism" remained to be seen.

5

From Sovereign to Vendor-State: How Delaware and Liberia became the McDonald's and Nike of Corporate Law

The globalization of finance and post-industrialism in its mature form create a series of challenges for the traditional twentieth-century nation-state. Basic notions of sovereignty and territoriality have come into question, as ensuring the safety of products assembled through far-flung supply chains, or patrolling virtual borders on the Internet to keep out (or tax) forbidden products, strain the capacities of traditional states. Consider the example of PartyGaming PLC, the company behind some of the Internet's largest gambling sites. PartyGaming.com was built by American entrepreneurs with prior experience in the online pornography industry, and it derived 90% of its revenues from US customers. Its business seemed to directly violate US state and federal law, and its business plan acknowledged as much. But it was incorporated and headquartered in Gibraltar, its servers were housed in Canada, and when it went public in 2005, it did so on the London Stock Exchange, outside the reach of US regulators. By studiously avoiding physical and jurisdictional contact with the US, PartyGaming's founders became overnight billionaires, albeit expatriates unable to set foot in the US without risking arrest.[1]

Cross-border finance shares some features with Internet gambling. For decades Switzerland has offered anonymous banking to wealthy customers seeking to keep their finances discreet. During the 1990s, thanks to the Internet, cross-border discreet finance went retail, as the IRS estimated that as many as 2 million Americans had opened credit card accounts with banks in offshore tax havens like Antigua and the Cayman Islands to access funds concealed from the US government. The financial traffic ran both ways: criminal organizations in Russia set up dozens of shell corporations in Delaware to launder funds looted from the former Soviet Union, aided by banks domiciled in the US. Business-friendly Delaware, which gets one-quarter of its budget from incorporation and related fees, allows the creation of corporations over the Internet without requiring the names of their owners or directors, a decided convenience for mobsters. As the state's Assistant Secretary of State put it, "They're choosing to incorporate in Delaware for the cachet of the fact that Coca-Cola and McDonalds and lots of large multinationals incorporate here. So in many ways, we are sort of victims of our own renown."[2]

Legitimate businesses were also attracted to virtual homes in the US. By 2000, hundreds of foreign companies had secondary share listings on US stock markets, including all but two of the twenty-five largest global corporations. Overseas entrepreneurs learned that they could bypass local investors and sell shares directly in the US, and thus dozens of Israeli startups skipped Tel Aviv to go public on Nasdaq. Finance had become even more detached from place, with the ironic consequence of spreading the American SEC's jurisdiction around the world: firms that list in the US thereby become subject to US securities regulations, including the corporate governance provisions of the Sarbanes–Oxley Act.[3]

On the other hand, the diffusion of the OEM model throughout manufacturing meant that global supply chains extended well beyond the reach of US regulators. As the virtual center of a nexus-of-contracts, the OEM corporation may rely on expansive production chains that ultimately draw on dozens or even hundreds of suppliers around the globe. In 2007, American pet owners were hit with a wave of sick cats and dogs that had been inadvertently poisoned by additives in their foods. The toxic chow was traced to a Canadian company that manufactured for over 100 brands, from the Wal-Mart house brand to high-end designer labels like IAMS and Science Diet. The Canadian vendor in turn had relied on overseas suppliers whose ingredients included melamine, a cheap industrial filler that is chemically similar to protein. And in 2008, several hundred serious injuries and at least eighty-one deaths were attributed to tainted batches of Baxter Health's blood thinner heparin, whose raw ingredients—made from pig intestines—came from countless mom-and-pop suppliers in China. The US Food and Drug Administration conceded at the time that it had conducted only thirty inspections of the more than 3,000 foreign drug suppliers in the previous year, and that its budget was nowhere near sufficient to conduct large-scale inspections.[4]

The result of the globalization of finance and production, in short, is that much economic activity is outside the territorial control of states; indeed, territorial boundaries are effectively meaningless for many products, leaving states at the limit of their capacity to raise revenues and keep their citizens safe.

States are left with the dilemma of how to generate revenues and make good on their promises when post-industrialism has detached physical territory from economic activity. On the revenue front, an industry of well-staffed accounting firms and consultancies finds increasingly ingenious ways to help clients evade state control and taxation. George Bush put it piquantly in a 2008 appearance on Fox News deriding the Democratic presidential hopefuls: "If they're going to say, oh, we're only going to tax the rich people, but most people in America understand that the rich people hire good accountants and figure out how not to necessarily pay all the taxes and the middle class gets stuck." The idea that it was fruitless to attempt to collect taxes from the wily rich was an oft-repeated theme by members of the Bush administration.[5] And corporate resources for tax avoidance far outstrip those of rich people, as hinted by the prevalence of virtual offshore subsidiaries and off-balance-sheet entities—Enron alone had thousands of them. Yet demands in the corporeal world for infrastructure and citizen safety have not gone away. Thus, like OEM corporations, states—particularly the United States—increasingly turn to outside suppliers to perform the work of government. During the years of the Bush Administration, annual spending on federal contracts doubled from $200 billion to $400 billion, and contractors took on tasks that ranged from providing armed security for diplomats in Iraq to reconstructing New Orleans to hiring, managing, and investigating other contractors. Indeed, if the corporation is a nexus of contracts, then the Federal government under Bush had become a "nexus of contractors."[6]

In light of this dilemma, basic questions about the purpose and function of the state are up for negotiation. One answer, popular in business circles, is that states' "core competence" is the business of law, providing a framework for contractual relations. The classic Hobbesian state has a contract with its citizens to protect them from physical harm. But in practice, law is primarily about contracts and property relations. In his 1913 book *An Economic Interpretation of the Constitution of the United States*, Charles Beard stated: "Now, most of the law (except the elemental law of community defence) is concerned with the property relations of men, which reduced to their simple terms mean the processes by which the ownership of concrete forms of property is determined or passes from one person to another." (In a post-industrial economy, of course, "concrete forms of property" are often highly abstract virtual goods, like collateralized debt obligations.) Sociologist Arthur Stinchcombe further notes that "most law practice is law on economic claims deriving from contract and property and has more to do with the contract clause in the Constitution than with the Bill of Rights."[7]

In their function of creating and administering frameworks for contracts, states are therefore service providers—specifically, business service providers, like Accenture or PricewaterhouseCoopers. And in a post-industrial economy, as long as the counterparties agree, the law that governs contracts can "reside" anywhere. This has two implications. First, states need not be monopoly providers. Indeed, like local bookstores, states implicitly face competition from virtual competitors: most significant public companies in the US incorporate in Delaware, which can be done over the Internet without setting foot in the state. Second, entrepreneurial states can draw on their distinctive status as sovereigns to compete as exporters. Thus, states can raise revenues by marketing products—incorporation, registering ships or aircraft, tax shelters—to distinct niches in the global business community. By providing an anonymous incorporation product for money-launderers over the Internet, for instance, Delaware is to financial crime what Amazon.com is to literature.

Post-industrial corporations play a central role in driving this dynamic. Corporations are chartered by states as legal fictions, but their organizers have great discretion over where they incorporate and can shop among jurisdictions around the world. Microsoft incorporated a subsidiary in Nevada to hold the rights to its copyrights and other intellectual property—unlike Microsoft's home state of Washington, Nevada does not tax royalties on IP. The Nevada subsidiary in turn was the parent of an Irish subsidiary holding the extremely lucrative licensing rights to various Microsoft products sold throughout Europe. Royal Caribbean Cruises, a Miami-based corporation catering to American vacationers, avoided US income taxes by incorporating in Liberia, making it a foreign shipper under both US and Liberian law. And Bermuda is the corporate home of hundreds of American corporations and subsidiaries, including Ingersoll-Rand, Tyco, and Accenture. Aided by accounting and consulting firms, companies are discriminating consumers of the goods and services that states have to offer. For services that entail a physical location, such as a plant or a server-farm, firms haggle with states and play them against each other, as in a Moroccan bazaar. For virtual goods, like legal homes for IP subsidiaries, firms can shop around among competing vendors, as in a shopping mall.[8]

For years, the proposed liberal strategy to respond to globalization and the disappearance of manufacturing jobs in the US was to focus on training and education of the nation's workforce in order to move to the higher end of the value chain. For instance, Robert Reich in *The Work of Nations* suggested expansive public education as a means to ready workers for jobs as (relatively) high-paid symbolic analysts. The global value chain of a Logitech wireless mouse illustrates how this might work: the $40 retail price is divided among suppliers in Malaysia, China, and the US ($14), an assembler in China ($3), distributors and wholesalers in the US ($15), and Logitech ($8), whose main function in the US is marketing. The US "symbolic analyst" jobs pay many times what the Chinese assembly jobs pay. But increasingly the highest value-added components—the intellectual property (designs, patents, trademarks)—are "housed" in Bermuda and Ireland.[9]

The result of this dynamic is that some states increasingly come to resemble shareholder-value-driven corporations in their relations with finance, corporations, and other actors. In order to serve corporate customers, they exploit their core competence (sovereignty, or a large installed base of lawyers) and contract out non-essential tasks, while guided by signals from finance. In the most extreme form, we may be seeing a "grey goo scenario." This phrase originally described a hypothetical danger of nanobots—tiny molecular robots created to, say, break down the chemicals in oil spills—that become self-replicating to the point that they end up devouring all life on Earth.[10] States initially chartered corporations to serve public purposes, but corporations have transcended states and become autonomous and self-replicating. Whether states are destroyed, or merely re-purposed, is a central question of the early twenty-first century.

This chapter describes changes in the nature of the state and how they are related to changed relations with corporations and finance. I begin with a brief discussion of the nation-state in the twentieth century, drawing on Philip Bobbitt's account of the history of the state since the Renaissance. I then describe competition among states in a federal system—in particular, the US and its experience with corporate law. Next comes a discussion of how states articulate themselves with footloose corporations and market-based finance. I analyze the emergence of the vendor state and what happens when sovereign governments see themselves as business service providers. I then argue that, as vendors, states have increasingly taken on the mien of shareholder-oriented corporations in how they raise capital and build relations with investors, manage their investment portfolio, manage their brand, and outsource non-core functions. Although the evidence is largely anecdotal, it suggests that states and corporations are becoming increasingly parallel in their strategies and structures.

The nation-state in the twentieth century

We take the nation-state for granted, but it is a relatively recent development in historical terms. According to historian Philip Bobbitt, "It may seem to us today altogether natural that states should occupy fixed and contiguous places on maps, but that . . . was not always the common conception. And it may also seem obvious that the geographical division of the world into states should fit the division of mankind into nations. But this too was not always so."[11] *Nations* are cultural groupings, often rooted in common ethnicity. In his dissection of the rise of nationalism in the nineteenth and twentieth centuries, Benedict Anderson famously defined the nation as "an imagined political community—and imagined as both inherently limited and sovereign."[12] Through an act of imagination members of nations were bound by a feeling of fraternity with strangers that made them willing to kill and die for an abstraction, the nation. *States*, on the other hand, are governmental organizations that have international recognition and a sanction to use physical violence, but they need not correspond to a "nation" or a "people," and for most of history they have not. In Bobbitt's telling, the nation-state was predominant only during the twentieth century, and its days may be numbered, to be succeeded by a "market-state."

Bobbitt describes five successive state types that evolved in the West from the Renaissance onward—each a constitutional archetype with its own central functions and bases of legitimacy. In Bobbitt's account, a primary function of a state is to raise revenues and organize to fight wars, and thus successful state types are those that are appropriately formatted to survive armed conflict according to the technology and warring style of the time. The *princely state* originated in northern Italian merchant cities during the fifteenth century to provide security in the face of military threats from new mobile artillery, which city walls alone were not sufficient to address. States had administrative, military, and revenue-raising functions, and successful models spread by mimicry among competing city-states. *Kingly states* were largely defined by the Peace of Westphalia of 1648, which many see as the origin of the contemporary state system. Each state was sovereign within its own territory, and legally equal within the society of states. States were characterized by a permanent bureaucracy, a standing army, and a centralized system of taxation geared towards maintaining the ability to wage war. In some cases there was an identity of the monarch with the state: as Louis XIV famously put it, "L'état, c'est moi." *Territorial states* maintained standing armies, but recruited them to fight not for king but for country, overseen by a limited monarchy. As exemplified by Frederick the Great of Prussia, the state was involved in the management of the economy beyond just taxation. Territorial states were succeeded by *state-nations*, whose approach to military mobilization and conflict was typified by Napoleon's France. State-nations characterized the imperial powers of the nineteenth century, as Western states subjected distant peoples and territories to metropolitan control.

Nation-states match the conception of a people, a nation, to the state. The nation-state was an accomplishment that primarily took hold in the second half of the nineteenth century and ultimately created a grand conflict in the twentieth century between three nation-state types—fascism, communism, and parliamentarianism—which Bobbitt calls the "long war," stretching from the First World War to the end of the Cold War in 1990. The nation-state of the twentieth century was characterized by several key features. Sovereignty was tied to territorial borders and the state's ability to defend them. Legitimacy was based in part on popular consent, which was necessary to raise armies of sufficient size to engage in large-scale war, such as the two world wars. Nation-states also took on the expectation that they would provide public goods and enhance the material welfare of their people, which meant a more-or-less engaged management of the economy.

Each of the three contending state types addressed these functions in characteristic ways related to their ability to engage in war. The typical nature of twentieth-century war, in contrast to armed conflicts of the past, was "total war," society against society (rather than army against army, as it was for Napoleon). The goal of total war is to deplete a society's willingness and ability to fight, which often meant making war on a society's civilian population and its industrial capacity (for instance, through the bombing of cities and industrial centers within their territory). Fascism, communism, and parliamentarianism were thus more-or-less viable configurations of elements for making total war. State types were also connected to economic systems. The parliamentarian nation-state, in particular the US, complemented and enabled corporate capitalism in the twentieth century, due in part to the requirement for large-scale mass production to support total war. The US was uniquely well suited to total war due to its vertically integrated manufacturers and its oceanwide distance from enemies. This advantage was on display in the Second World War, when automotive mass production was transformed into an "arsenal of democracy."

Commentators have asserted that the nation-state is increasingly obsolete because it is ill-suited to the contemporary global situation. Bobbitt argues that, for most of the twentieth century, only a state could threaten the basic security of another state because of the need for funds, armies, and equipment on a grand scale to fight a total war. Potential enemies were therefore a countable number of other nation-states that could be monitored, bargained with, and fought. But if the primary external threat to security is weapons of mass destruction wielded by rogue states, or even non-state actors, this makes defense of territorial integrity difficult or impossible. And within states, threats can come from guerrillas, warlords, criminal gangs, or terrorists with retail access to powerful weapons. "The mobilization of the industrial capacity of the nation is irrelevant to such threats; the fielding of fast tank armies and fleets of airplanes is as clumsy as a bear trying to fend off bees."[13] Thus, states' ability to make credible claims to legitimacy through protection of the safety of its citizens is undermined.

The decline of the nation-state does not mean the end of states, but simply that a different kind of state is likely to succeed the nation-state as the predominant type. States are still necessary for their economic function and the governance of property relations: after all, intellectual property is only "property" if there is a state to define and defend property rights. But states need not continue to have the familiar features of the twentieth-century nation-state. Their form and function has clearly changed over time, and will do so again. Bobbitt describes the "market-state" as an emerging alternative. In contrast to the nation-state, which sought to enhance the economic security and material wealth of its people, the market-state seeks to expand the opportunities available to its members, which need not result in security.

I argue here that a predictable response for a revenue-hungry state to the decline of the traditional nation-state model is to become a vendor—a service provider operating in a particular business niche, competing with other vendor-states. The state's ability to provide services for its citizens (or consumers) depends on its ability to compete effectively economically. This idea is not original. States have a history of business-like tactics to pursue economic goals, for instance, mergers and acquisitions to expand their legal product offerings.[14] But the vendor-state model is particularly relevant under post-industrialism, as the practical implications of jurisdictional choice are expanded. A vendor-state competes in a global market: it recognizes distinct business niches that states can serve but that other vendors (like corporations) cannot. Sovereigns can register ships and enable them to fly their flag, a requirement for global shipping. They can create securities laws that provide assurances to issuers and investors. They can enable banks and other business institutions attached to states. And they can provide tax homes that are recognized by other sovereigns. Inter-state conflict among vendor-states in this case is over economics, not territory, and the nature of this competition is directly analogous to competition among other business vendors. In this sense, the vendor-state model differs from the market-state described by Bobbitt: economic competition, not military conflict, is the central dynamic driving this state.

Federal states as economic competitors
The concept of a vendor-state is not such a radical change from prior convention; rather, it highlights different aspects of what states do in

their relations to business and the economy. In federal systems such as the United States, sub-national states have a long history of friendly (and not-so-friendly) competition over jurisdictional dominance in the economy. And even when states are not in explicit competition, they are often in implicit competition, creating an effective marketplace of laws. The notion of competition in a legal marketplace is therefore a recurring theme among scholars of law and economics, if not among civil servants.

Political economist Charles Tiebout introduced a model of market competition among local governments in 1956. Tiebout argued that the national government did not face a market test to determine proper expenditures on public goods, but that local governments did. The federal government is (or was) a monopolist with a captive audience, but local governments faced relatively mobile "consumers" for their offerings of fire and police protection, parks, beaches, school systems, and so on. City dwellers bound for the suburbs can choose among municipalities based on their combination of features and prices (taxes); local governments compete not by adapting to the preferences of their installed base of consumer-voters, but by attracting the optimum number of residents. Local governments were not the only ones in competition. At the time Tiebout was writing, state governments in the American South were in the third decade of their campaign to lure Northern manufacturers with a combination of cheap labor, low taxes, and no unions, eventually resulting in a shift in the center of gravity for American industry. Governments acted like economic competitors, whether their marketplace was recognized or not.[15]

In the case of corporate law, the US has well over a century of experience with the "shopping mall" model of competing states. Under American federal law, contracts made in one state are generally recognized in other states, including the creation of a corporation. Thus, incorporation has long been detached from physical domicile: companies can incorporate wherever they like, regardless of where their operations are housed. This has long been described as generating a competition among states—either a "race to the bottom," or a "race to the top." In the race to the bottom scenario, managers choose to incorporate in the state offering the most lax laws that enable them to loot the corporation with impunity. The winning state should therefore be the one that mandates corporate jets for all CEOs. In practice, however, things don't work out that way: Delaware has about a 60% market share among the largest corporations, yet its laws are not particularly tilted toward management. Rather, Delaware is distinguished more by the quantity of its case law (which is vast), and the customer orientation of its judiciary, which is generally regarded as quick, efficient, and unsurprising.

Revisionists described the competition among states in corporate law as, instead, a race to the top: states compete to provide the law that best facilitates creating shareholder value. The flywheel in this model is the stock market: for the reasons described in previous chapters, corporate managers seek to enhance their company's share price, and the stock market is highly attuned to aspects of corporate governance such as the character of corporate law in a firm's state of incorporation. Thus, firms incorporated in shareholder-hostile states (e.g. Pennsylvania, where corporate law encourages boards to take stakeholders into account) receive lower valuations than firms in shareholder-friendly states like Delaware. Managers know this, which encourages them to choose wisely when they incorporate; and state legislatures know this as well, which encourages them to pass laws attractive to their shareholder-oriented corporate clientele. Yale law professor Roberta Romano calls this the "genius of American corporate law": although the federal system was not designed to be a "market," it has that effect, creating beneficial competition among suppliers. Moreover, the federal competition model can potentially be exported to other federated systems, such as the EU, and to other aspects of law within the US, such as securities regulation.[16]

Re-revisionists have argued that the "race" analogy is highly flawed: the revenues available from the incorporation business are trivial to states other than Delaware, and thus the motivation to race is largely absent. Similarly, revenues from registering ships may be modest for large states, compared with Panama or Liberia. But the nature of the model suggests that there is a logic to interstate competition in some cases. Delaware will not pass egregiously shareholder-hostile law because of the counterweight of the stock market and the state's heavy budgetary dependence on corporate fees. Similarly, Liberia's rules for flagging ships face a counterweight in the insurance industry, as legitimate shippers will not choose a flag of convenience that limits their ability to get insurance. The implication is that interstate legal competition is not inevitably a race to the bottom: in some cases, countervailing forces exist to provide rules to the contest. On the other hand, some forms of interstate competition are clearly destructive, such as the competition to attract corporate facilities by providing lucrative tax breaks and infrastructure. In the first case, law is provided off-the-rack by vendor-states such as Delaware; in the second case, individual governmental bodies compete by being custom tailors to their business customers.[17]

It is also true that, among the American states, Delaware has embraced the vendor model most enthusiastically, becoming in essence the McDonald's of corporate law. In addition to providing anonymous shell corporations for Eastern European gangsters, Delaware has taken the lead in providing a home for intellectual property (IP) subsidiaries aimed at circumventing state-level corporate income taxes. Delaware does not collect income tax on royalties for out-of-state companies, and thus dozens of them set up Delaware subsidiaries to house patents, trademarks, and copyrights. The Delaware subsidiary—in effect, a brass plate in downtown Wilmington—charges hefty licensing fees to its corporate siblings, thereby reducing the earnings that would otherwise be subject to state income taxes where they actually operate. Major retailers including Toys R Us, Burger King, Gap, and Home Depot have all set up Delaware IP subsidiaries, prompting several states to launch lawsuits against the device (which perhaps contributes to the steep decline in the proportion of state revenues coming from corporate taxes in recent decades). Jonathan Chait of *the New Republic* voiced the frustration of Delaware's "competitor" states in a 2002 article titled "Rogue State": "Delaware's image as small and inoffensive is not merely a misconception but a purposeful guise. It presents itself as a plucky underdog peopled by a benevolent, public-spirited, entrepreneurial citizenry. In truth, it is a rapacious parasite state with a long history of disloyalty and avarice."[18]

The federal competition model is not limited to the US. In the European Union, the European Court of Justice has ruled in recent years that a company may, in effect, incorporate in a different country from its seat (that is, the primary home of its business operations). Although no "Euro Delaware" has arisen, legal observers anticipate seeing the evolution of new combinations in Europe as competition in corporate law becomes a live possibility.[19] As with the US, an EU competition model would be a form of regulated competition—member states are bound with a superordinate authority, so the "race" has a referee. Increasingly, however, the kinds of interstate competition we observe face no such overarching authority, as the states involved compete not within a federation, but as independent contractors.

Finance, post-industrialism, and interstate competition

The nation-state model is premised on the concept that states defend territorial, physical boundaries and are sovereign within them. In its relations with the economy, the state can govern trade and activities within its borders; in the US, sub-national governments also regulate aspects of the economy. But location (physical or virtual) is central to taxation. It is also central to notions of the corporation's place in society. When Pennsylvania's legislature passed its statute protecting "local" companies from unwanted takeovers, it charged the corporate board with attending to the effects of its actions on "communities in which offices or other establishments of the corporation are located." But in a post-industrial economy, much of the value added is via intellectual property, which can legally reside anywhere, and a corporation need not own or manage the establishments where the work is done—or even know where they are. The $40 retail price of a Logitech mouse primarily reflects its design, brand, and patents; at $3, the assembly of the final product by a Chinese supplier is a fairly trivial component of the value chain. And now even the dog food industry follows the OEM business model; since dozens of brands are all made by the same foreign manufacturer from the same ingredients, the price of the food is evidently driven by the value of the brand.

The widespread use of the OEM model by shareholder-oriented corporations means that the effective boundaries of corporations and states are flexible. Corporations do not carry a passport, and they do not exist anywhere in territorial space. They are simply a financial device. It was easier to overlook this when manufacturing companies actually made physical objects. As we saw in Chapter 3, NCR's attachment to Dayton, Ohio, was integral to its business, and its socially responsible behavior paid dividends, not least in the goodwill of the community. But what does a brass-plate IP subsidiary housed in Wilmington owe to the people of Delaware? Paradoxically, while corporations are increasingly untethered from particular physical locations, they are also called to take greater responsibility for actions beyond their corporate boundaries, including those of their suppliers and the states with which they do business. Nike is expected to vouchsafe employment practices of its overseas assemblers and those of their suppliers—perhaps back to the leather tannery. Baxter Health's use of a Chinese manufacturer for ingredients in heparin left it vulnerable to tainted supplies several links back in the supply chain. Unocal was sued by Burmese villagers in US courts under the Alien Tort Claims Act—created in 1789 to allow suits against pirates, among other things—for violating human rights by working with the Burmese government in building a pipeline, a suit which Unocal settled in 2004.[20]

Much as corporations might yearn for statelessness, they still require states to govern contracts and protect patents. States also provide other essential business services, such as a domicile for tax purposes. Even IP subsidiaries need to reside in a recognized nation—preferably one with a tax treaty with the US. As a result, one of the ways that states compete is by providing more-or-less friendly legal frameworks for intellectual property and other virtual goods. The attraction of a virtual domicile depends almost exclusively on the nature of its legal product offerings. And while a plausible case can be made for a "race to the top" in federated systems facing a superordinate authority, the case is far less certain in other international races among states, as we will see.

Financial markets further reinforce the competitive impact of corporate state-shopping by putting states in competition for financial capital for both public and private uses. States have long relied on international banks to give them loans, making bankers potentially powerful supranational actors. In *The Great Transformation* Karl Polanyi describes the role of *haute finance* in maintaining international peace during the late nineteenth and early twentieth centuries, with bankers acting as transnational mediators and providing loans to states contingent on their good behavior—particularly smaller states in "backward regions."[21] International commercial banks grew to be major sources of external capital for low-income countries through the 1970s, providing about two-thirds of the net private capital flows to developing countries between 1980 and 1982. But after the 1982 debt crisis, triggered by Mexico's suspension of its debt payment, commercial banks substantially retrenched their lending to the developing world, thus kicking off the so-called "lost decade" in economic development.[22] In response, and with the encouragement of the IMF and World Bank, states increasingly turned to markets for financing and implemented liberalizations enabling foreign investment.

A new understanding of the role of the state in the economy—broadly if inaccurately labelled the "Washington Consensus"—led to a new role for foreign investment, particularly market-based investment. "Emerging markets" (a term coined by the International Finance Corporation's Antoine von Agtmael shortly after the debt crisis) now compete for foreign direct investment (FDI) from multinationals, portfolio investment from Western institutional investors, and sovereign debt from Wall Street—as do well-established markets such as the US. In each case, the state is the relevant financial unit, as debtor and manager of the economy.

One of the most vivid manifestations of this new role for states is the extensive spread of stock exchanges around the world since the debt crisis. In 1980, fifty-nine nations had indigenous stock exchanges, overwhelmingly residing in rich economies in Europe and North America. This number doubled in the subsequent twenty-five years, coming to include nearly every nation in the former Soviet bloc as well as countries across Asia and the Pacific (Bhutan, Mongolia, Papua New Guinea), Africa (Namibia, Malawi, Uganda), Latin America (Guatemala, Guyana), and the Middle East (Qatar, United Arab Emirates, Lebanon). Research evidence suggested that stock markets enhanced economic growth in low- and moderate-income countries, particularly when embedded in an appropriate set of legal and corporate governance institutions. Stock markets allowed liquid investments and could stimulate entrepreneurship and economic development. Of course, many exchanges failed to take root: Swaziland's exchange saw a total of fifty transactions for its five listed companies in 2000. But others grew spectacularly: by 2007, the Shanghai Stock Exchange achieved a total capitalization of over $3 trillion, on a par with those of the world's largest industrial economies. (The Industrial and Commercial Bank of China, the country's largest, was worth one-third of a trillion dollars in late 2007, far more than Citigroup.)[23]

The effect of "installing" financial markets can be profound. Stock markets simultaneously provide a channel for capital from savers to businesses and an instrument for taking the pulse of an economy and making projections about the future. They can also guide companies by providing a kind of economic compass, as when companies orient their strategies toward shareholder value. And they can be a fulcrum for broader kinds of change. The creation of a speculative "shareholder culture" virtually overnight in China is a remarkable shift, given that the Shanghai Stock Exchange was closed after the Communist Revolution in 1949 and only re-opened in 1990.

Early enthusiasts imagined that the spread of stock markets to dozens of new countries would result in a kind of corporate McDonaldization, with the American system of shareholder capitalism franchised around the world. The practice of cross-listing company shares on American markets, which hundreds of companies did during the late 1990s, seemed to reinforce this idea. Such firms are subject to US securities laws and regulations, including the demand for particular formats for corporate governance. The evidence, however, has not borne out the prediction of worldwide standardization. With the possible exception of Israeli companies, most US-listed firms are indistinguishable from their domestic counterparts in the size and structure of their corporate boards, the level of concentration of their ownership, and their appeal to foreign institutional investors. Indeed, in many cases, such as the two dozen Chilean firms quoted on the New York Stock Exchange, listing in the US seemed to be more of a status symbol for their domestic investors than a sign of commitment to American-style shareholder capitalism.[24] It appeared, in short, that the American-style public corporation with dispersed ownership was an orchid that only thrives in a distinct institutional climate, rather than bamboo that would out-compete the indigenous forms. Regardless of whether states embrace full-on shareholder capitalism, however, it is clear that financial markets have achieved a broad reach around the globe and shaped the role of the state in the global and local economy.

The emerging vendor-state

Whether out of choice or necessity, states increasingly find themselves in competition as vendors to a corporate and financial clientele. States compete for many types of consumers: for foreign direct investment, for portfolio investment, for taxes, for incorporation. What is the likely outcome of this competition? In the case of federal competition—interstate competition with a referee—we may see a beneficial race to the top, as arguably happens with corporate law. But what about less constrained interstate competition?

The competition to provide so-called flags of convenience for ships was an early version of interstate rivalry rooted in the sovereignty business. Ships are governed by the laws of the country in which they are registered, which—as with a corporation—need bear no particular relation to where they operate. Thus, flying a "flag of convenience" refers to being "flagged" by a government that has created a ship registry amenable to shipowners. Prior to the twentieth century, it was common to fly the flag of one's own country, which had certain advantages when the sea was contested. But during the early decades of the twentieth century,

American shipowners began to register ships in Panama, which had more amenable labor laws from the perspective of shipowners (as well as no prohibition on alcohol—unlike the US). American oil companies created a ship registry for their oil tankers in Liberia after the Second World War—Liberia's flag looks much like the American flag at a distance—and within a few decades a number of other states began flagging vessels for profit as the volume of international shipping exploded with containerization.[25]

Panama and Liberia are #1 and #2 in registered ships, but under international law, even landlocked countries can register ships, and there is no international body to provide binding standards—the US, characteristically, has failed to ratify the UN Convention on the Law of the Sea, which might provide some international oversight. During the early 2000s, Bolivia earned $1 million per year for registering about 300 ships, promising "Immediate registration, total tax exemption, no restrictions in respect to size and age of the vessel and no restrictions as to nationality of ship owner or crew."[26] Moreover, the doctrine of "innocent passage" means that foreign ships can sail unhindered through territorial waters as long as they are not an immediate threat to the adjacent state. Ships can change name and nationality while en route; as the ship ages and its safety declines, it might register in ever-more-lenient countries.

William Langewiesche's *The Outlaw Sea* describes the consequences of the nautical race to the bottom: "By shopping globally, [shipowners] found that they could choose the laws that were applied to them, rather than haplessly submitting to the jurisdictions of their native countries... What's more, because of the registration fees the shipowners could offer to cash-strapped governments and corrupt officials, the various flags competed for business, and the deals kept getting better."[27] One consequence is that global shipping has gotten very cheap. The vast majority of the world's international trade in physical goods is carried on containers aboard perhaps 40,000 effectively stateless merchant marine vessels, and the de facto deregulation of the seas has helped make this economical. It is economical, however, in part because labor and safety standards are somewhat "relaxed." Langewiesche documents a number of disasters at sea (as well as rampant piracy and opportunities for terrorism) that deregulation of the seas has enabled. An elderly ship called the *Kristal*, owned by an Italian family through a Maltese holding company, was carrying a 28,000-ton load of molasses from India to Europe for a British sugar company in February 2001 when it broke in half and sank off the coast of Spain. Its captain and chief mate were Croatian and the crew came primarily from Pakistan (for the grunt jobs) and Spain (for the more skilled positions); communication among crews was primarily in English. Eleven members of the *Kristal*'s crew were lost when the rusty vessel sank, a predictable consequence of the combination of cost pressures and deregulation faced by contemporary merchant ships. Osama bin Laden is also alleged to own a navy of twenty such merchant vessels, all protected from bother by flying the flag of a sovereign nation.

Bermuda was in the vanguard of providing an appealing offshore legal home for insurance companies and, later, other types of corporations. The genesis of its position as a top-selling vendor, however, had little to do with state-level business strategy, at least initially. Executives of American International Group, once the world's largest commercial insurer and now 80% owned by the US government after a multi-billion dollar bailout in September 2008, helped craft the laws that made Bermuda an attractive jurisdiction for insurance businesses over several decades. The first was in 1947, when the Parliament passed a special statute exempting AIG from a local ownership requirement and from taxes on income outside the country (subsequently extended to other foreign firms). An AIG executive based in Bermuda advised local politicians on the features of laws that American insurance companies would find attractive, such as permissive rules regarding how insurance premiums are invested. AIG executives also served as representatives of the Bermuda government in negotiations with the US over a tax treaty in the mid-1980s which included a provision allowing US income tax exemption for insurers legally domiciled in Bermuda. This treaty subsequently prompted a boom in Bermuda-based insurance subsidiaries. Today Bermuda is the self-styled "risk capital of the world," home to hundreds of insurance companies and subsidiaries that operate in the US and elsewhere.[28]

Bermuda's other product offerings include incorporation and air-craft registry. During the 1990s, accounting firms pitched the notion of Bermuda IP subsidiaries to technology, software, biotech, and pharmaceutical companies as a means to shelter foreign income from taxes. IP subsidiaries entail an American corporate parent transferring ownership of intellectual property (patents and trademarks) to a Bermuda subsidiary. Other foreign subsidiaries then pay royalties for the use of the IP to the Bermuda subsidiary, thus shielding the income from US taxes until the point that the income is repatriated to the US (if ever). Dozens of US companies set up such subsidiaries, although the precise number is difficult to determine.[29] In a move to induce some of these companies to repatriate more of their parked foreign profits in 2004, Bush signed into law the "American Jobs Creation Act," a tax bill with a variety of treats for multinationals, including a one-time break that allowed foreign profits to be taxed at a modest 5.25% rate. Contrary to the name of the bill, however, it appeared that little if any of the repatriated income was used to create jobs; Colgate-Palmolive, for instance, repatriated $800 million at the same time that it was closing one-third of its American factories and eliminating 12% of its workforce.[30]

Some corporations went further than merely creating IP subsidiaries, by reincorporating the parent company itself in Bermuda. Bermuda corporations came to include New Hampshire-based conglomerate Tyco International (1997), Ingersoll-Rand of New Jersey (2001), and Houston-based electrical equipment maker Cooper Industries (2002). Although some in Congress questioned the patriotism of such companies, sympathetic members of the Bush Administration placed the blame for "corporate emigration" squarely on the American tax system: the Treasury Department's chief of tax policy stated, "We may need to rethink some of our international tax rules that were written 30 years ago when our economy was very different and that now may be impeding the ability of U.S. companies to compete internationally." While Congress was considering bills to limit the appeal of reincorporating in tax havens like Bermuda,

Tyco retained Viagra pitchman Bob Dole to lobby for its cause, evidently with some success.[31]

If the corporation is a legal fiction, then the major accounting firms would seem to be the Philip Roths of the genre, encouraging firms to create simulacra of themselves in tax havens around the world. Moreover, their own consulting arms seem inevitably to incorporate in Bermuda. One of these was Accenture, formerly the consulting arm of Arthur Andersen. The firm hired a platoon of lobbyists to argue that, parentage notwithstanding, Accenture had never been an American company, and that its operations in forty-seven countries demonstrated its intrinsic globalness. PricewaterhouseCoopers Consulting (PwCC Ltd.) also briefly organized in Bermuda, although it was acquired by IBM before going public.[32]

Bermuda exemplifies the old-school island vendor-state, but Nauru provides the parody form. A tiny island nation in the South Pacific, with the smallest land mass of any country outside Europe, Nauru was blessed with an abundant natural resource that made it rich, namely, bird guano—or more specifically the phosphate contained in millennia worth of bird droppings. After decades of mining its phosphate-rich interior, the island was left nearly barren by the 1990s, leaving the country with nothing else to trade. But as a sovereign nation, Nauru found a new business as an international banking center, chartering banks at $5,000 (Australian) apiece. As with Delaware, the best customers for these anonymous banks appeared to be elements of the Russian mafia, alleged to have laundered $70 billion in illicit funds through Nauru before the island nation was sanctioned in 2001. Two years later, Nauru was cut off from the US financial system due to persistent concerns about money laundering. Shortly thereafter, Nauru fell into bankruptcy, forced to sell its only assets (commercial property in Australia) to pay its debts, and ended up effectively in receivership under Australia.[33]

The point of this discussion is not that other states are likely to turn into Bermuda, or Nauru. But the existence of interstate competition for law changes what states can do and how the role of the state is conceived—even the US cannot be indifferent to Bermuda, or Nauru.

According to the IMF, there are now dozens of competing vendors along the lines of the Cayman Islands, and the model has spread fairly broadly, with different states staking out different niches. Industry segmentation also takes place within the US: Delaware gets the bulk of the incorporation business, but Nevada has come to specialize in certain kinds of businesses such as energy. Eighty Canadian-headquartered firms are incorporated in Nevada, as are a half-dozen Hong Kong-based companies.[34] Even tiny niches can find a willing vendor. Montana has developed a modest business for local lawyers in creating shell corporations for buyers of recreational vehicles seeking to avoid state taxes. Many states charge sales tax on RVs, which can run into thousands of dollars, and others charge hefty annual licensing fees. Montana levies neither fee, and accordingly has found it lucrative to create Montana corporations to act as holding companies on behalf of elderly RV enthusiasts. Some retirees have no fixed address; thus, Montana may be particularly effective at capturing their business.[35]

Blessed with a jurisdictional Mall of America, many multinational corporations have adopted a "legal masala" model, fine-tuning the domicile of each aspect of the value chain from their places of incorporation, to where they stash their patents, to where they register their corporate jet. Multinationalism is centuries old, of course, and companies have long experience extending the reach of their products around the world. What is different about the legal masala approach is that companies may not be identifiably "American" or "French," in spite of the connotations of the brand. Accenture's claim to have no fixed nationality is not wrong. Recall our familiar example of Tommy Hilfiger, which was headquartered in Hong Kong, incorporated in the British Virgin Islands, held its annual meeting in Barbados, listed its shares on the New York Stock Exchange, and contracted manufacturing to vendors in Mexico and East Asia. (There is also a person named "Tommy Hilfiger," who lives on Long Island.) Hilfiger is no more American than teenagers who wear Polo shirts, Hilfiger pants, and Timberland shoes are citizens of Ralph Lauren. In this context, even a country's physical territory and population are part of the façade. A Dublin-based law firm that markets its nation's legal products through a Palo Alto office noted that multinationals find it increasingly attractive "to unbundle the traditional value chain and locate appropriate profit generating functions in Ireland." Why Ireland? Unlike Bermuda and the Cayman Islands, which may have a hard time conveying the impression of a tangible business behind the brass plate to tax authorities, Ireland has infrastructure for the "construction of profit-generating centres defensible by reference to functions, risks and tangible assets of the Irish operation."[36]

States adopt the corporate model

If corporations adopted models of bureaucracy from governments and armies in the late nineteenth century, then post-industrial states increasingly repay the favor by coming to look more like shareholder-oriented corporations. From the process of raising capital on Wall Street, to managing relations with investors, to overseeing contractors and managing their brand, states reflect the sensibilities of vanguard corporations—particularly those that have perfected the OEM model.

Raising capital   States have always faced the prospect of raising funds, particularly when war required revenues beyond what could be generated from taxation. The advantage of funding wars via market-based finance rather than tax increases became evident to England at the end of the seventeenth century during the wars with France. Due to the expense of new military technologies, as sociologist Bruce Carruthers puts it, "War had become as much a test of financial strength as of military power."[37] Moreover, an absolute monarch such as Louis XIV could force his subjects into penury through taxation, but an English monarch needed the permission of Parliament to raise taxes. This limited how much citizens could be squeezed and necessitated the creation of financial market infrastructure for issuing government debt. English monarchs learned that they had to make credible promises to potential creditors to raise debt: taxpayers can be coerced, but lenders must be persuaded. Thus, the English learned from the Dutch how to sustain long-term government debt with the aid of markets.

The ability to raise debt financing is still an indispensable capability for successful states, and after the virtual disappearance of bank-based financing after 1982 for so-called emerging markets, states frequently had to rely on Wall Street to raise funds. (Indeed, in Wall Street parlance, "corporates" include any business or governmental entity that seeks to access the capital market.) As with corporations, the cost advantages of market-based finance over other forms of governmental debt became widely recognized around the world. As a result, states came to work with Wall Street bankers just as corporations did, with similar rules for "relationship-building." (There is, of course, a thin line between "relationship building" and "bribery" in this context, as the various "pay to play" scandals involving state and municipal government officials and their banking friends illustrate.[38]) And using the markets for debt places states into a position directly analogous to corporations in how they deal with their investors.

Investor relations   Along with a reliance on market-based finance comes a need for investor relations. Emerging markets in particular are at the mercy of their significant creditors, such as the institutional investors that hold their bonds. The Pacific Investment Management Company, or PIMCO, a California-based unit of German insurer Allianz, is one of the biggest investment managers focused on fixed income securities (bonds) and runs the largest bond fund in the US. PIMCO has the largest share of emerging market bonds, at about 7.5% in 2004, and the firm's holdings were big enough to have a substantial influence on the structure and price of debt offerings among developing countries. PIMCO's primary manager for emerging markets, formerly with the IMF, was a familiar figure among finance ministers around the world, to whom he was happy to offer advice—such as when and how to make debt offerings, how big they should be, and at what price. Investor interests also benefit from the influence of the United States government. After Indonesia's transition from the Suharto dictatorship to democracy in the late 1990s, US representatives ensured that the harm to American financial interests would be limited: according to the US embassy's chief political counsellor at the time, "Protecting the interests of major investors and creditors was at the center of the table in everything we did … Concerns about stability made it to the margins. Concerns about human rights, democracy, corruption never made it onto the table at all."[39]

Attending to investor relations was not limited to emerging markets. The Clinton Administration was particularly attuned to the financial markets in the 1990s, from the staffing of positions in the Treasury Department to the rationales for specific policies. Like a CEO who tunes to CNBC to see how his latest strategic announcement played with Wall Street, Clinton was famously attentive to the instant polls of the financial markets. For example, in arguing for fast-track trade authority, Clinton said this: "If it passes, I think it will have a very positive impact on the stock market here and around the world." A Clinton speechwriter asked Clinton's top economic advisor Gene Sperling, "When you were a little kid watching Bobby Kennedy and dreaming of social justice, did you ever imagine whispering in the President's ear, 'Sir, there was a big bond rally today'?" Perhaps no administration in history was more intimately attuned to the concerns of Wall Street. For an administration whose motto was "It's the economy, stupid," financial markets provided a second-to-second guidance system for policy.[40]

By the late 1990s, the financial news media began to routinely report financial market reactions to political events around the world. A *New York Times* article of March 13, 1999 opened, "One day after the abrupt resignation of Germany's most powerful left-wing political boss, German financial markets soared in euphoria… The German stock market surged 5.4 percent." In contrast, "Taiwan shares posted their largest plunge in nine years Friday, falling 6.4% amid uncertainty over Sino-Taiwan relations" after Taiwan's leadership indicated that the "one state" fiction of its relations with the PRC were no longer acceptable. In India, "After two trading sessions of huge losses, bargain hunters emerged to bid shares up 8 percent on the Indian exchange on Tuesday, encouraged by reports that Sonia Gandhi was reluctant to become the prime minister… On Monday, the index fell more than 11 percent, after a 6 percent tumble on Friday, on anxieties that the left-backed Congress party, led by Mrs. Gandhi, would hamper economic modernization and stop the sale of government-owned enterprises." In the meantime, brokers and investors had led street protests against Mrs. Gandhi.[41]

Investor sentiment can not only respond to a state's "business strategy," but drive it as well. In the Philippines, President Joseph "Erap" Estrada was elected in a popular landslide in May 1998, but his administration quickly lost the confidence of the foreign investors through a series of corruption scandals. Foreign direct investment plummeted, the stock market tanked, and the peso declined substantially in value. In response, a committee of the nation's wealthy elite, including directors from the country's top five business groups, began a campaign to depose Estrada and replace him with a more investor-friendly model. Stock traders and executives mounted street protests, and bankers took out newspaper ads demanding Estrada's resignation. To promote the impression of popular support for their movement, elites provided catering to bring farmers and laborers out to their protests; some gave their servants time off from work to march. With the aid of an impeachment trial, protests ultimately swelled into a replay of the "People Power" movement that had ousted Ferdinand Marcos fifteen years before. Estrada was ultimately forced to resign by the Supreme Court in January 2001, albeit through extra-constitutional means supported with threatening moves by the Philippine military. It was as if the Board of Directors of Philippines Inc. had fired the CEO after he had lost investor confidence, sending in security guards to escort him from the premises.[42]

A year later, the Philippines was again rattled by restive investors. This time, it was CalPERS, the California Public Employees Retirement System, which brought trouble. CalPERS had hired a consulting firm to help it assess the suitability of foreign markets for investment using a rating scheme, and an employee inaccurately classified the Manila Stock Exchange as having a manual entry system rather than a computerized system—which incorrectly put the Philippines on CalPERS' investment blacklist. When this became public, the Philippines exchange dropped over 3% in value, leading the country's Financial Secretary to lobby

CalPERS to repair its mistake before a contagion of divestment occurred. As an investment professional put it at the time, "CalPERS is seen as an industry leader and investment committees are saying, 'Well, if CalPERS is doing this, they must have a good reason.' "[43]

From some perspectives—particularly that of the *Wall Street Journal* editorial page—governing a country the way corporations are governed for shareholder value is not such a bad idea. By hypothesis, the market's price is always right. Matters of judgment can be resolved by observing the market's reaction, which estimates the future consequences of an action or policy, and the mechanisms of corporate governance are oriented toward this metric. As a result, those that manage states might profitably attend to financial market reactions as a critical form of opinion poll in the same way that corporate managers do. Holman Jenkins, columnist for the *Wall Street Journal*, argued that all states need a feedback mechanism to guide policy, and that financial markets (because of their ability to render unbiased estimates of the future impact of policies) should guide US policy. Elections are too infrequent to provide much guidance, and opinion polls are unreliable and involve too low a stake. But financial markets provide a continuous distillation of the aggregate opinions of well-informed players putting their own wealth at stake. Voters can be fooled, but financial markets cannot. Thus, "What we need is an investing strategy that would let the markets discipline the politicians, not the other way around."[44]

As quixotic as this might sound, there are signs that some voters have already adopted a shareholder orientation to politics—a theme we take up again in the next chapter. Puzzled about why Clinton managed to maintain highly favorable evaluations from voters even as he was being impeached for matters regarded as personal, pollsters discovered that he was seen as a successful economic manager, and that personal peccadilloes were largely irrelevant. As one put it in describing suburban Chicagoans, "Voters weren't electing a president. They were electing a CEO." And just as investors evaluate stocks according to their perceptions of other investor sentiment (Keynes's famous newspaper beauty contest), voters evaluate candidates based on their perceptions of how the candidates are perceived by other voters, with "electability" being a primary concern. In 2004, a biographer of Keynes said "This is a political market, and everyone is not choosing on the merits of the individual but on whether they think he's a winner or not." This is perhaps not a surprising development, given that most households were shareholders by the turn of the twenty-first century, and many had adopted the cognitive style of investors.[45]

Making investments Like corporations, some states have also become major investors—not simply in sovereign debt, but also in corporate shares. Sometimes this happens inadvertently, as when the US Pension Benefit Guarantee Corporation—created as part of the Employee Retirement Income Security Act of 1974 (ERISA) to insure corporate pensions—ends up holding shares in bankrupt firms whose underfunded pension plans become its responsibility. The PBGC became a major shareholder in the American airline industry due to a series of airline bankruptcies in the mid-2000s, owning large stakes in USAir, United, and Delta Airlines, and there was some expectation that it would become a significant shareholder in the auto industry if trends in pension funding and bankruptcy continued there.[46]

Sovereign wealth funds (SWFs) have become an even more significant source of equity investment, particularly among American commercial and investment banks. SWFs invest on behalf of pools of government funds, which can accumulate through pension savings (e.g. Chile), sales of commodities (especially oil—Abu Dhabi, Norway, Kuwait, Russia), or foreign exchange reserves generated through exports (Singapore, China, Korea, Malaysia). SWFs traditionally followed extremely cautious approaches to investment, focusing on safe government securities such as American treasury bills. During the 2000s, however, several SWFs became increasingly aggressive in seeking higher returns by buying corporate shares around the world. In terms of their assets under management, SWFs are larger than all hedge funds and private equity combined; the twenty largest SWFs alone are estimated to manage over $2 trillion. SWFs were largely ignored when they invested primarily in sovereign debt. But the funds rose to overnight prominence when a few of them became Wall Street's largest shareholders during the credit crisis that began in 2007, as a number of banks required quick capital infusions not available elsewhere. Chinese government funds bought just under 10% each of Morgan Stanley and Blackstone; a Singaporean fund bought 9.9% of Merrill Lynch; and the Abu Dhabi Investment Authority made an investment convertible to 4.9% of Citigroup. The IMF estimated that foreign assets owned by SWFs would reach $12 trillion by 2012, creating a formidable new force in the world economy. The dark side of this, according to uber-investor Warren Buffett in his 2004 letter to shareholders of Berkshire Hathaway, could be to turn the US into a "sharecropper society," driven by its persistent trade deficits to sell off its most important capital assets to foreign funds.[47]

Mergers, acquisitions, and divestitures Some governmental units also pursue mergers and spinoffs. In a number of cases in the US, cities have merged with their surrounding counties to save funds on redundant services and engage in more efficient regional planning. Indianapolis, Houston, and Kansas City all managed to merge with their counties, and Pittsburgh, Cleveland, and Fairbanks have contemplated it as well— although such moves are often unpopular with voters. Buffalo, New York, pitched the idea as part of its brand-building: through a merger, Buffalo would become tenth largest city in the US, a potential economic advantage.[48]

Naomi Klein describes a remarkable move in the opposite direction. Residents of a wealthy enclave outside Atlanta elected to incorporate as their own city, Sandy Springs, in December 2005 to effectively secede from surrounding Fulton County, hiring CH2M Hill, a construction and consulting firm, to build and run the city government from the ground up. Other county residents soon followed suit, creating the cities of Milton and Johns Creek in December 2006—all relying heavily on the same contractor to run their municipal services. Residents of the three new cities were contemplating a move to create a new Milton County and formally secede from the less-affluent Fulton.[49]

States and the OEM model   Many of the states adopting a corporate model have taken a page from the OEM ("original equipment manufacturer") corporation's playbook. OEMs such as Nike or Hewlett-Packard typically focus on design and marketing and contract out most or all of the actual production tasks. One of the OEM's signature strengths is in building and managing the brand. Thus, a British marketing consultant who had previously worked with Nestle and Coca-Cola opened Place-brands to help countries build their brand more effectively, stating that "Marketing is at the heart of what makes rich countries rich." He argued that bringing in foreign investment and tourists was just as critical to national economic development as building transportation systems and a functioning civil service, and that brand management was the key to wooing foreigners. Brand management can be tricky for some countries. Croatia, one client, was best known among its European neighbors for its collaboration with the Nazis and for its interminable struggles with Serbia. Thus, efforts focused on highlighting Croatia as a Mediterranean country and a market-based democracy. Slovenia's major problem was that consumers confused it with Slovakia, which (unlike Slovenia) does not have Alps or a majestic coastline. A good logo helps—consider Spain—but other factors, such as English-speaking staff at hotels and generosity in foreign aid, also go far to convey an appealing brand image. Tony Blair's UK joined the trend by marketing itself as "Cool Britannia," with the Prime Minister stating "I'm proud of my country's past, but I don't want to live in it." National brand management is not as new as its name might suggest: an "imagined community" is, in some sense, just a brand, a calculative identity that serves internal political ends, such as taxation and military recruiting. As the Placebrands website put it, "This 'brand equity' is what sustains the community, attracts and retains the people, businesses, events, visitors and institutions that the place needs in order to grow and prosper."[50] But in the past, building and managing national identity was not contracted out to marketing consultants.[51]

Like OEM corporations, states—particularly the US and its sub-national governments—have increasingly turned to contractors to perform critical government tasks. Of course state contracting has a very long history prior to the advent of the nation-state. Rome sold the rights to collect taxes to tax farmers, and city-states hired mercenaries. But beginning with the Clinton Administration's "Reinventing Government" initiative, which shrank the Federal civilian workforce by 350,000, the US Federal government came to rely on contractors to an unprecedented degree. The Federal Activities Inventory Reform Act of 1998 (FAIR) promoted outsourcing by requiring Federal agencies to open activities that are not "inherently governmental" to bidding by outside contractors.[52] The Act was more than effective at shifting government work from public to private. As the *New York Times* described it in February 2007,

> Without a public debate or formal policy decision, contractors have become a virtual fourth branch of government. On the rise for decades, spending on federal contracts has soared during the Bush administration, to about $400 billion last year from $207 billion in 2000, fuelled by the war in Iraq, domestic security and Hurricane Katrina, but also by a philosophy that encourages outsourcing almost everything government does. Contractors still build ships and satellites, but they also collect income taxes and work up agency budgets, fly pilotless spy aircraft and take the minutes at policy meetings on the war. They sit next to federal employees at nearly every agency; far more people work under contracts than are directly employed by the government. Even the government's online database for tracking contracts, the Federal Procurement Data System, has been outsourced (and is famously difficult to use).[53]

There are legal limits to what contractors are allowed to do, at least in principle: they are not allowed to perform "inherently governmental" functions. According to the Office of Management and Budget,

> As a matter of policy, an 'inherently governmental function' is a function that is so intimately related to the public interest as to mandate performance by Government employees. These functions include those activities that require either the exercise of discretion in applying Government authority or the making of value judgments in making decisions for the

> Government.... Inherently governmental functions... do not include
> functions that are primarily ministerial and internal in nature, such as
> building security; mail operations; operation of cafeterias; housekeep-
> ing; facilities operations and maintenance, warehouse operations, motor
> vehicle fleet management and operations, or other routine electrical or
> mechanical services.

These are regarded as "commercial activities" and therefore appropriate
for contractors.[54]

During the Bush years, contractors went well beyond operating cafete-
rias to take on core governmental functions, from protecting diplomats
to managing other contractors. As the *Times* noted, Lockheed Martin
gets more federal money each year than the Departments of Justice
and Energy, and the government employs far more contractors than
federal employees (although the precise number of contract employees
is unknown). The American war in Iraq was perhaps the apex of the
practice of turning "inherently governmental" work over to contractors. Contract employees were hired to work at Abu Ghraib prison,
apparently in conflict with the Army's explicit policy, and some of them
were alleged to be "directly or indirectly responsible" for the abuses
there. Blackwater, DynCorp, and Triple Canopy have all taken on tasks
that seem to meet basic definitions of mercenary armies, without the
accountability of actual governmental armies. Blackwater was allegedly
responsible for the deaths of dozens of civilians in Iraq—most famously,
seventeen killed in Nisour Square in Baghdad—but managed to evade
charges, aided by a 2004 Coalition Provisional Authority order (Order
17) that rendered US government contractors immune from Iraqi law.
The medieval French practice of *privilege*—private law, applicable only
to certain persons—had found a home in Iraq. An under-secretary of
state explained Blackwater's continued lucrative business with the US
government: "We cannot operate without private security firms in Iraq.
If the contractors were removed, we would have to leave Iraq."[55]

The elaboration of an entire sector of contractors performing "inherently governmental work" at sites around the world makes clear that

there is nothing particularly sacred about states as organizations, and that there are alternative forms that can accomplish many of the same functions. By the same token, non-state actors can underlay imagined communities. Moreover, with retail access to high-powered weapons, including weapons of mass destruction, they can act with the lethal force of a state: consider Al Qaeda, for whom geography is relatively unimportant to its terrorist operations. There are plenty of vendor-states willing to use their sovereign status to flag ships and planes, register shell corporations, and provide homes for banks to launder funds, from Liberia to Delaware. With the ready availability of contractors to perform civil, military, police, and financial functions, the ingredients for an OEM state are available off the shelf.

Regulatory masala

Americans are accustomed to thinking about corporations operating in nested legal units—municipalities, states, and nations—with a constitutional basis for resolving antinomies. This is the familiar "layer cake" of a federated legal system, with relevant regulatory bodies potentially subject to capture by those within their jurisdiction. But in the "legal masala" model, in which corporations fine-tune their jurisdictions, firms can end up facing multiple, potentially conflicting regulations. About ten large German firms are listed on the New York Stock Exchange, which makes them subject to American securities laws and corporate governance requirements, such as the Sarbanes–Oxley Act (SOX). But while SOX requires that audit committees be staffed only by "outsiders" on the board, German law requires labor representation on boards and committees. Regulatory harmonization is not impossible, but it is not trivial.[56]

A more intriguing prospect is that, just as corporations are not bound by states, so laws are not bound by territory. Hundreds of foreign firms are listed on American securities markets—particularly Nasdaq for high-tech firms and the New York Stock Exchange for established companies—which means they are subject to regulation by the SEC and by the American Congress. This includes meeting strict accounting standards and observing extensive disclosure requirements (e.g. a relatively detailed annual report). Disclosure requirements extend to investors in such firms: a Finnish citizen or group that accumulates 5% of the shares of a Russian firm that lists on the New York Stock Exchange is in principle required to disclose their control intentions and the size of their stake to the Securities and Exchange Commission, which makes these disclosures available to the public. Moreover, all securities issuers are subject to the Foreign Corrupt Practices Act of 1977, which bans paying bribes to foreign officials, as well as a number of other statutes not directly tied to securities issuance. Prosecution for violations has historically been rare; however, during the 2000s the SEC brought charges against Royal Dutch/Shell, Dutch supermarket chain Ahold, and Italian dairy producer Parmalat, and settled an investigation of French water and media conglomerate Vivendi Universal. European critics refer to the SEC's new international activism as "US regulatory imperialism," and European firms were increasingly vocal about the declining cost-benefit tradeoff of listing in the US.[57]

But European Union standards are another form of implicit global regulation. EU regulators scuttled the proposed merger between GE and Honeywell on antitrust grounds in 2001. EU privacy standards limit the kind of datafiles that can be assembled, which meant that General Motors was unable to assemble a corporate-wide online telephone directory because it violated EU privacy regulations. EU environmental standards have changed the way American and Japanese electronic products are assembled to meet the criterion that the product can be recycled by the company after its use. And the EU's ban on importing genetically modified crops has changed the economic prospects for African farmers. GE's CEO referred to the EU as the "global regulatory superpower," setting the standards that multinationals seeking to sell in the world's largest market—and their suppliers—must meet.[58]

Corporations parallel states

Yet corporations are not without their own resources in addressing regulatory constraints. Ironically enough, they are becoming more like states, and their executives more like politicians with respect to their various constituencies. The demands for increasing "transparency" and "accountability" in corporate governance, and the power of shareholders to focus attention on shareholder value, have lent greater visibility to executives. At the same time, calls for greater corporate social responsibility expose executives to a potentially conflicting set of demands. As commentators have noted, the job of a CEO is increasingly politicized, demanding a set of skills and activities more like those of political leaders. Carly Fiorina, at the time CEO of Hewlett-Packard, was a regular feature at the annual Davos conference where elites from business, government, and academia meet. Asked how she could take time out from running a vast multinational, she stated, "The day when business and government were totally separate spheres is over. Public policy and business practice are inextricably linked." This is particularly true for regulated businesses and those with a heavy intellectual property component—finance, telecoms, pharmaceuticals, health care, technology—because these businesses rely on the actions of states for their survival.[59]

Multinationals now require foreign policies. Due to new uses of the Alien Tort Claims Act of 1789, which allows non-US citizens to file suits in US courts for violations of international law, a number of American corporations have been sued in the past decade for human rights abuses around the world. Burmese villagers sued Unocal for human rights violations due to the actions of the Burmese government; DaimlerChrysler was sued over the disappearance and torture of union leaders in Argentina; Texaco was sued on behalf of Nigerian villagers; and Chiquita was sued on behalf of victims of Colombian paramilitaries allegedly hired by the firm. Over three dozen cases were filed under ATCA between 1993 and 2006. And in May 2008 the US Supreme Court allowed a suit to go forward charging more than fifty multinationals with aiding and abetting the former apartheid regime in South Africa.[60]

Multinationals are also expected to conduct programs of foreign aid, addressing social problems that are beyond the scope of states. In a January 2001 appearance before the US Chamber of Commerce, UN

Secretary General Kofi Annan urged American corporate leaders to make use of their vast resources and capabilities to take on the role in fighting the AIDS epidemic that states—particularly failed states in sub-Saharan Africa—could not:

> I come to you, the leaders of American business, representatives of one of the greatest forces in the world, but one which has yet to be fully utilized in the campaign against AIDS/HIV. It is high time we tapped your strengths to the full ... Business is used to acting decisively and quickly. The same cannot be said of the community of sovereign states. We need your help – right now ... Together, I believe we can succeed – if only because the costs of failure are simply too appalling to contemplate.

His call was notably unsuccessful—only about two dozen major American businesses joined the UN-sanctioned Global Business Coalition on HIV/AIDS, the preferred vehicle for business action against AIDS.[61] But there is reason to expect that, as the balance of economic power shifts toward corporations and the technology of monitoring becomes more elaborated, such calls will become increasingly frequent. If trends continue, in the future states, corporations, and non-state actors will be on an increasingly even plane, in which their similarities will often seem more important than their differences.

6

From Employee and Citizen to Investor: How Talent, Friends, and Homes Became "Capital"

During the 1920s, a booming stock market drew in millions of new investors with no prior experience in the ways of financial markets. The number of shareholders in the US doubled from 2.4 million in 1924 to 5 million in 1927 and doubled again to 10 million by 1930, leaving the ownership of the largest American corporations highly fragmented— and a large part of the American public about to learn a hard lesson in finance. The dispersion of stock ownership, coupled with the increasing concentration of economic assets in a few dozen large corporations, had birthed a new kind of economic system, a "corporate system" in Berle and Means's terms, which was unlike the competitive private enterprise system of the previous century. Two hundred companies controlled half the assets of the corporate sector, and if trends in consolidation contin- ued, they would control it all by 1959. Corporations run by autonomous professional managers were becoming the dominant social institutions in America, with the rest of society revolving around them like moons around a planet.[1]

Berle and Means, along with subsequent critics, described the corpo- rate system as analogous to feudalism, and under pressures from labor and the Federal government the corporate system came to evolve its own standards of *noblesse oblige* over time. The biggest employers were also those most recognized for their vanguard personnel policies: middle- class pay, employment security, job ladders, and retirement and health plans for their employees. They were like feudal welfare states—"modern manors," in the words of Sanford Jacoby—providing a gravitational pull on the lives of their members and surrounding communities.[2]

Sociologist Charles Perrow described what had come of this process in the ensuing decades: "[T]he appearance of large organizations in the United States makes organizations the key phenomenon of our time, and thus politics, social class, economics, technology, religion, the family, and even social psychology take on the character of dependent variables ... organizations are the key to society because *large organizations have absorbed society*."[3]

But since the early 1980s, the trend toward greater corporate concentration has reversed. This is particularly evident in the case of employment, as the fraction of the workforce employed by the largest corporations—particularly manufacturers—continued its long slide. GM's unionized US workforce in 2008 was one-sixth what it had been in 1985, and in February of that year the company offered to buy out all remaining hourly workers in hopes of hiring lower-priced replacements, following the same move by Ford the previous month. By that point Wal-Mart, with 1.4 million US "associates," employed more Americans than the dozen largest manufacturers combined, while seven of the ten largest US employers were in retail or fast food—industries not well known for providing generous pay and career mobility. In 1973 Daniel Bell wrote, "One can say, without being overly facile, that U.S. Steel is the paradigmatic corporation of the first third of the twentieth century, General Motors of the second third of the century, and IBM of the final third." Clearly, Wal-Mart is the paradigmatic corporation of the early twenty-first century.[4]

Some commentators saw the decline of "corporate feudalism" as the worrisome loss of America's corporate-sponsored social welfare system. Others applauded the advent of a free-agent nation: the corporate serfs would be dependent no more, free to arrange their own work schedules, health insurance, and retirement savings. The feudalism analogy here is instructive. The end of medieval feudalism was a time of massive social dislocation and turbulence, as estateless "free labor" lost the familiar world of the manor for a new life as proletarians. The rise of market society in England left former agricultural laborers to fend for themselves in an uncertain world whose rules were obscure and where the old mutual obligations were gone. The new market society provided no legible social map to replace the old world and its familiar structures—a new map had to be created. Jean-Christophe Agnew describes how the Elizabethan theater of Shakespeare and his colleagues mirrored the market, providing a metaphor and a means to apprehend a new culture in which everything was for sale and market transactions rewarded those good at artifice. All the world was now a marketplace, and we were all simultaneously buyers, sellers, and spectators. The dominant idiom imagined market transactors as actors in a theater.[5]

In twenty-first-century America, *investment* became the dominant metaphor to understand the individual's place in society and a guide to making one's way in a new economy. George Bush referred to this nascent system as an "ownership society," but its denizens were more like investors, or even speculators, than owners. The smart money knows better than to own assets outright: savvy investors diversify their risk and avoid leaving all their eggs in one basket. Through portable pension plans, complex home mortgages, and investments in human capital and social capital, investor-citizens managed a portfolio containing many species of assets. Indeed, one could recognize the sophisticated investor by the ribbons running along the bottom of her laptop: Fidelity to track her 401(k), Zillow.com to monitor home prices in her neighborhood, US News to update the value of her college degree, and Facebook to assess the worth of her social capital (formerly known as "friends").

But at the end of the first decade of the twenty-first century, much of the standard wisdom of the investment enthusiasts seemed utterly discredited, and only the metaphor lingered on.

Individuals with money to invest for college or retirement were advised to buy and hold a broad equity index fund as the most prudent vehicle for long-term savings. But the stock market crash of early 2000 destroyed $7 trillion in value, and the S&P 500 in late 2008 was far below where it had been a decade earlier. Investors who had bought a standard index fund in the late 1990s were in much worse shape financially than those who had put their money in a government-insured savings account.[6]

Shoppers for homes were encouraged to stretch to buy the biggest house they could afford, because house prices always go up, making a highly leveraged home the best investment for the long run. But the burst of the housing bubble in 2007 showed that, like the stock market, house prices do not always go up, and indeed they could decline catastrophically. It was estimated that by 2009 nearly one-quarter of mortgage holders would owe more on their home than it was worth. For millions, the financially prudent response was to pack up and move on before the neighbors noticed.[7]

Young people were told to invest in their human capital by studying for a degree that prepared them to be a symbolic analyst—a computer programmer, securities analyst, engineer, or other cognitively oriented job—because these were the high-value-added occupations of the future. But thanks to a newly flat world, they increasingly found themselves competing with equally qualified offshore providers available for a much lower wage. Symbolic analysis turned out to be highly portable.[8]

And with a housing market in free-fall and career employment an anachronism, the ties that bound stable communities together were increasingly frayed, as some former homeowners left behind friends, neighbors, and empty houses with mortgages that were beyond their means, one step ahead of the debt collectors calling from New Delhi.[9]

This chapter surveys how the society of organizations was replaced by the portfolio society, and how talent, personality, friends, family, homes, and community all became kinds of securities. I first describe how changes in the organization of production and the structure of corporations have changed the nature of the employment relation and economic mobility. I then describe the theory of the ownership society, focusing in particular on equity and home ownership. Share ownership is thought to change people's perceptions of their political interests and to have a broader educational function, but while the evidence supports the former, it is decidedly mixed on the latter. I also describe the rise and fall of the US mortgage bubble and its lingering effects on the meaning of home ownership and community, arguing that securitization has unexpectedly given homeowners the mindset of investors, to the detriment of their surrounding communities.

The dis-integration of the corporation and the end of corporate feudalism

In the opening paragraph of their 1932 book, Berle and Means compared the new corporate system to feudalism:

> The corporation has, in fact, become both a method of property tenure and a means of organizing economic life. Grown to tremendous proportions, there may be said to have evolved a "corporate system"—as there was once a feudal system—which has attracted to itself a combination of attributes and powers, and has attained a degree of prominence entitling it to be a dealt with as a major social institution.

The largest and most prosperous companies had adopted an approach to personnel management that sought to promote loyalty and employment stability through a range of practices recognizable today: promotion ladders, pension benefits, profit sharing, and implied guarantees of long-term employment. Critics had previously referred to this new system as a form of paternalism or even social engineering, claiming that it encouraged an unhealthy dependence on the corporation; in any case, the Depression made such practices unaffordable for all but a few employers.[10]

With the success of organized labor in the late 1930s and the greatly increased demand for committed employees during the 1940s, many of the vanguard policies—employment security, health care benefits, pensions—became standard corporate practice in the postwar era. Internal labor markets, in which jobs are structured into ladders and positions above entry level are filled by current employees, became a widespread approach to white-collar employment. Commentators in the 1950s lamented the conformity of the organization man in his gray flannel suit and worried about the slow death of individualism and creativity that a corporate career seemed to entail. But for better or worse, as

Richard Sennett points out, careers in pyramidal bureaucracies provided a life narrative, a vision of the future, and encouraged the discipline of delayed gratification. Bureaucracy may have been an iron cage, but it was also a reliable map. And in a nation with a muted welfare state, economic security was largely bound up with careers in companies.[11]

The lords of the corporate manor were also bound by obligations to the broader community that surrounded it—what we would today label "corporate social responsibility." Carl Kaysen in 1957 described the expectations that faced the modern corporate elite: "Its responsibilities to the general public are widespread: leadership in local charitable enterprises, concern with factory architecture and landscaping, provision of support for higher education, and even research in pure science, to name a few." Commercial banks held a special obligation: because they were geographically constrained to operate within a single state, or even a single city, they became uniquely tied to the well-being of the local business community and took a lead in guiding local philanthropy. And "business community" was an apt term, as the heads of local businesses were more likely than not to be acquainted with each other, through serving on the same corporate and nonprofit boards and through memberships in the same social clubs. Dense local networks made it easier to maintain local standards of good corporate behavior; for instance, Minneapolis-St. Paul became famous for its "5% Club," in which local businesses pledged 5% of their net income to charity.[12]

The dis-integration of production is doing to the corporation as a locally embedded social institution what the market economy did to the feudal manor. Chapter 3 described the bust-up takeovers of the 1980s, in which businesses formerly housed within a single corporate parent were split up into free-standing units. By the early 1990s, as outsourcing began to take off, business writers described a new "modular" or "hollow" or "virtual" corporation in which production was scattered across a network of specialist organizations. This was in some sense a return to the past: prior to Ford's expansive approach to vertical integration—owning the supply chain all the way back to iron mines, oak forests, and rubber plantations—vertical dis-integration was the norm across many manufacturing industries, including auto making. What is different now is the scale and the geographic breadth of the new system of dis-integration, and its implications for the old sense of corporate obligation.[13]

Our discussion of the OEM corporation highlighted how the production of goods, from cellphones and PCs to dog chow and blood thinner, is routinely divided up and contracted out among a geographically dispersed value chain. But dis-integration is not limited to manufacturing: the service value chain can also be divided and fine-tuned across a set of separate organizations and individuals. Mortgages, for instance, were traditionally vetted by a local bank's loan officer and held on the bank's balance sheet until the loan was ultimately paid off, with funds for the loan coming from local depositors. More recently, the vast majority of home mortgages in the US crossed multiple organizational boundaries. A self-employed mortgage broker might work with a buyer to locate an appropriately priced loan, which would then be originated by a free-standing finance company in California, which in turn would sell the mortgage to a Wall Street bank that would bundle it together with several thousand other mortgages into a pool that would be divided into bonds and sold to overseas investors—or, perhaps, to yet another Wall Street bank, which would bundle them together with other mortgage-backed bonds into a "collateralized debt obligation," to be organized as a limited liability company in the Cayman Islands and serviced by yet another legally separate organization. In this example, most of the value chain resides in the US. But as Tom Friedman points out, with high-speed Internet connections around the world, standardized software, and broad agreement on English as the language of business, it is increasingly easy to outsource service tasks electronically to wherever in the world they can be done most cheaply.[14]

Outsourcing is no longer limited to just companies. Web-savvy individuals can send tasks like editing video from a family vacation, planning a wedding, or math tutoring for the kids to overseas vendors—with Skype and a high-speed connection, "face to face" meetings no longer require physical proximity. The OEM household is increasingly within reach, with the mundane low-value-added tasks of parenting outsourced to low-cost labor while parents focus on the high-value quality time. And like the brand-focused OEM company, parents can now hire outside vendors for "baby branding," to make sure that their progeny have names that will convey the right image to their eventual consumers on the labor market.[15]

The implication of this new "flat world" frontier is that perhaps 40 million jobs in the US are at risk of offshoring, according to economist Alan Blinder. If it can be transmitted electronically, it can be offshored. Examples of occupations at risk include computer programmer, call center operator, tax preparer, radiologist, securities analyst, and mortgage originator—what Blinder calls "impersonal services" (as opposed to personal services in which "touch" is required or highly valued). Notably, it is not the *level of skill* that distinguishes "offshoreable" jobs, but the *means of their delivery*, which implies that—unlike in the past—a high level of human capital is not sufficient to provide job security. (In response to Blinder, Greg Mankiw, former Chairman of Bush's Council of Economic Advisers, pointed out that the chance of massive overnight unemployment due to offshoring was small, and anyway offshoring traffic can work both ways: it is entirely possible that foreign firms might choose to locate their call centers or tax accountancies in the US, leading to a bonanza of new employment for competitively priced US workers.)[16]

Early on in the process of dis-integration, it seemed that China had become the world's workshop for low-priced goods, and India the world's call center.[17] But both China and India are far more economically diverse, for better or worse, and even industries normally considered immune to offshoring are not. Construction, for instance, seemed to be the quintessential local industry, but London's Verbus Systems found a way to assemble modular hotel rooms in metal containers in China and send them by kit for final stacking on-site, like Legos. With this system, a company director said, the firm "can build a 300-room hotel anywhere on the planet in 20 weeks." And vanguard "service" industries that would have been incomprehensible a decade ago are quickly rationalized and offshored before they even exist in the US. An especially surreal example is online "gold farming," in which participants in multiplayer games on the Web such as World of Warcraft gather points ("gold") in virtual worlds that can be sold for real cash to American and other players seeking a head start on the game. As with other sweatshops in China, such as in the textile industry, the hours are long, the workers live on company dorms, and they are paid a piece rate that works out to roughly 30 cents per hour. It is estimated that over 100,000 workers in China are employed in the gold-farming industry—for comparison purposes, the US textile mill industry employed about 150,000 persons in 2008.[18]

More broadly, geography has become largely fungible, and the trends in dis-integration are not limited to India and China. The crews of state-less merchant vessels are a model of national and ethnic diversity, as are their Byzantine systems of ownership, incorporation, and flagging. And the business plan for SeaCode received a great deal of attention in 2005 by proposing to buy a used cruise ship to house an "offshore" software factory, to be parked 3.1 miles from Los Angeles in international waters. The labor force, which would be the "crew" for business purposes and governed by the labor laws of Liberia (or wherever it chose to register), would be close enough to allow inspection by clients, but just far enough to avoid having to find US visas (or receive American-sized wages). The company's founders claimed that they had received job applications from around the world.[19]

Faced with this menu of options for organizing production across organizational and geographic boundaries, companies have grown savvy about sourcing by where the value is added. For instance, when IBM worked with a Texas electric utility to create a computerized "smart grid," it drew on research scientists in New York, software developers in Bangalore, engineering equipment specialists in Miami, on-site organizers flown in from Pennsylvania, and a set of subcontractors for some of the hands-on work. Sometimes this sourcing process benefits US workers: nearly 5 million Americans work for foreign affiliates, and Indian IT firms are expanding their US presence. But outside corporate decision-making is less intrinsically attuned to local considerations.

For instance, research shows that corporate charitable donations and community involvement are overwhelmingly concentrated in a company's headquarters city, within shouting distance of its executives, and thus corporate relocations are particularly hard on the local non-profit community.[20]

All this is not to imply that the new organization of business inevitably plays to the advantages of multinationals. The logic of the OEM model means that the barriers to entry in many industries are surprisingly low. The availability of off-the-shelf parts and standardized services makes it easy to assemble a global value chain with minimal start-up cost, and, in many industries, putting together a business has become analogous to a large-scale Ikea project. In the airline industry, for instance, contractors can be hired for essentially every task required to license and operate a startup, including writing the application for the FAA, selling tickets, staffing the boarding gate, and piloting the plane. The frequent turnover in industry participants means that there is a large supply of used jets waiting to be re-painted and leased to a new airline, while surviving airlines will gladly offer services to their new competitors, including employee training, food service, and aircraft maintenance. Similarly, some of the largest vendors of flat-screen televisions are startups that buy components from the same suppliers as the well-known consumer brands and undercut them on price, just as happened with the personal computer industry. Analysts estimate that one could start a no-frills cellphone manufacturer for roughly $10 million using off-the-shelf parts. And even cars are no longer out of reach for generic manufacturers. One Chinese startup ramped up to producing 180,000 cars within just six years of beginning production. The firm's founder stated, "How to make cars is no longer a big secret. The technologies are widely used and shared." Tellingly, Ford Chairman William Clay Ford Jr. responded, "It's easy to build a car. It's harder to build a brand."[21]

One outcome of this process of rampant corporate dis-integration seems clear: for the vast majority of the US workforce, jobs and career ladders will no longer be attached to particular companies in particular places for extended periods. In this sense, corporate feudalism is over.

Employment and income in a post-corporate economy

With the lost expectation of long-term attachments between firms and their employees, corporations are losing their place as primary mediating institutions that inform people's perceptions of their economic and political interests. Carl Kaysen described the ideal-typical employer seeking to turn its employees into "members" in 1957: "The whole labor force of the modern corporation is, insofar as possible, turned into a corps of lifetime employees, with great emphasis on stability of employment" and thus "Increasingly, membership in the modern corporation becomes the single strongest social force shaping its career members." As Peter Drucker likewise put it, the corporation "determines the individual's view of his society."[22] At the time that both wrote, the largest employers in the US were manufacturers and AT&T, firms in which specialized skills and firm-specific knowledge encouraged the creation of long-term commitments between firms and employees. The emblems of this long-term commitment were the defined benefit pension plan, for which employees became eligible after years of service to the firm, and plans guaranteeing health care benefits for retirees.

Today, the biggest American employers are in retail and fast food, where tenures are relatively short and few employees look forward to a company-funded retirement. Table 6.1 shows the median employee tenure and age for the ten most-tenured industries in the US, according to the 2004 Current Population Survey. Survey respondents were asked how long they had worked for their current employer, among other questions. The industries with the most-tenured employees are in manufacturing and agriculture, where the average employee is in his or her 40s. Recall from Chapter 3 that this list of industries contains most of the top employers in 1960 and 1980. On the other hand, the least-tenured industries include food service and retail, where seven of the ten largest employers operate today (Table 6.2). There are several possible reasons for this striking disparity, of course, and without data on individual careers over time we cannot disentangle them. If appliance manufacturers or petroleum refiners stop hiring, or lay off employees based on low seniority, then their average employees will simultaneously

Table 6.1. *Ten industries with the most-tenured employees in 2004*

Industry	Median tenure (yrs)	Median age
Agriculture	14	47.0
Utilities	13	45.0
Petroleum and coal products mfg	11	45.0
Forestry, logging, fishing, hunting	10	44.0
Electrical equipment, appliance mfg	10	46.0
Public administration	9	45.0
Transportation equipment manufacturing	8	44.0
Beverage and tobacco products	8	38.5
Paper and printing	8	43.0
Primary metals and fabricated metal prods.	7	43.0

Table 6.2. *Ten industries with the least-tenured employees in 2004*

Industry	Median tenure (yrs)	Median age
Internet publishing and broadcasting	0.5	42.5
Food services and drinking places	1.5	26.0
Private households	2.0	40.0
Retail trade	3.0	38.0
Motion picture and sound recording	3.0	34.0
Rental and leasing services	3.0	36.0
Administrative and support services	3.0	40.0
Social assistance	3.0	41.0
Arts, entertainment, and recreation	3.0	38.0
Accommodation	3.5	40.0

grow older and more tenured. On the other hand, if retailers go on a hiring binge, then their average employee will be less tenured. But it is notable that the average retail employee is 38, even though the industry's median tenure is just three years. We cannot easily project how long these retail employees will continue with their current employer, but— in contrast to, say, auto manufacturing in its heyday—it is difficult to see this as a long-term career choice. And whether or not employees do end up staying with their present employers for extended periods, it appears that their perceptions of job security are relatively low. Political scientist Jacob Hacker, author of *The Great Risk Shift*, reports that survey respondents in 2005 were about three times as likely to agree with the statement "I am frequently concerned about being laid off" compared with respondents in 1982, even though unemployment in 2005 was half what it had been in 1982.[23]

The expectation of relatively short-term employment is reinforced by the decline of "defined benefit" corporate pension plans and their replacement by "defined contribution" (typically 401(k)) plans. The traditional corporate pension was a defined benefit (DB) plan, in which increasing years of service with the company were rewarded with increasing pension payments at retirement. DB plans require the employer to set aside sufficient funds and invest them in a suitable fashion to make good on their promises to employees. From the employee's perspective, the plan is "the GM pension," and retirees have little reason to probe into its details, as long as the checks clear. In contrast, 401(k) plans entail accounts that are owned by the employee, not the employer. Workers are able to contribute a portion of their salary tax-free, and their contribution is often partially or fully matched by their employer. The employer provides a structure for the plan, typically offering several options for where to put the money (equity mutual funds, bond funds, company stock). Seniority, and even continued employment, do not affect the plan directly, making them effectively portable in the event that the employee changes jobs. Since 1982, when the tax status of 401(k) plans was clarified, there has been a sea change from DB plans to 401(k) plans, and many established DB plans have been frozen such that workers no longer accrue benefits. In 1981, 81% of employees in corporate pension plans had a DB plan, a number that declined to 38% by 2003.[24] GM froze its DB pension plan for salaried workers in 2006, switching employees over to a less costly 401(k), and dozens of other large employers have done the same. In response to these developments, young workers entering the workforce have taken to heart the idea of at-will employment; few seem to expect to find job security with a corporate employer, and "community" is more likely to be sought outside the workplace.[25]

According to enthusiasts, the new knowledge-based innovation economy would make up for the greater insecurity it brought by providing opportunities for self-realization through creative work. Edmund Phelps, who won the Nobel Prize in Economics in 2006, compared the benefits of the free-wheeling American system with its sclerotic European counterpart:

> Instituting a high level of dynamism, so that the economy is fired by the new ideas of entrepreneurs, serves to transform the workplace— in the firms developing an innovation and also in the firms dealing with the innovations. The challenges that arise in developing a new idea and in gaining its acceptance in the marketplace provide the workforce with high levels of mental stimulation, problem-solving, employee-engagement and, thus, personal growth.

Notably, it is through one's work that this must happen, as "most, if not all, of such self-realization in modern societies can come only from a career ... If a challenging career is not the main hope for self-realization, what else could be?"[26] Phelps imagined a nation of Howard Roarks, bold individualists scaling Maslow's pyramid to fulfillment, while their European counterparts were atrophying during their endless mandatory vacation time.

But for many reporting on the frontline of employment in the US, the nature of work has become increasingly brutal, as documented by a spate of recent books with titles such as "Nickel and dimed," "The disposable American," and "The big squeeze." The new world of work is described as a high-tech corporate panopticon whose members are more

like *1984*'s Winston Smith than Howard Roark. Standardization is pervasive in many service industries, and the manufacturing assembly line has
been succeeded by "enterprise systems" software that allows centralized
monitoring and control and generates detailed productivity and time
usage information—say, how long one spends on a bathroom break.
In this nightmare world, cheerful obedience is valued far more than
creativity and specialized skills.[27] If GM was the synecdoche for industrial capitalism in the US, then Wal-Mart stands in for post-industrial
capitalism, combining low wages, meager benefits, tight control, and
enforced cheer, starting with the singing of the corporate anthem in the
morning (or whenever one's computer-assigned shift begins). Wal-Mart
is often accused by critics of single-handedly speeding up the offshoring
of American manufacturing through its requirement that suppliers meet
the "China price," but it has spawned at least one new industry that has
yet to be offshored: Wal-Mart bashing. And for the firms that have taken
out "dead peasant's insurance" on their rank-and-file workers, as Wal-
Mart did on hundreds of thousands of employees during the early 1990s,
their incentives to maintain long-term ties with employees are decidedly
mixed: it is a plain statement of fact that many workers were literally
worth more to their employer dead than alive.[28]

Corporate dis-integration can have an unanticipated effect on occupational mobility: by contracting out "non-core" jobs, these jobs become
separated from the ladders that once offered a means to move up
within an organization. Outsourcing traditional entry-level positions—
working in the mailroom, or in maintenance—can leave their occupants
stranded without an obvious place for promotion. Thus, researchers find
that young men entering the labor market in the 1980s and 1990s were
more than twice as likely to remain in low-wage jobs ten years later
compared to those that entered the labor market in the late 1960s and
early 1970s.[29] Even those that are employed by vanguard employers with
a commitment to employee training may have an unpredictable career
path. Companies seeking to maintain career ladders face the uncertain
task of predicting what skills they will require in the future. IBM, for
instance, annually identifies a dozen "hot skills" likely to be in demand

in the coming three years, such as in Linux programming or genomics, and spends lavishly on employee training to insure that its workforce is prepared for economic shifts. And in some cases, employees of globalizing firms are fortunate to find themselves in occupations and industry segments in which their employers' global presence reaps benefits.[30] But those who guess wrong can find themselves specializing in an obsolete job, or one easily outsourced to a lower-cost competitor. With no clear career ladder and little sense of what skills will be valuable in the future, it is difficult to plot out a life trajectory, and the ride is getting bumpier. Jacob Hacker argues that year-to-year income volatility has gone up substantially since the 1970s, with the implication that the typical family is significantly more likely to see their income drop by half from one year to the next than they were in prior decades. His estimate of a 17% chance of such a potentially catastrophic drop is controversial among economists, but it appears that the chances of such a drop have indeed increased over time, fueling perceptions of economic insecurity.[31]

The decline of corporate career ladders corresponds with lower economic mobility and greater social inequality more broadly. First, corporations with internal labor markets used to provide a direct means of mobility through internal promotions. But without a corporate ladder to enable promotions, class mobility has stalled in the US. Indeed, the image of the US as a land in which the son of a janitor can, through hard work, grow up to be CEO is belied by systematic research documenting that intergenerational mobility—doing better than one's parents—is far less likely in the US than is generally believed, particularly compared with Europe. Half of the children of poor parents in the US grow up to be poor themselves, while 40% of the children of high-income parents will themselves become high-income adults. By contrast, in Denmark childhood poverty is rare, but even poor children rarely grow up to be poor.[32] It is difficult to know how much of America's low level of social mobility is due to lost job ladders, but the relation is suggestive.

A more direct link is between corporate hierarchy and broader income inequality. At first glance, the organizational pyramid is the very image of inequality in income and status, but traditionally the gradations among levels were held to reasonable proportions by systems of job evaluation such as the Hay System, which were intended to maintain perceptions of equity in compensation. The Hay System and its ilk limited just how high or low pay could go within a hierarchy, as compensation at the top was linked to the number of hierarchical levels below. As a result, the heyday of the Organization Man was also the high point of relative economic equality in the US. Now, income inequality has reached levels not seen since the 1920s, with the top 1% earning 21.2% of all income in the US while the bottom 50% earned just 12.8% in 2005. High CEO compensation is part of this divergence in income, but extreme incomes at the very top are more attributable to "unconstrained" earners that are outside of the corporate ambit: in 2004, it is estimated that the top twenty-five hedge fund managers collectively earned more than the CEOs of all firms in the S&P 500 combined.[33]

By the early years of the twenty-first century, there was an emerging consensus among business leaders that America's reliance on corporations as social welfare agencies had become too costly to maintain. This was particularly evident in "rust belt" industries, where health and retirement benefits promised in flush times were no longer economically sustainable and had become a drain on corporate competitiveness. In 2002, when its underfunded pension plan was taken over by the government, Bethlehem Steel had five pensioners for every active employee, and more to come. When GM's CEO announced plans to freeze pension benefits in 2006, he stated: "Most of the companies we compete with ... have a different benefits structure. A significantly greater portion of their retirement is funded by a national system." Indeed, by late 2008 the total market value of the General Motors Corporation, at less than $2 billion, was a tiny fraction of the value of the portfolio held by GM's pension funds in other companies. A succession of bankruptcies had led several corporate pension plans to become the obligation of the federal Pension Benefit Guarantee Corporation, including those of several steel companies, auto suppliers, and three major airlines (Delta, US Airways, and United), and analysts predicted more to come. As Alicia Munnell of Boston College described it, "Our employer-based social-welfare system is collapsing." The proportion of firms offering health benefits dropped from 69% to 60% between 2000 and 2006, and major employers—including GM and Ford—renounced health care coverage of retirees in favor of "health retirement accounts."[34] Corporate employers were rapidly abandoning their old "paternalism," leaving current employees and retirees to rely more on personal savings and Federal programs such as Social Security—an uncertain bet at best.

The standard response to economic uncertainty is to boost one's savings to provide a cushion in the event of emergencies, such as medical expenses or unexpected drops in income, and to put away more money for retirement. In the US, however, household savings actually became *negative* in 2005 for the first time since the Great Depression—that is, household spending exceeded after-tax income. This paradox was explained by the Economic Report of the President for 2006: households were relying on increases in asset values, and in particular rising home prices, to fund their consumer spending. The sophisticated American credit markets had simply made it much easier for homeowners to refinance their mortgage and extract some of the value of their rising equity (all of it, in fact) as it increased year to year, or to take out home equity lines of credit secured by the value of their house. The Report aimed to reassure its readers by pointing out that a negative household savings rate was not a problem for the US, but a positive feature: only in a country with such exemplary capital markets would citizens be comfortable saving so little. The bedrock of ever-rising home prices, and the availability of mortgage refinancing, allowed households to smooth out their consumption even without the cushion of savings, in contrast to high-saving countries such as Japan, Germany, and China.[35]

The "ownership" alternative

If a bureaucratic career with a corporation is no longer feasible, what other societal systems are in place to provide order and stability to households and neighborhoods? The Republican answer was asset ownership. Individual ownership of financial assets would wean people from dependence on corporations and the government and provide a school for virtue and economic literacy. George Bush outlined his vision of an "ownership society" in his second inaugural address in January 2005:

> To give every American a stake in the promise and future of our country, we will bring the highest standards to our schools, and build an ownership society. We will widen the ownership of homes and businesses, retirement savings and health insurance - preparing our people for the challenges of life in a free society. By making every citizen an agent of his or her own destiny, we will give our fellow Americans greater freedom from want and fear, and make our society more prosperous and just and equal.

The replacement of defined benefit plans with 401(k)s was already a step in this direction, but Bush's vision was more expansive: privatized Social Security accounts invested in the stock market, expanded home ownership for buyers with no money down, and market-invested health savings accounts that could revert to cash for those that made it to retirement in good health.[36]

Bush had long been a believer in the magic of asset ownership. Home ownership, according to Bush, could be transformative: "Just like that, you're not just visitors to the community anymore but part of it—with a stake in the neighborhood and a concern for its future."[37] A long line of previous American presidents had expressed the same idea: home ownership was good for individuals, families, and societies, and it merited governmental promotion. Calvin Coolidge stated, "No greater contribution could be made to the stability of the Nation, and the advancement of its ideals, than to make it a Nation of homeowning families." Herbert Hoover claimed that home ownership makes "a more wholesome, healthful and happy atmosphere in which to bring up children." And Franklin Roosevelt argued that "A nation of homeowners, of people who own a real share in their own land, is unconquerable."[38]

Researchers have documented that those who own rather than rent their home are different on a number of "citizenship" dimensions— controlling for obvious confounds, they are more likely to join nonprofit groups, to vote in local elections, to know the names of their Congressional representative and the head of their school board, and even to plant gardens. And the children of owners do better than those of renters: they stay in school longer, and daughters of homeowners are less likely to have children when they are teenagers than daughters of renters.[39] A difficulty with such studies is that the kinds of people who become homeowners are different in a number of ways from the kinds of people who become renters, and thus it is hard to know if it is ownership *per se* that has these beneficial effects. Ideally, researchers would be able to do a double-blind study that randomly assigned some people to renting and others to owning and assessed the effects several years later. In fact, an ingenious study of Argentine families who illegally settled a neighborhood on the edge of Buenos Aires comes close to doing just this. Through a fluke in how the government sought to compensate the land's original owners, some squatters came to own the titles to their homes, while others did not. Those that were "titled" subsequently adopted a range of bourgeois virtues, in comparison to their untitled neighbors. They were more likely to believe that hard work would pay off; they had fewer kids, and their kids had better school attendance. Their homes were also assessed to be better built and maintained. According to the researchers, those with titles came to see their house as an insurance and saving tool.[40] The implications of this work would seem to be that broader home ownership has great benefits for society and merits a host of economic supports.

It is fortunate that home ownership has so many collateral benefits, because buying a house is a rather poor investment over the long term. In 2006 Robert Shiller compared very lengthy time-series data for Amsterdam, the US, and Norway, and concluded that, over time, house prices essentially stay flat after controlling for inflation. Examining data on US house prices from 1890 to 2005, he says, "It's notable that until the recent explosion in home prices, real home prices in the United States were virtually unchanged from 1890 to the late 1990s." Writing of the dramatic upturn after 1997, he states: "The magnitude of the current boom is practically unique in history, making it difficult to predict what comes next based on historical examples." In other words, absent a hyperactive trade in mortgage-backed securities, one does not see a substantial housing price bubble—or even upward movement in house values, net of inflation.[41]

The Argentine squatters came to own their homes through the stroke of a pen. But it is not just ownership that can mold one's virtues: participation in finance can itself serve as a means of self-betterment and a prod to further education. Adam Smith's most abused metaphor described how an invisible hand guided market participants to provide for the well-being of others about whom they may care little: "It is not from the benevolence of the butcher, the brewer or the baker, that we expect our dinner, but from their regard to their own self interest." And participating in a market for assets can also have an educational and moral function. This theory informed the early thrifts in the UK and the US that allowed people to buy homes by drawing on the savings of their neighbors. A commentator in 1811 wrote, "A man who has earned, saved, and paid for a home will be a better man, a better husband and father, and a better citizen of the republic." Another said in 1925: "Thrift is a disciplinarian. It breeds virility. It strikes at sensuality, self-indulgence, flabbiness. It teaches the heroism of self-denial, temperance, abstemiousness, and simple living. It is the way to success and independence. It makes for happy homes, contented communities, a prosperous nation."[42]

As forms of financing become more elaborated, the potential educational benefits multiply. The concept that their short-term savings were tied up in the long-term mortgages of their neighbors seemed to stretch the comprehension of thrift depositors in the movie *It's a Wonderful Life*. But home buyers today—at least those that take the time to parse their loan documentation—may have to learn about exchange rates, the Federal Reserve Bank, and LIBOR, thus attuning them to currents in the broader world economy. Eastern European buyers who live outside the Euro zone are particularly prone to such benefits, as a large proportion of them borrow the funds for their home purchases in foreign currencies with low interest rates—one-third of home mortgages in Poland, and half in Hungary, are denominated in foreign currencies. Much like bankers, these buyers implicitly operate in the "carry trade," exposed to currency risks such that their monthly payments go up or down according to prevailing exchange rates. The practice is not limited to Eastern Europe: one London businessman took out a mortgage on a second home in Florida denominated in yen. Perhaps never before in history has monthly household spending been so directly connected to the actions of central banks.[43]

On the other side of the market, with advances in information technology and finance, more and more retail investors could be owners of more and more kinds of assets from around the world. Since finance had "split the atom of property," people could own—in some microscopic way—thousands of different assets, from corporate shares to municipal bonds to life insurance settlements on their elderly neighbors.

Does stock ownership make you smarter?

The advent of the 401(k) plan and the expansive growth of retail mutual fund investment provided a test of the hypothesis that participating in finance makes one smarter and more virtuous. In spite of a long-standing popular "equity culture" in the US, stock ownership has traditionally been the domain of the wealthy. The number of shareholders declined by about half during the Great Depression, after the high point reached on the eve of the 1929 crash, and by the early 1950s only about one household in ten had money invested in the stock market. Shareholders tended to be richer, older, and more educated than non-owners, and they tended to buy shares only after having accumulated a substantial amount of savings. Professionals and the self-employed were also well-represented among shareholders. The proportion of households owning shares eventually crept up to 20% by the early 1960s—about where it had been at the onset of the Depression—where it stayed for almost two decades.[44]

During the late 1970s and 1980s, however, the cost of investing in mutual funds declined substantially along with the effective interest rates on bank-based savings accounts, and a large proportion of households began to put their savings in money market funds (typically invested in commercial paper) and, eventually, equity mutual funds (invested in the stock market). Moreover, the IRS clarified the tax treatment of defined contribution pension plans beginning in 1982, which encouraged employers to switch from traditional defined benefit plans to 401(k)s. In a typical 401(k) program, employees are offered four or five mutual funds where they can contribute part of their pre-tax income, often with a partial matching contribution by their employer; the income is not taxed until it is withdrawn, typically at retirement. Brand-name mutual fund families (Fidelity, Vanguard, T. Rowe Price, and so on) are the most common options, and several of these funds act as plan administrators as well. Once the employer has made its contribution, the 401(k) is essentially the property of the employee, and its value fluctuates with that of the fund(s) it is invested in. Thus, 401(k)s encourage stock investing even for those with little or no savings. Most 401(k) providers offer tools for employees to track their investments (e.g. customized websites), and surveys suggest that a large proportion check the value of their portfolio once per week or more—many as often as daily.

Due in part to the reduced cost of mutual funds and the advent of 401(k) plans, the proportion of households invested in the stock market increased from 20% in 1983 to 52% in 2001. Household savings seemed to migrate from bank savings accounts, to money-market accounts, to equity mutual funds. Steve Fraser notes that "More was invested in institutional funds between 1991 and 1994 than in all the years since 1939," providing the raw material for a stock market boom in the 1990s. The increase in market participation was greatest among the young, as nearly half the households headed by someone under 35 held shares in 2001 (compared to one in eight in 1983). This expansion of ownership prevalence was described by advocates at the Federal Reserve Bank and elsewhere as a "democratization of ownership." But it was decidedly a *representative* democracy, not a direct democracy, as investment was overwhelmingly channeled through intermediary institutions—in particular, mutual funds. This left almost three-quarters of the average large firm's ownership in the hands of institutional investors by 2005. Thus, the proportion of households owning shares directly held steady at roughly 20%, where it had been since the 1960s, while the number owning shares through intermediaries such as mutual funds increased to over half. Whereas the modal stockholder in 1952 held shares in only one company—often the household head's employer or a local utility company—the predominant pattern of ownership now was of highly diversified funds. That is, households typically owned a slice of the over-all market, and thus their fortunes were tied to business in general rather than to particular firms.[45]

Yet while ownership had become widespread, the amounts at stake were not particularly large for the typical household. According to the Federal Reserve's triennial Survey of Consumer Finances, 69% of house-holds owned their homes in 2004, with a median value of $160,000. In contrast, the median stock portfolio among households was worth $24,300 in 2004 (down from $36,700 in 2001), which was less than the average increase in home value during the previous three years—or, indeed, less than the cost of a new car. Stock ownership, in short, was spread wide but not deep in the US.[46]

Evidence on individual investor behavior provides little support for the idea that finance educates its participants, at least at a retail level. Individuals are more prone to buying stock when they have higher incomes, higher education, and more liquid assets, and thus on aver-age shareholders have achieved higher levels of education than non-shareholders. In the aggregate, however, retail investors tend to pile into stocks in the wake of price increases, not in anticipation of them (that is, they are "momentum investors"), and then suffer in the sub-sequent downturn. This happened in the 1920s and the 1990s and, to a smaller extent, the 1960s—each time, a market boom drew in mil-lions of new investors, which was followed by a long market slump that punished those that got in late. Indeed, an apocryphal anecdote has it that, after receiving a stock tip from his shoeshine boy in 1929, John D. Rockefeller—America's first billionaire—pulled his fortune out of the stock market, in time to avoid the crash. His rationale: when one's shoeshine boy is giving insider stock tips, it's time for the smart money to bail out.[47]

The statistics on the investment patterns of 401(k) buyers also sup-port a cautious assessment of the wisdom of household investors. As

401(k)s are the main form of retirement savings for 42 million people, investing wisely is essential to their future well-being. Yet the evidence on how effectively they invest is not encouraging. First, millions of those eligible for 401(k) plans do not invest at all—forsaking both tax savings and, in many cases, employer matches, thereby leaving free money on the table. Second, standard financial wisdom outlines a few simple rules that apply fairly broadly: young people and others with a relatively long time horizon should weight their investments toward equities, which are riskier in the short term but have superior payoffs over the long term; older people should re-balance in favor of fixed-income investments (bonds) because they are safer, if lower in returns. The cardinal rule of investment in any asset class is to diversify, and to avoid concentrating too much risk in a single holding. And 401(k) participants violate all of these rules. A recent survey found that 43% of those in their 20s had *none* of their 401(k) assets in equity funds (although many of these were invested in balanced funds or company stock), while 16% of those in their 60s had 80% or more in stocks. Half of 401(k) plans offer the employer's stock as an investment option; among those, almost half their participants had more than 10% of their assets in company stock, and 10% had over 80% of their assets in company stock.[48]

The dangers of holding too much company stock in one's 401(k) became quite evident during the Enron meltdown: 60% of the value of the company's 401(k) was invested in Enron stock, which rapidly became worthless. Thousands of Enron employees were left both unemployed and with little or no retirement savings. The company had amplified the danger of such a loss by providing its matching contribution in Enron stock, which the employees were forbidden from selling until they reached age 50. More broadly, employees' 401(k) choices are shaped by what their employer makes available, which in turn is often driven by what pension consultant the employer hires. The SEC found that pension consulting, like much of financial services, was characterized by conflicts of interest due to the incentives consultants received from the money-managers whose products they recommend.[49]

An entire academic field of "behavioral finance" has evolved around the foibles of individual investors. Behavioral finance draws on the psychological study of cognitive biases to document the characteristic ways in which individual investors deviate from what is rational. The evidence of self-defeating bias is vast; conversely, at least one study showed that individuals with a particular form of brain damage which moots the influence of emotions on risky choices actually make better investment choices.[50] Some behavioral finance scholars have come to recommend a form of "soft paternalism" to gently ensure that, if investors choose the default option in a 401(k) plan, they will be taken care of.[51]

China's stock market bubble shows just how quickly the dynamics of behavioral finance can develop at a national level. The Shanghai Stock Exchange was closed from the Chinese Revolution until 1990 and had a relatively listless start. But during the mid-2000s, as the Chinese economy boomed, the market took on its own animal spirits. The Exchange's composite index increased by 600% from June 2005 to October 2007, achieving a total market capitalization of over $3 trillion—making it the fifth-largest in the world. Given the very high personal savings rate in China, the raw materials for a bubble were in place, and investors opened brokerage accounts at a rate of 100,000 per day at the market peak, ultimately reaching 100 million accounts. As prices surged, investors seeking to take advantage of the boom began to fund stock purchases with second mortgages and credit cards. In contrast to the US, individual retail investors rather than institutions dominated the trade in shares. One account described the retail trading scene: "Brokerages are set up like casinos. Investors drink tea, smoke and chat as they make trades on computers lined up like slot machines. Instead of dropping in coins, they swipe bank cards to pay for shares." The fact that non-professional traders dominate trading led to some colorful anomalies in pricing. Many Chinese retail investors rely on investment theories not widely recognized in the West; for instance, the number 8 is considered lucky, and thus stocks whose ticker code includes the digit 8 receive higher valuations, and those with a double 8 are particularly prized. Such theories inevitably become self-fulfilling, as Keynes might have predicted: if investors believe that other investors will highly value particular kinds of stocks (those with a number 8, say, or those whose names end in "dot-com"), then it becomes true. At least, that is, until it is no longer true: like all bubbles, the China stock market bubble could not last forever, and by June 2008 the Shanghai market had lost half its value since peaking the previous October.[52]

Stock ownership and politics

If stock ownership does not perform the educational function its proponents claim, it may have other effects. Perhaps 401(k) holders do not become Alan Greenspan, but several Republican theorists hoped they might become more like Ayn Rand in their political views. Of course, the theoretical link between property ownership and political interests is virtually axiomatic, and a foundational assumption of the US Constitution. In *The Federalist # 10*, James Madison stated:

> Those who hold and those who are without property have ever formed distinct interests in society. Those who are creditors, and those who are debtors, fall under a like discrimination. A landed interest, a manufacturing interest, a mercantile interest, a moneyed interest, with many lesser interests, grow up of necessity in civilized nations, and divide them into different classes, actuated by different sentiments and views.[53]

Could buying a mutual fund cause one to identify with the owning class? More pertinently, could it turn voters into Republicans? During the late 1990s, as commentators observed the rapidly increasing prevalence of stock ownership in the US, a handful of writers and activists in conservative publications answered in the affirmative, finding evidence for a correlation between stock ownership and political sentiments, even at relatively low levels of participation. Richard Nadler, in an article published by the conservative Cato Institute entitled "The Rise of Worker Capitalism," reported that free-market policies such as capital gains tax cuts were popular among shareholders compared to non-shareholders, independent of income, age, sex, race, and party affiliation. By the time of the 2000 election Nadler asserted, based on opinion polls, that "mass ownership of financial assets has midwifed a new birth of free-market opinion," and that the longer individuals were enrolled in a 401(k) plan, the more likely they were to identify as Republican. He argued that shareholding was a causal variable in this relationship through its effect on the kind of information shareholders attend to, and lamented that "It is this educating tendency of capital ownership that the GOP has been slow to grasp... The party has to actively recruit investor members— but it is failing abysmally in this task."[54]

In subsequent years, however, the Republican Party—led by the administration of George W. Bush—took the "investor class" model to heart. In 2003, Bush signed reductions in the capital gains tax and the dividend tax—policies that appealed explicitly to investors but drew little attention from non-shareholders—and during the 2004 presidential election campaign, he began to promulgate the theory of the ownership society, with the privatization of Social Security as its centerpiece. In Bush's plan, workers would direct a portion of their mandatory Social Security contributions into accounts invested in the stock market—a sort of national 401(k). Although putatively an effort to reform Social Security and to address shortfalls in decades ahead, analyses suggested that the transition to private plans would be phenomenally costly in the short run. But it had two potential electoral benefits that were recognized by its proponents on the right. First, current shareholders favored the idea, as they did other shareholder-oriented policies such as capital gains tax cuts, and shareholders were substantially more likely than non-shareholders to vote in elections. Second, as another commentator put it, "Social Security reform is the key goal of an investor-class politics, since it would bring almost the entire population into the class." In short, according to conservative activist Grover Norquist, privatizing Social Security would make the Republican Party "a true and permanent national majority" by creating a vast population of shareholder-Republicans.[55]

Research evidence suggests that Norquist and friends were not entirely wrong. According to analyses of surveys conducted by the American National Election Studies, shareholders were about 30% more likely than non-shareholders to identify themselves as Republicans in 1998, 2000, and 2002, after taking into account income, education, age, race, sex, and home ownership. Moreover, this figure jumped to 130% in 2004 in the wake of the shareholder-oriented tax cuts of 2003 and the campaign pledge to privatize Social Security. Over time, those that owned shares in 2000 turned Republican at a significantly higher rate than those that did not: 38% of shareholders called themselves Republicans in 2004, compared to 31% in 2000. (The proportions of non-shareholders calling themselves Republican was 18% in both 2000 and 2004, showing no increase.)[56]

It appears, however, that the "shareholder effect" was fairly narrow: shareholders favored policies that were economically favorable to themselves, but this did not spill over into full-throated support of free markets. Table 6.3 compares non-shareholders and shareholders on a set of attitudinal questions and voting in the presidential election of 2004, drawing on the American National Election Studies. Notably, there were no significant differences on a number of political questions that investor class proponents see as being influenced by stock ownership. Shareholders were just as likely as non-shareholders to agree that government is run by a few big interests, and that the gap between rich and poor has grown in the past twenty years. Perhaps more surprisingly, shareholders were indistinguishable from non-shareholders in their response to two "acid test" free market questions. One question asked this: "Recently, some big American companies have been hiring workers in foreign countries to replace workers in the U.S. Do you think the federal government should DISCOURAGE companies from doing this, ENCOURAGE companies to do this, or STAY OUT of this matter?" The correct free market answer is "Stay out of this matter," but 63% of shareholders stated that the Federal government should discourage companies from doing this. A second acid test concerns school vouchers. The survey asked "Do you FAVOR or OPPOSE having the government give parents in low-income families money to help pay for their children to attend a private or religious school instead of their local public school?" Here, the correct answer, and a particular hobbyhorse for Milton Friedman and followers, is "Favor,"

Table 6.3. *Percentage of shareholders and non-shareholders agreeing with each statement*

	Non-shareholders	Shareholders
Government is run by a few big interests	58	55
The gap between rich and poor has grown in past 20 years	79	79
... this is bad	57	62
I oppose school vouchers	63	69
The federal government should discourage companies from offshoring	63	66
The rich pay less tax than they should	61	58
I'll be better off financially in a year	39	36
The economy will get better in a year	34	34
The economy is worse since Bush became President	55	55
I approve of Bush's tax cuts	31	45*
I favor allowing Social Security funds to be invested in the stock market	36	50*
I approve the President's handling of his job in general	45	55*
I approve the President's handling of the economy	32	49*
Pre-election: intend to vote for Bush	39	50*
Post-election: voted	70	93*
Post-election: voted for Bush	40	56*

Note: From American National Election Study. Percentages with an asterisk are substantive differences, statistically significant at $p < .05$.

but 69% of shareholders opposed it—a slightly higher number than non-shareholders.

Shareholders, in short, were not doctrinaire devotees of free market policies, and were largely indistinguishable from non-shareholders on a range of attitudinal issues. But on policies explicitly targeted to shareholder interests—tax cuts and privatization of Social Security—shareholders were substantially more favorable to Bush than non-shareholders. They were more positive about Bush's handling of his job in general by 10 percentage points compared to non-shareholders, and on his handling of the economy they were 17 points higher.

In retrospect, predictions of a permanent Republican majority may have been slightly premature. Even well-off voters that might have voted for Bush in 2004 turned against the Republican Party in large numbers in subsequent elections, and by 2008 the majority of those making over $100,000 per year were rooting for a Democratic presidency. Evidently, political identity was not completely controlled by one's stock portfolio; issues of education, public infrastructure, war, and governmental competence might also play a role in voting. Discussions of "rebranding" the Republican Party were widespread among the punditry.[57]

It is perhaps unsurprising that the investor class model was short-lived, given its narrow pecuniary base. If the average shareholding family owned $24,000 worth of stock in 2004, as the Federal Reserve's survey suggested, then their economic interests were clearly more tied to their status as workers and homeowners. On the other hand, with the pervasiveness of financial news in the broad cultural environment, shareholders and others were deluged with information about how the market was doing on a day-to-day basis. Financial news networks proliferated along with business publications, and the *Wall Street Journal* became the second-highest circulation daily newspaper in the US. Moreover, the World Wide Web made financial information widely available, and most large mutual funds and 401(k)s established websites to make it easy to track one's portfolio—which roughly half of the investing public did once per week or more, according to one survey. Shareholders had a direct personal stake in how American capitalism (i.e. the S&P500) was doing on any particular day, albeit a small one. Perhaps it is not the amount of money at stake but its apparent objectivity that focuses attention on portfolio value as a gauge of well-being. It is hard to calculate with precision how policy choices on climate change affect my overall welfare; it is easy to look up how my 401(k) did the day a tax cut was announced.

And given the faith of some in the omniscience of financial markets, the conflation of "markets" and "democracy" is unlikely to end soon.[58] Electronic markets that allow speculators to bet on the outcomes of elections have a very good record at predicting their outcomes. Wall Streeters have bet on elections for at least a century, and apparently the probabilities that their betting reveals are fairly accurate. A columnist for the *Wall Street Journal* suggested that deregulating Web-based election markets would allow a more accurate advance read on electoral outcomes.[59] Given the effort, expense, and unreliability of actual elections, can a call by editorialists to turn over the selection of government officials to Wall Street be far behind?[60]

Mortgage bubble

A home truth that forms the basis of much public policy is that a house is a person's most prized asset, and that paying the mortgage takes precedence over almost all other outlays, with the possible exception of medical expenses. A second truth, based on decades of experience, is that, with rare local exceptions, home prices always go up. Mortgage securitization—a financial practice designed to make home ownership more affordable and accessible—has upended both of these truths by creating a bubble in housing prices unprecedented in American history. The bubble created trillions of dollars in paper wealth and fueled an economic expansion through its effects on household consumption. Millions of jobs were created in construction, real estate, finance, and home improvement. And then, very quickly, it burst, with consequences felt from neighborhoods in California and Detroit, to Wall Street, to villages in Norway that had invested in mortgage derivatives. Several players helped inflate the mortgage bubble.

Buyers, sellers, and appraisers At base, the "true" value of a house is uncertain. Unlike securities, homes are illiquid and have no underlying income stream, so the standard models of valuing capital assets do not work well. Houses are fundamentally worth what someone will pay for them. Thus, industry practice was to rely on appraisers to state a value based on what comparable houses had sold for recently. Given this slack, appraisers naturally face pressure from sellers and brokers to sign off on high valuations. Each gets paid only if a deal gets done, and appraisers—who rely on repeat business—have reason to maintain cordial relations with their clients. Notably, once a buyer has agreed to a price, all the pressure militates for higher valuations, not lower ones.[61] In light of the inherent uncertainty around fair valuation, even the stated sale price might not be the "real" price. In some markets, sellers and buyers are known to collaborate with real estate agents in inflating valuations through the practice of the "cash-back transaction," in which a buyer without sufficient savings pays 10% above fair value for the house, which the seller returns under the table for the buyer to use as a down payment—thereby further inflating prices in the neighborhood.[62]

Wall Street Local banks might be vigilant about inflated valuations in their town, but local banks are not where most mortgages end up anymore. As we have described previously, most mortgages are pooled with other mortgages and then divided into bonds to free up lenders to make more loans—a long-standing practice that created a stable, if boring, business for government-created companies like Fannie Mae and Freddie Mac. But Wall Street banks found ways to make mortgage-backed bonds more exciting by lowering the standards for borrowers and by creating exotic derivatives that were increasingly removed from the underlying assets (that is, homes). Subprime mortgages were generally those that did not meet the "standard" criteria of Fannie Mae and Freddie Mac: the borrowers had problematic credit histories, low down payments, less rigorous documentation of their assets and income, or the property they were buying did not conform in its size or configuration. With this added risk came higher interest rates.

The most infamous product created by banks was the collateralized debt obligation (CDO). CDOs buy chunks of dozens of mortgage-backed bonds, which in turn hold thousands of individual mortgages that may or may not be subprime. The CDO then issues several tranches of securities, each with different levels of risk and different payouts. As with other underwriting jobs, banks receive a fee for underwriting a CDO, perhaps equal to 1–1.5% of the size of the issue (which will typically be in the $1 billion range). CDO managers—free-standing businesses that handle the flow of funds in and out of the CDO—also receive a management fee, perhaps 0.1% per year. The market for CDOs was initially large because their top tranches were seen as safe, thanks to their certification by independent ratings agencies, and relatively remunerative compared to other "safe" instruments.[63]

The high fees available for underwriting mortgage-backed bonds and CDOs, coupled with the global demand for them, encouraged Wall Street firms to maintain a steady deal flow from originators (e.g. Countrywide Financial). But the competition for deal flow resulted in a contagion of declining standards among banks. At some point, everyone that needed one already had a mortgage. Thus, as the number of creditable borrowers went down, banks began to accept shakier subprime mortgages for a higher fee, which encouraged the finance companies that supplied the banks to issue shakier mortgages, which encouraged the brokers that supplied the finance companies to accept lower standards from applicants.

Brokers The advent of subprime mortgages changed the nature of the bubble, as even the creditworthy began taking out subprime loans. High-interest subprime loans made up 29% of the total loans originated in 2006, and were spread all across the country, even in wealthy communities in which credit scores are typically high. The prevalence of subprime loans was due in part to a compensation structure that rewarded brokers for putting borrowers in loans at higher rates than they qualified for. The higher the interest rate that buyers agree to, the higher the premium paid to brokers by finance companies. In most states, brokers were not legally obligated to put borrowers in the best mortgage available to them, inducing a "buyer beware" marketplace in which ethical standards could be somewhat relaxed. The rapaciousness of brokers was in some cases encouraged by the credulity of borrowers: a survey by the Mortgage Bankers Association found that half of borrowers could not recall the terms of mortgages they had taken out within the previous twelve months. Even for the biggest purchase of their lives, individuals in the midst of an ever-rising housing market were prone to making poorly informed—or intentionally misinformed—financial deals. Still other buyers seemed to be treating their mortgage as a quick bridge loan, to be refinanced at a better rate later.[64]

In later years of the bubble, subprime lenders began approving loans based on just a credit score, with no verified income and no verified assets. At the time, the assumption based on recent historical precedent was that house prices would go up enough to allow refinancing, so that even "under-qualified" borrowers could be fobbed off on the next lender. By 2006, 44% of subprime borrowers did not fully document their income and assets, up from 17% earlier in the decade.[65] In some cases, brokers themselves fraudulently filled in details on loan applications without the knowledge of the borrowers. But the loans were approved, and the brokers got their commissions; the mortgage companies got their cut; the Wall Street bank got its fee for underwriting the bond; and the rating agency got its fee for evaluating it.

Rating agencies Evaluating the riskiness of packages of mortgages and CDOs fell to three main bond rating agencies: Standard & Poor's, Fitch, and Moody's. Bond rating agencies grade bonds according to their risk of default, using variations on a system that grades bonds from AAA (the lowest risk, comparable to Treasury bonds) to C. Many investors cannot buy bonds that do not have an "investment grade" rating from one of these three Federally recognized agencies. Thus, bonds are typically designed to achieve such a rating, or else they are not marketable. There is an intrinsic conflict of interest in the industry: issuers, not investors, are the ones that pay the agencies, and the agencies only get paid if the bond gets the desired rating. Thus, the rating process can seem more like a negotiation than a test, and issuers can engage in "ratings shopping" among the three agencies to ensure that at least one gives them the desired rating.

The explosive growth in securitization, which we described in Chapter 4, was a substantial source of new business for ratings agencies. No longer limited to boring corporate and municipal bonds, the rating agencies were evaluating the exotic cutting edge in financial instruments, which provided a large inflow of new fees. Thus, Moody's went public in 2000, and its profits surged 900% thanks to the expansive frontier of new business. It was also a source of potential strain. Given the flow of deals on Wall Street, an analyst at a ratings agency might have a day to evaluate a mortgage-backed bond based on a giant spreadsheet with information about several thousand underlying mortgages and borrowers. From this information, and a statistical model for predicting the risks of individual loans based on what other home borrowers had done in the past, analysts were charged with assessing the risk of the aggregated securities. The task, essentially, was to make an educated guess about how likely home buyers were to make their payments on time, or to pay off early, or to default at various points in time. That was the source of risk in mortgage bonds.

The underlying model of mortgage-buyer behavior was based, inevitably, on what buyers had done in the past. Buyer behavior, however, changed during the bubble. The best predictor of default was no longer the size of people's first mortgage, nor their credit scores, but the size of their first and second loans combined. Creditworthy borrowers with adequate incomes were defaulting on mortgages, which was unprecedented. According to a Moody's analyst, "It seems there was a shift in mentality; people are treating homes as investment assets." In other words, like investors, home buyers found it sensible to abandon properties on which they owed more than it was worth, just as one would not exercise a stock option that was underwater. Yet this is just the kind of thing that homeowners had never done before. As a Moody's managing director put it, to rely on their old model of buyer behavior was "like observing 100 years of weather in Antarctica to forecast the weather in Hawaii."[66] Philosopher David Hume's problem of induction had come to the financial markets: the laws of nature had changed, making the future unpredictable from the past. As a result, masses of bonds were rapidly downgraded from AAA to junk.[67]

Speculators and fraudsters The ready availability of mortgages with little money down, and a contagion of declining loan standards in a market where house values had nowhere to go but up, opened the doors to rampant speculation and fraud. According to the National Association of Realtors, 28% of buyers in 2005 were investors, and far more in some "hot" markets like Naples, Florida. Buyers were literally treating houses like investments that they were buying to flip, like a day trader betting on an IPO. Some buyers even bought properties on eBay, where thousands of residences were listed for sale and many were bought, sight unseen, by prospective mini-Trumps who aimed to pass them on like penny stocks to the greater fool.[68]

With compliant brokers, eager sellers, appraisers paid by the deal, and loan standards that no longer required documentation of income or assets, mortgage fraud was easy. In some neighborhoods, fraud accounted for perhaps half of the foreclosures; in the meantime, the houses' overstated values briefly inflated the value of their neighbors. Harried mortgage issuers were faced with demands for rapid turnaround on loans, perhaps allocating fifteen minutes between receiving closing documents by fax and releasing the funds to the borrower. In a newly fast-paced business, mortgage companies relied on free-standing brokers as "external loan officers," expecting them to fulfill the functions of a bank loan officer. But traditional bank loan officers were employees of the bank, expecting to be around long enough to be held accountable for their work. If buyers missed payments within the first three months, bankers were likely to get a talking-to. Brokers, on the other hand, were undoubtedly on to another line of work, in online gold farming, or wind-power sales.[69]

Regulators If the housing bubble was obvious to those paying attention, then why didn't policymakers intervene to deflate it? One possible reason is that rising prices helped prop up the economy. Because the US has sophisticated means to get cash out of homes through refinancing and equity lines of credit, American homeowners became unusually prone to the "wealth effect," that is, spending in a fashion commensurate with their overall wealth rather than just their current income. The wealth effect is why Americans don't save—or at least didn't save prior to 2008. As the cliché has it, owners were treating their homes as an ATM, making up for income shortfalls to fund their expenditures. Of those with mortgages 45% refinanced them between 2001 and 2004, and one-third of these borrowed more than the amount refinanced (that is, extracted equity) for home improvement or to pay off other debts, according to the Fed's 2004 Survey of Consumer Finances. The amount of money involved grew quite large: Alan Greenspan and James Kennedy estimated that home equity withdrawals went as high as $840 billion per year from 2004 to 2006, equal to about 9% of the nation's disposable income. Of that, as much as $300 billion went toward personal consumption. It was hard to find an organized constituency that opposed rising home prices and easy credit; certainly, the 70% of households that owned their homes (or "owned" their homes) were not likely to reward politicians that brought the party to an end.[70]

Entire industries were being stoked by the mortgage bubble: From 2003 to 2006, it is estimated that almost one-quarter of the new jobs added were in housing-related industries, including construction, home improvement, and real estate-related occupations. The *New York Times* estimated near the top of the bubble that there were 400,000 mortgage brokers working in 50,000 firms, and their trade association reports that there were 1.2 million real estate agents. There were about as many real estate agents in the US as employees in the Computer and Electronic

Product Manufacturing industry, and twice as many mortgage brokers as those working in Apparel Manufacturing.[71]

Even as the housing market began to cool, households did not substantially increase their savings rate, and consumer spending continued apace. Many consumers had been trained to expect that they could refinance the mortgage or take out a line of credit to fund major expenses, just as the Economic Report of the President promised.[72] And in spite of the signs of impending difficulties, foreign investors continued to provide funding due to the attractive rates paid by mortgage-backed securities and their derivatives. From Abu Dhabi and China, to Germany and Norway, bonds backed by US mortgages continued to find eager buyers. After all, Americans don't default on their mortgages, and those three conservative bond rating agencies had certified them as safe.[73]

Mortgage meltdown

It couldn't last forever. It was clear that, even as house prices increased dramatically, home equity (the value of the home minus the mortgage debt still owed) was not keeping up. Through multiple refinancings and equity lines of credit, homeowners were continuing to expand their mortgage debt, which rose at an even faster pace than house prices. Even those nearest to retirement no longer owned their homes outright. By early 2008, homeowners' share of their equity sank to the lowest level on record—less than half, on average, compared to 80% in 1945. And a trickle of foreclosures began to turn into a flood, signaling that a massive devaluation was underway. Once prices began to drop, it triggered a downward spiral in which homeowners that were unable to make their payments could not refinance, because the imputed value of their home had dropped, which put them into foreclosure, which in turn further lowered the prices of neighboring houses. Within a few months, foreclosure rates rapidly surged, particularly in the former industrial heartland of the Midwest and the "bubble states" of California, Florida, Nevada, and Arizona.[74]

The rising rate of foreclosures affected homeowners, neighborhoods, and the cities that relied on their taxes to provide services. Many foreclosures were concentrated in cities like Las Vegas or Miami, which had seen huge increases in housing values. But even Detroit, which already had the highest foreclosure rate in the nation, was further laid low by the mortgage meltdown. During the bubble, entrepreneurial brokers had targeted existing homeowners with advertisements for mortgage loans that would yield the brokers high fees—particularly if they were high-interest subprime loans. Many homeowners used the proceeds to fund costly home improvement projects intended to enhance the resale value of their homes. But once the foreclosures started, the prospects for resale were bleak, and a hard-hit city was hit hard once again. As a Detroit real estate agent put it, "Nobody's going to want to buy into a neighborhood with 20% foreclosures. You end up with no neighborhood."[75]

Early estimates of the costs of the meltdown ranged from $400 billion to perhaps $4 trillion in lost real estate wealth. Cascading declines in home values could in turn cost nearly $1 trillion in lost property taxes for state and local governments.[76] Even Norwegian villagers lost municipal services due to turbulence in the American mortgage market. The 18,000 citizens of Narvik found that a multi-million dollar loan backed by their future energy revenues had been invested in Citigroup CDOs that had lost tens of millions in value, forcing cutbacks in budgets and employment.[77] It was like a financial version of the butterfly effect: Detroit homeowners' fates were linked to the London Interbank Offered Rate, while childcare for Norwegian villagers depended on the mortgage payments of Florida real estate speculators.

Beyond the financial effects, the mortgage bubble had transformed the *meaning* of homeownership. Trained to think like investors through their disintermediated mortgages, many individuals now regarded their homes as just another class of asset in their portfolio. They had received the message of the portfolio society: they were *investors*. The CEO of Bank of America said, "There's been a change in social attitudes toward default ... We're seeing people who are current on their credit cards but are defaulting on their mortgages." They are "homeowners in name only.

Because these people never put up much of their own money, they don't act like owners."[78]

This phenomenon was not limited to those with low income or poor credit. Credit scores no longer distinguished those who could be relied on to pay back their debts, as even those with high scores were willing to abandon a house with negative equity. According to one debt collector in India, "People are walking away from their homes and hanging onto their credit cards, because this is their lifeline".[79] Financially, this was not irrational: 10% of homeowners with a mortgage in early 2008 owed more on their house than it was worth, and this number was expected to go as high as one in four. As a result, millions were effectively trapped in their homes. If they had to relocate for their job, they faced a choice between coming up with funds to cover the shortfall between the sale price of the house and the amount remaining on their mortgage, or abandoning their home to foreclosure.[80] Given this choice, in many cases the smart money abandons the option.

When a home becomes an asset class, the presumed societal benefits of home ownership become more dubious. If, as Bush described it, renters are like visitors to a community, and owners are genuinely part of it, with a stake in its future, how are we to regard the situation of those whose mortgages are underwater? According to the *Wall Street Journal*, "These days, bankers and mortgage companies often find that by the time they get the keys back, embittered homeowners have stripped out appliances, punched holes in walls, dumped paint on carpets and, as a parting gift, locked their pets inside to wreak further havoc. Real-estate agents estimate that about half of foreclosed properties to be sold by mortgage companies nationwide have 'substantial' damage." Many banks found themselves in the strange position of offering cash payments to those they were about to evict to leave quietly without trashing the house.[81]

Political responses were complicated by the nature of the crisis. It's easy to blame rapacious brokers and Wall Street. Some critics blamed Fed chairman Alan Greenspan for failing to step in when he had a chance to police predatory lending practices. But the regulation of mortgage finance was a mad patchwork, and most major mortgage finance companies were concentrated in California, whose state legislature had lovingly nurtured the home-grown (and largely unregulated) industry. George Bush emphasized the virtues of home ownership and sought to lower the financial barriers to buying a house—normally a politically popular program (particularly for homeowners, who tend to vote Republican). But in retrospect, those barriers were there for a reason.[82] Within a few months of the start of the mortgage crisis, entire neighborhoods from southern California to Detroit were left dotted with empty houses in foreclosure, like a real estate rapture.

Some homeowners who were current on their payments blamed their neighbors for taking on too much debt—particularly those whose homes went into foreclosure, bringing down neighborhood property values. A Treasury department presentation on the crisis echoed this "blame the homeowner" approach, stating that "Homeowners who can afford their mortgage but walk away because they are underwater are merely speculators"—a remarkable sentiment from an organization that had recently put up billions to bail out Bear Stearns, which surely meets most definitions of a "speculator." On the other hand, through no fault of their own, millions of homeowners were seeing their most valuable asset plummet in value, and foreclosures in the neighborhood had spillover effects on blameless neighbors. Entire neighborhoods were at risk, which clearly required a thoughtful government response. But the Bush administration was loath to reward mere speculators, or to create a precedent for bailing out those that had been financially reckless (Bear Stearns, Fannie Mae, Freddie Mac, and AIG notwithstanding). How to distinguish the "worthy" borrowers who fell into hard times, and therefore merited help, from the unworthy speculators? The answer to this conundrum was a long time in coming. Going forward, Harvard law professor Elizabeth Warren proposed a "Financial Product Safety Commission" to help protect consumers from some of the dangers of the new finance, but it was clear that any such initiative would have to wait for a Democratic administration in 2009.[83]

The mortgage crisis calls to mind a parallel. In 1958 Chairman Mao sought to increase harvests in China with his "great sparrow campaign." Sparrows were seen to eat grain, and so grain harvests could be increased by mobilizing the population to kill as many of them as possible. The campaign was wildly successful, killing millions of sparrows. Unfortunately, it turned out that sparrows ate relatively little grain; rather, they were the primary natural predator of locusts, which do eat grain. Without sparrows, the locust population exploded and the grain harvests plummeted, creating a massive famine. Mortgage-backed securities originated from a financial program created by the government to make home ownership affordable and to make mortgages available to those that might not otherwise have access to them. But through a combination of lax regulation and Wall Street innovation, the spread of mortgage securitization had resulted in the largest number of people losing their homes in American history.

Aftermath of the bubbles

The successive bubbles in the stock market and in housing made it clear that the economic well-being of households faced unexpected perils in the new century. But if the workplace and the government could no longer be relied on to provide economic security after the era of corporate feudalism, where could individuals turn? The answer implied by the ownership society was that financial innovations would help households find a way to make it through the crisis. JG Wentworth began running a television advertising campaign featuring angry-looking people yelling out their windows: "It's my money, and I need it now!" The pitch was for "structured settlements" in which individuals who have been awarded an insurance payout signed it over to the firm in return for a lump-sum payment. Some similar innovations skated illegality—veteran's pensions, for instance, cannot legally be signed over to others, but dozens of firms with military-sounding names advertise openly in periodicals oriented toward veterans. Along the same lines, payday lenders have found that Social Security beneficiaries—retirees or the disabled—are a reliable source of income, and many have created programs in which monthly Social Security checks are deposited directly into accounts controlled by the lenders, who then allocate an allowance to the beneficiary. Effective annual interest rates as high as 400% have been reported for some of these products. And why not? An industry spokesman stated, "It certainly wouldn't be right for the business to discriminate against them for whatever the source of their income is." After all, David Bowie had issued bonds based on his future royalties—why not Social Security recipients? Similar pitches were made to lottery winners and others with a reliable stream of payments. In the meantime, credit card debt reached almost $1 trillion outstanding.[84] In the Book of Matthew, the Parable of the Talents ends: "For unto every one that hath shall be given, and he shall have abundance: but from him that hath not shall be taken away even that which he hath" (25: 29).

Finance had hit America like a tornado hits a trailer park, leaving disruption in its path from the workplace to the neighborhood to the voting booth. In the next chapter, I speculate on what comes next.

7

Conclusion: A Society of Investors?

In his book *The Great Transformation*, economic historian Karl Polanyi described how nineteenth-century Britain attempted a society-wide experiment in free markets that had never been done before or since. Adam Smith had claimed that people possessed an intrinsic propensity to "truck and barter" and that markets were in some sense fundamental to the human condition. Yet the anthropological evidence showed that this was not true: markets played little part in pre-modern societies and were regarded with great suspicion throughout the Middle Ages in Europe due to their disruptive effects. In order for markets to work effectively in an industrial economy, Polanyi argued, labor, land, and money had to be re-conceived as *commodities*—objects produced for sale on a market—even though they quite evidently were not. He referred to this practice as the "commodity fiction" and argued that its acceptance had wide-ranging consequences, becoming a "vital organizing principle in regard to the whole of society affecting almost all its institutions in the most varied way." The commodity fiction had followed from industrialization: "The extension of the market mechanism to the elements of industry—labor, land, and money—was the inevitable consequence of the introduction of the factory system in a commercial society." Thus, in industrializing Britain, "human society had become an accessory of the economic system."[1]

Post-industrialism and the pervasiveness of finance in the US have created a *portfolio society*, and in a portfolio society it is the "capital fiction" that dominates. As the American economy has come to orbit financial markets like planets around the sun, entire categories of social life have been securitized, turned into a kind of capital. It is not the company or the government that will take care of us in our old age, but our 401(k). Home is not simply a place to live, but an option on future housing price increases. We now refer to education, talent, and personality as "human capital"—not ironically, but as an obvious fact. Friends, families, and neighborhoods are now "social capital," investments that might pay off down the road. And just as the commodity fiction became an "organizing principle of society" in the wake of the Industrial Revolution in England, the capital fiction describes social organization in post-industrial America. The individual's place in an ownership society is as an investor, buying and selling securities for their economic and social portfolios.

The societal adjustment to the Industrial Revolution took generations. The industrialist and early socialist Robert Owen described the consequences of industrialization for society in 1817: "The general diffusion of manufactures throughout a country generates a new character in its inhabitants; and as this character is formed upon a principle quite unfavorable to individual or general happiness, it will produce the most lamentable and permanent evils, unless its tendency be counteracted by legislative interference and direction." Britain's experiments with free markets ultimately ended in societal backlash, as the squalid world of Dickens was more palatable in print than in real life. In the wake of the stock market bubble and its burst, and the mortgage bubble and its implosion, we are observing some of the early consequences of post-corporate, post-industrial social organization in the US. The character of any societal backlash remains to be seen.

In this final chapter, I review the argument that has unfolded over the previous six chapters and engage in some speculation about what finance has wrought for the United States.

Finance and the transition from manufacturing to service

Managed by the Markets makes one large argument: that the shift from a manufacturing to a service (or post-industrial) economy in the United

States has been decisively shaped by finance. The first chapter described the advent of post-industrialism, which I argue is an almost inevitable consequence of productivity growth in manufacturing. The US has seen a steady decline in the proportion of the labor force employed in manufacturing since 1944, when it reached its apex at 45% of the total private labor force. By late 2008, manufacturing employment had dropped below 10%; during the Bush years alone, roughly 4 million manufacturing jobs—more than one in five—had disappeared. Although this was widely blamed on offshoring, a more fundamental factor was growth in productivity, enabled in large part by information technology. It simply takes fewer people less time to assemble a car or a computer than it used to, with the implication that large-scale employment in manufacturing was unlikely to ever return. Employment for the foreseeable future will be concentrated in services; Wal-Mart, not General Motors, is now the prototypical American employer. A consequence of this shift is that long-term attachments between employees and firms, which were relatively common among large manufacturers, are largely a thing of the past, with important consequences for individuals, households, and communities.

Information and communication technologies (ICTs—particularly computers, the Internet, and wireless telecommunications) have also revolutionized the practice of finance, as described in Chapter 2. It is now much cheaper to rely on financial markets for many kinds of financing that used to be done through banks, from the short-term cash needs of businesses to thirty-year home mortgages. ICTs have also opened up opportunities for innovations in products and businesses from the mundane (mortgage brokerage) to the macabre (insurance payoffs for the terminally ill). By making things tradable that were not before (e.g. streams of insurance payoffs), finance has had broad and often unexpected effects on both buyers and sellers.

Public corporations in the US have a long history of dealing with issues of accountability and control that arise out of being financed by markets. *Corporate governance* describes the system of institutions used to keep order in public corporations, in particularly by orienting those that run them toward share price. Chapter 2 gives a brief outline of the theory of corporate governance in the US and the central place it gives to share price as a privileged kind of knowledge. The same level of institutional elaboration that guides public corporations has not yet spread to other things traded on financial markets. The chapter also describes the idea of finance as a technology, and argues that finance is an inherently *social* technology, prone to particular kinds of disasters not seen in physical technologies.

The third chapter provides a brief history of the large US corporation during the twentieth century. Early in the century, corporations were regarded with suspicion as unnatural, soulless amalgamations of power and resources. A few vanguard corporations pioneered personnel practices and public relations campaigns intended to give themselves an aura of "institutionality"—they were interested in making a contribution to society, not just in making a profit, and they maintained extensive bonds with their employees. Over time, as ownership became dispersed and regulations changed the character of the employment relation and the status of organized labor, the largest corporations became relatively autonomous from finance, and their professional managers increasingly acted as if their earlier PR were true. They became "soulful corporations" (or perhaps feudal corporations), with obligations to their employees and their broader communities as well as their shareholders. The US during the corporate-institutional era was a *society of organizations*, in which lives were largely lived in and through organizations. Corporations took on the role of miniature welfare states, providing wage stability, health care coverage, and retirement security. This system largely disappeared with the bust-up takeover wave of the 1980s and the triumph of the shareholder value movement. By the late 1990s, there was widespread agreement on all sides that the corporation existed to create shareholder value. As a consequence, corporate organization in shareholder-oriented firms became increasingly dispersed—more like a network or "nexus of contracts" than a social institution, exemplified by the so-called OEM (original equipment manufacturer) model. The late 1990s stock market bubble and its burst, and the subsequent revelation of various scandals that infected the relations between corporations and Wall Street, called into question the effectiveness of the model of corporate governance described in Chapter 2.

Banking and the financial services industry more broadly have been transformed by the shift to markets, as we saw in Chapter 4. Commercial banks, once the locally based anchors of urban business communities, consolidated into a small handful of enormous entities that were largely national in scope during the 1990s and 2000s. Due to the advent of securitization, many banks have been transformed into portals for financial markets, with more tenuous ties to particular places and clients. The financial landscape has seen both conglomeration, as businesses previously separated by law have been combined (e.g. commercial banking and investment banking), and disaggregation, as formerly unified businesses have been separated (e.g. originating, holding, and servicing loans). New kinds of industries have arisen, along with new forms of competition; for instance, hedge funds have grown into competitors with Wall Street, and mutual funds now compete with pension managers. Mutual funds grew to enormous size and potential influence due to the growth in retail investment and defined contribution pension plans; a small handful of fund complexes now hold the largest concentration of corporate ownership in American history, although they generally avoid exercising their power overtly.

The boundaries around *finance* as an industry became increasingly porous during the 1990s and 2000s, as many kinds of firms earned much of their profit in financial activities even if they were nominally in non-financial industries (e.g. GE, GM, Enron). Importantly, although "Wall Street" lives on as a term, Wall Street is now everywhere, from the hedge funds of Greenwich to the retail banks of Charlotte to the abandoned mortgage companies of Orange County. Moreover, and in sharp contrast to the turn of the previous century, it is impossible today to point to a handful of banks that are somehow "in charge," as the consequences of the mortgage implosion for finance firms and their executives demonstrated. "Wall Street" became collectively powerful yet also highly dispersed.

Finance and ICTs are also transforming states from sovereigns to vendors, as I argue in Chapter 5. The twentieth-century state was generally tied to a particular territory and nation, with its own base of local corporations, but many states today face a market of mobile corporations able to fine-tune the jurisdictions governing their corporate form, intellectual property, securities, labor, and other contracting. In the eyes of many shareholder-oriented corporations (and scholars of law and economics), "sovereignty" is a kind of business services industry, and states are in competition with each other to provide sovereign services, from incorporating tax-avoiding IP subsidiaries to chartering corporate jets. In the US, Delaware is the most evolved vendor when it comes to corporate law; for instance, Russian crime rings are evidently attracted to its online incorporation product for their money-laundering needs. As business competitors, many states have adopted the strategies of OEM corporations such as Nike, relying on contractors for services outside of their core competence and hiring consultants to help them develop an appealing brand image. At the national level, the US has vastly increased the use of contractors for basic tasks of government, from collecting taxes to protecting diplomats, leaving the federal government itself largely drained of talent for some of its essential work.

Finally, Chapter 6 describes the implications of finance-driven post-industrialism for households. The end of "corporate feudalism" and its system of long-term attachments between firms and employees has left households to fend for themselves in an economy tied in myriad ways to finance. With job security and career ladders a thing of the past, individuals have been urged to think of themselves as investors in human capital and social capital rather than as employees. Companies can no longer be relied on to provide health care coverage or retirement security. Thus, individuals increasingly find themselves tied to the stock market through their 401(k) pension plans and through the use of mutual funds as outlets for their savings. Households are also tied to financial markets through mortgages, which are overwhelmingly bundled with other mortgages and turned into securities.

Whether by choice or not, the end of corporate feudalism has meant that "employees" have been turned into free-agent day traders, a role for which many are not prepared. Optimists on the political right saw this as the beginning of an "ownership society" in which widespread share ownership would transform America into a land of free market-loving Republicans, an investor class highly attuned to the workings of the market and its wisdom. But the burst of the "new economy" bubble highlighted the risk of trusting one's savings to 401(k)s and mutual funds, while the collapse of the housing market made clear the dangers of mortgage securitization. We have lost the security of corporate feudalism, but do not yet have a new safety net in place.

Where are we now?

When Daniel Bell wrote about the advent of post-industrialism in 1973, he described it as an interstitial time, having the unsettled sense of being between eras. Industrialism had its own logic and its own form of social organization, but being "post" gave little sense of the next phase of social organization. Subsequent decades have resolved some of this uncertainty: in the US, finance has been a shaping force in working out the social implications of the time after industrialism. The old institutions of corporate industrialism have largely disappeared; finance-inflected institutions are taking their place.

Of course, it did not have to happen this way. The relative decline in manufacturing employment may have been inevitable, but the centrality of market-based finance to social organization was not. No one would describe Japan or Germany, or India or Brazil, as a "portfolio society." Corporations do not exist to create shareholder value in Japan, foreign investors notwithstanding: a Japanese vice minister for Economy, Trade, and Industry stated in a speech in 2008 that shareholders are "stupid, greedy, adulterous, irresponsible and threatening... They are the type of people who just sell the stock if they get mad," and certainly did not merit being the predominant beneficiaries of the corporation.[2] Corporations were still social institutions with societal obligations in Japan. And Germany has only about 650 public corporations—fewer than Malaysia or Hong Kong, and a small fraction of the number of public corporations in Japan or the US. Few people in such settings would confuse their home with a stock option, or see their children as "social capital." Portfolio thinking seems to be peculiarly attuned to America's distinctive economic organization.

Much the same was true for the mass-production mindset of the previous century. Peter Drucker at mid-century described how the production methods of the auto factory had become the operating logic for American society, from medical research to farming and from the education of children to the invasion of Normandy. Mass production had simply become how rational people did things. Yet elsewhere in the world, manufacturing had taken a rather different evolutionary path, with industrial districts comprising networks of firms taking the place of the vertically integrated corporation.[3] As Robert Owen's quote above highlights, people's experiences of the workplace and the organization of the economy shape their perceptions of the social world. The portfolio society makes sense in the US in a way that it may not elsewhere.

This book has argued that finance as a worldview has much the same status in the US today that mass production did in the twentieth century. In 1958, individuals were organization men, cogs in the corporate machine; now they are investors on a virtual exchange floor, surrounded by financial news and opportunities for trading. To view stocks, bonds, education, jobs, friends, and neighborhoods as investments in a portfolio implies that they are, in some sense, a "position," not a commitment. Investments are ephemeral; sophisticated investors diversify rather than concentrating their investment in particular positions. Richard Sennett has written about the consequences of this approach to jobs for human development, describing it in terms of the "corrosion of character." It is hard to sketch out a life narrative in one's career in a world of temporary employment, when this year's hot skills (say, mortgage brokerage) are obsolete next year. And if a house is a fungible financial investment rather than a tie to a neighborhood, what becomes of community?

This sense of fragmentation and ephemerality are, of course, the hallmarks of postmodernism. (The word may still seem alien, but the idea is not.) Fredric Jameson describes the spectacle and contrived depthlessness of postmodern art and architecture and how they reflect a particular structure of feeling abroad in the culture. The idea that surface is all there is—there is nothing more real or true deep down (or, indeed, that there even is a "deep down")—seems perfectly suited to a world of OEM corporations, where a primary source of the value of something is its brand, its "story," rather than the thing itself, and thus the production of the thing itself—cars, computers, blood thinner, dog food—can be contracted out. Recall the comment by Henry Ford's great-grandson, Ford's current Chairman: "It's easy to build a car. It's harder to build a brand."[4]

Wall Street contributes to this depthlessness and spectacle by its high valuation of intellectual property and expectations about the future relative to tangible property. When Sara Lee's CEO announced the company's plan to "de-verticalize" and focus on brand management rather than production, he said, "Wall Street can wipe you out. They are the rule-setters. They do have their fads, but to a large extent there is an evolution in how they judge companies, and they have decided to give premiums to companies that harbor the most profits for the least assets. I can't argue with that." And this last comment—"I can't argue with that"—hints at the link between postmodernism and finance: their connection to American pragmatism, a theme initially explored by geographer David Harvey that I turn to next.[5]

Finance and cynical pragmatism

I have asserted that in a portfolio society, nearly everything can be viewed as an investment. The individual's place in society is that of an investor in a market, trading with other investors. But the financial worldview also has implications for how we think about knowledge and the nature of truth. We touched on this in Chapter 2 when discussing prediction markets and the efficient markets hypothesis—the idea that financial markets have privileged access to truth and provide the best available estimate of what the future will bring. As we saw, legal theorists take an explicitly pragmatist approach to financial markets and corporate governance. To these scholars, it doesn't matter if the efficient market hypothesis is literally true as long as it is the best available approximation to truth. The related idea, that corporations should maximize shareholder value, "is not premised on the conclusion that shareholders do 'own' the corporation in any ultimate sense, only on the view that it can be better for all of us if we act as if they do," as William Allen put it.

Financial markets in this approach play a role similar to that of other deities in guiding behavior. "If behaving as though we had free will or God exists gets us results we want, we will not only come to believe those things; they will be, pragmatically, true."[6] Thus, if we all agree to the stipulation that what the market says is right—or at least that it makes sense to defer to the market—then the market's price will be, pragmatically, true. Moreover, true theories of corporate strategy and structure are those that create shareholder value, operationalized in terms of the inerrant movements of share price—a fairly literal version of William James's view that beliefs are to be judged by their effects, their "practical cash value."

While financial markets may or may not have unequaled access to truth, they have brought about a kind of quasi-pragmatism in the corporate world that is echoed in several different domains, with potentially noxious consequences. Chapter 3 described the ways in which executives defer to the market in choices about corporate strategies and structures. Given the nature of their compensation, tied as it is to share price, there is no point in executives complaining about the market's faulty theories or its alleged short-termism, as they did in the 1980s. In this kind of setting, "The very idea of Truth—with a capital T, something beyond what is merely persuasive to all concerned [i.e. the stock market]—is a fifth wheel, inoperative except that it occasionally comes loose and hits a bystander."[7]

But the scandals during the "new economy" bubble made clear that being guided by market reactions can lead to something closer to sophistry than to pragmatism—perhaps "cynical pragmatism" is the right label. Companies about to go public were fortified by affiliations with investors, venture capitalists, law firms, auditors, investment banks,

and alliance partners intended to testify to their unobservable underlying quality—apparently with great success.[8] Investment banks helped
organize these "optics." For example, if a particular alliance would help
the first day pop, then banks could hand out friends-and-family shares to
potential alliance partners. If impressive "hook" investors were needed,
then they could be brought in on appropriate terms. If an objective-
seeming analyst following was needed, then banks could compensate
analysts at other firms to maintain their coverage. It was not especially
difficult for the attentive executive or banker to engineer the kinds
of affiliations needed to persuade the market. And executives quickly
caught on to the value of the rhetoric of corporate governance and
the kinds of tactics that the market found persuasive. Gestures to the
financial markets ranged from whom they appointed to the board, to
how they announced strategic initiatives, to what kinds of actions could
be announced but then subsequently forgotten. They also learned the
comedian's art of timing: grants of stock options should be given out just
before good announcements, or just after bad announcements. To a surprising degree, managing for shareholder value looked like performance
art, giving a new twist to performance-based pay.

The cynical pragmatism of the corporate world is now widespread,
although how much of it can be blamed on finance is of course debatable.
Journalist Ron Suskind described a particular political variant of this
approach in the Bush Administration:

> In the summer of 2002, after I had written an article in Esquire that the
> White House didn't like about Bush's former communications director,
> Karen Hughes, I had a meeting with a senior adviser to Bush. He expressed
> the White House's displeasure, and then he told me something that at the
> time I didn't fully comprehend—but which I now believe gets to the very
> heart of the Bush presidency.
>
> The aide said that guys like me were "in what we call the reality-based
> community," which he defined as people who "believe that solutions
> emerge from your judicious study of discernible reality." I nodded and
> murmured something about enlightenment principles and empiricism.

He cut me off. "That's not the way the world really works anymore," he continued. "We're an empire now, and when we act, we create our own reality. And while you're studying that reality–judiciously, as you will–we'll act again, creating other new realities, which you can study too, and that's how things will sort out. We're history's actors... and you, all of you, will be left to just study what we do."[9]

Through frequent repetition, the Administration had managed to convince much of the American public that Saddam Hussein was responsible for the attacks of 9/11 and that he possessed weapons that were an imminent threat to the United States, in order to justify the invasion and occupation of Iraq; enough of the voting public was convinced of these pseudo-facts that Bush went on to win re-election shortly after the article appeared. If an informed electorate agrees, then it is, pragmatically, true—the reality-based community notwithstanding. (The idea of "framing" and "narratives" went on to do big business among Democrats, in the spirit of "If you can't beat them, join them.")

Science is not immune either, particularly if money is involved (as it usually is these days). For many pharmaceutical companies, "true" is what persuades the FDA to approve a drug and what convinces doctors to prescribe it. At the extreme, science is a branch of marketing. Journal publishers were alarmed to discover that pharmaceutical companies such as Merck retain a small army of ghostwriters to write up journal articles that they then shop around to reputable scientists to act as senior authors. Prior published research can speed a drug's way through the approval process and make it easier to market to physicians. Merck allegedly had dozens of academic articles about its drug Vioxx ghostwritten and then published under the names of prominent academics, who benefited by more lines on their CVs. Vioxx was later removed from the market after it was discovered that it increased the risk of heart attacks and strokes, leading to a multi-billion dollar lawsuit settlement.[10]

Litigation consultants have also been known to game the scientific system by covertly funding publications that support the views that they seek to prevail in court and recruiting "authors" for maximum impact.[11]

Oliver Wendell Holmes said that the law, in practice, is what a judge says it is. By the same token, scientific truth, in practice, is what makes it through the journal review process. Lamentably, judging academic work by whether it persuaded reviewers to accept it for publication, or whether it gets cited in other academic works, often seems to take the place of engagement with the quality of the work itself.

Yet while politics, science, justice, and academia echo the quasi-pragmatist approach to truth observed in finance, finance itself seems increasingly besieged by questions about the credibility of its basic numbers. In mid-February 2008, Bear Stearns was selling for $85 per share. One month later, it was sold to JP Morgan Chase for $2 per share (later revised upward), with a government sweetener to ease the deal—a total price less than what Bear's headquarters building would fetch. In what sense did Bear have a true intrinsic value? And how much can we trust the market to figure out what that value is? Pricing anomalies have become increasingly less anomalous. Although American securities markets are prized for their transparency and accessible prices, the surprising suddenness of the mortgage meltdown revealed that many prices are, in effect, pure guesswork. "Today, 'way less than half' of all securities trade on exchanges with readily available price information ... More and more securities are priced by dealers who don't publish quotes." As a result, "Large parts of American financial markets have become a hall of mirrors."[12] Banks across Wall Street found themselves struggling to determine the value of their own assets; given the way that bankers are compensated, it is unsurprising that employees at Bear Stearns, Credit Suisse, Lehman Brothers, Merrill Lynch, Morgan Stanley, and elsewhere had been found to have inflated the value of their holdings.[13]

And it was not just murky securities like CDOs that had implausible values: LIBOR, the London Inter-Bank Offered Rate, to which trillions of dollars in debt is pegged, was called into question in 2008. LIBOR is calculated daily based on reports from panels of banks on what it would cost them to borrow a "reasonable amount" for a particular duration in a particular currency (e.g. the dollar panel consists of sixteen large banks); it is intended as the average rate that banks would charge each other for short-term loans. Loan contracts are commonly written in terms of LIBOR—for instance, a thirty-year mortgage might be priced at LIBOR plus three percentage points. But LIBOR began to diverge significantly from other indicators of what banks would have to pay in 2008, which implied that banks were not being forthright in their reports. Honest reporting by the banks risked giving the appearance that they were in financial trouble, and appearances of financial weakness can quickly become reality, as bank runs demonstrate. The prospect that LIBOR was cooked was not trivial: "Payments on nearly $90 trillion in dollar-denominated mortgage loans, corporate debt and financial contracts rise and fall according to LIBOR's movements."[14]

Even the most basic national statistics that everyone takes for granted—unemployment, inflation, GDP—have come under scrutiny. Apostate Republican Kevin Phillips summarizes critiques that suggest that all three numbers have become increasingly dubious in the US as "Pollyanna creep" has set in. Policymakers have strong incentives to make the numbers look good, and through a series of adjustments over the years, the numbers have come to look better than they should. Those who were out of work and no longer looking—"discouraged workers"—were no longer classified as unemployed; those in the military were reclassified as "employed;" and so on. Phillips concludes: "Based on the criteria in place a quarter century ago, today's US unemployment rate is somewhere between 9 percent and 12 percent; the inflation rate is as high as 7 or even 10 percent; economic growth since the recession of 2001 has been mediocre, despite a huge surge in the wealth and incomes of the superrich, and we are falling back into recession."[15]

Conclusion: Where next?

Finance has become like a religion in the US, with adherents willing to accept its core tenets on faith. Pragmatists are willing to defer even without a particularly strong faith. But in light of the spectacular failures of finance in the past decade, it is perhaps time to re-assess our faith-based economic system.

Finance has created sophisticated tools for risk management and has the potential to address a number of social problems: affordable housing and education, insurance against the unexpected. But as this book has argued, finance can bring collateral damage in the form of changed worldviews. When citizens see themselves as investors, the results can be benign or disastrous. Recent experience has highlighted both possibilities, and it is not clear if the investment metaphor will survive the global financial crisis that was precipitated by American mortgage financing.

The stunning productivity of the agriculture and manufacturing sectors—the roots of post-industrialism—should be a cause for celebration. The ancient Greeks would have seen the current moment as a turning point in human history, where only a tiny fraction of the population's hours are needed to produce all of the food, clothing, shelter, and material goods people need to live comfortably. Surely we were on the verge of a society devoted to a life of art, literature, and contemplation. Instead, Americans face economic anxiety and chronic insecurity about the future. Houses are going into foreclosure, food prices climb ever higher, and millions of families are one medical crisis away from bankruptcy. Why is there such a disjuncture between the economy's capacity to produce and the lived experience of Americans?

The answer, in short, is that societal institutions have not yet adjusted to the new post-industrial, post-corporate economy. Instead, we have made a collective wrong turn, creating a set of institutions that fail to take care of basic needs at the societal level. In this closing section, I highlight the five most pressing societal problems for the next decade that this book has raised.[16]

Less mobility, more inequality   One of the consequences of the "end of corporate feudalism" described in the previous chapter is that the pathways to economic mobility can seem obscure and almost random for much of the population. When employment was concentrated in large organizations with standardized employment practices, it was feasible to start at an entry-level job and work one's way up. An ambitious janitor's son, through education and hard work, had a shot at a comfortable middle-class life by climbing the corporate ladder. Now the exemplars of career employment—AT&T, GM, and others—are mere echoes of their former selves. "Ma Bell" has been swallowed by one of her babies (SBC), and "Generous Motors" is doing its best to jettison the bulk of its North American workforce; climbing a ladder to prosperity is no longer seen as an option. Economic mobility happens through processes that are difficult to decode—few of us know how to open a hedge fund, or how to found a business that Microsoft will want to buy. As a result, the prospect of climbing out of the class one is born into has declined steeply in the US, particularly relative to other rich countries.

The end of corporate feudalism has also coincided with an enormous increase in the level of economic inequality in the US, as those at the top pull ever farther away from the rest. Top earners in prior times tended to be those that ran corporations, and bureaucratic employment practices placed a limit on just how stratospheric their compensation could be relative to their fellow employees. But stock-based pay for corporate executives, and the extreme compensation practices in financial services, have created what some call a new Gilded Age. Inequality in the US has reached a level not seen since the 1920s, and one that is almost never observed in advanced democracies today.

The legitimacy of the American economic system, and its relatively high level of inequality, has long been sustained by the belief that economic mobility is possible for those willing to work hard. But to the extent that inequality increases and mobility is stalled, the fairness of the entire enterprise is called into question. This demands relatively large-scale institutional renewal.

Educational insecurity With the loss of career ladders and with the accompanying expectation that attachments to any particular employer will be short, it is hard for average citizens to know how to prepare themselves and their children for the future. The traditional answer has always been education: a college degree is the ticket to well-paid white-collar employment and economic security. But with the increased "offshoreability" of many of the white-collar jobs that were supposed to provide security, this advice now rings hollow. If high-skill jobs such as programming computers, decoding genomes, designing cars, diagnosing X-rays, doing taxes, and analyzing securities can all be done wherever the labor is cheapest, what kind of education should one seek? Alan Blinder's answer is that personal "high-touch" services are relatively immune to offshoring. Training to be a home health aid for elderly baby boomers, or a personal trainer for investment bankers, might lead to a secure job. On the other hand, boomers may not have saved enough for retirement or managed to secure health care coverage. And finance is eminently off-shoreable, as demonstrated by the top Wall Street bankers that decamped to London in the wake of the mortgage crisis in order to be closer to the international business.

It is possible that the unpredictability of future employment recommends training to be a "flexible generalist"—what used to be called liberal education—but with regular updates for discrete skills as they become valuable. This is a model of education common in medicine, and perhaps a variant of this will become more widespread—at least once an appropriate business model is worked out. But, given the effects of the financial crisis on the private student loan business, this may require further governmental intervention in the short run to be feasible.

The end of the corporate safety net   America's reliance on corporations as functional substitutes for the welfare state is coming to a fitful end. Under corporate feudalism, the standard employment package included health insurance and some measure of retirement security, a dispersed system that covered a large portion of the population in its heyday. Providing such benefits is no longer feasible for many employers, at least to the degree that it had been, which is likely to leave many employees and retirees without adequate coverage.

There is relatively broad consensus that businesses, especially new ones, cannot shoulder this burden if they seek to be competitive. But without a safety net for employees and their families, businesses are disadvantaged relative to global competitors from countries with government-sponsored healthcare and retirement coverage. Indeed, one of the reasons entrepreneurs are able to take risks with new ventures is because they often have a spouse with company-sponsored health insurance. The corporate safety net had a broad catchment area that extended well beyond its own employees.

The "ownership society" suggested that this responsibility could be ceded to individuals, through personal accounts for education, health care, and retirement. But the experience of the past decade demonstrates that individually based solutions simply will not work. Large numbers of those offered access to employer-organized retirement savings programs either fail to enroll, or make choices that don't make sense economically, such as investing a large part of their retirement savings in their own employer, as at Enron. This is not because these individuals are not smart, but because the effort it takes to become well-schooled in financial planning is large, and typically takes a backseat to other forms of on-the-job training (learning to be a parent, to maintain a house, to stay healthy, to set up a wireless network, to program in HTML). Similarly, legions of smart people signed on to dumb mortgages, and paid a high price. Maintaining a social safety net in a post-industrial economy, in short, is a social task best done by the collective–in other words, by government.

Dangerous financial services The mortgage crisis has made clear that poorly regulated finance can bring about spectacular damage. Robert Shiller compares the mishaps arising from the technology of finance to the early development of other kinds of technologies—boiler explosions, plane crashes, and so on. But with the possible exception of nuclear power, it is hard to think of another technology in which "accidents" lay waste to entire neighborhoods the way that the mortgage crisis has. Even nuclear meltdowns tend to have their effects locally; the toxic clouds from the mortgage crisis have spread from Orange County and Detroit to Zurich and Norway. The broad yet irregular deregulation of finance has created a financial services industry rife with conflicts of interest and malign incentives, which the mortgage crisis brought into high relief.

Two decades after Reagan, Americans are still loath to regulate industry. The case against regulation in finance is that efficient markets are a flywheel for the economy, and that, as long as prices are right, the apparatus of corporate governance will adjust to ensure that the rest of the system works to create value. But many securities don't have active or transparent markets and they are thus extremely difficult to put an accurate price on. Even publicly traded corporations can be hard to value: was Bear Stearns truly worth $85 per share, as in February 2008, or $2 per share, the price JP Morgan Chase initially agreed to pay a month later? Generally, the appropriate regulatory answer is "Who cares, as long as the risk is borne by those doing the buying and selling?" But the dangers of financial technologies are not limited to the contracting parties: home foreclosures generate externalities for neighbors, cities, and distant investors. The collateral damage from widespread foreclosures can be enormous, as homeowners and investors around the world can attest.

Such externalities, of course, are a classic rationale for government regulation of markets. A comprehensive plan for financial regulation is a bit beyond the scope of this book. Minimally, however, Professor Elizabeth Warren's concept of a Financial Product Safety Commission is a judicious first step toward protecting members of the public.

The brain drain from government to contractors The previous set of issues all suggest a central role for government in addressing collective social problems arising out of the post-industrial transition in the US. But a final problem is that the government may not be up to the task of broad institutional renewal. The rise of the OEM state has meant that many of the most critical tasks of government are performed by contractors. Moreover, employees of contractors often make far more than their Federally employed counterparts. The result is the prospect of a large-scale brain drain, in which the most skilled Federal employees decamp for the private sector. Indeed, for many, government service has become a brief internship preceding a move to the private sector, not a long-term career. The extent of the damage to Federal government competence from this decade-long outsourcing process is hard to assess, but there are certainly vivid examples that citizens of New Orleans and Baghdad might point to.

In short, government is needed to help create a new set of institutions to address the void created by the end of corporate feudalism and the rise of financialization. But after the past decade of government outsourcing, it is perhaps less equipped than ever to accomplish this.

My aim in writing this book was to sketch a map of how finance and post-industrialism have reshaped contemporary American society. This chapter has assessed some of the grim consequences. Our discussion has been perhaps morose but not hopeless. It is possible that, in the wake of the contemporary economic crisis, the time is finally here for a re-constitution of America's social institutions for a post-corporate world. The Great Depression yielded a stable set of institutions that worked well for generations during the ascendancy of the corporate-based manu-facturing economy. Those institutions arose from progressive reforms that stemmed from a reconceptualization of the role of government in managing the economy through spending on public works, maintaining labor stability (the Wagner Act, the National Labor Relations Board), regulating financial markets (the Securities Exchange Act, the Banking Act), and providing a safety net for the aged (Social Security). In order to alleviate the problems facing us today, a similar reconceptualization is necessary.

On November 4, 2008, the citizens of the United States elected Barack Obama to be their forty-fourth President. His election reflected a stark repudiation of his predecessor's policies. Up until the financial crisis that began in late 2007 and metastasized in 2008, George W. Bush had followed a traditional conservative playbook that eschewed broad regula-tion of the financial sector. Meanwhile, the manufacturing sector hemor-rhaged jobs and the American system of employer-based health care and retirement security began to unravel, with nothing available to replace it. The remarkable speed with which the economic crisis spread from finance to the real economy, and the depth of the damage it caused, made evident just how ill-conceived the "ownership society" concept had been. Tying the well-being of society to financial markets and under-regulated financial institutions had resulted in an economic meltdown that voters blamed on Bush and his Republican Party. To outside observers, the Bush Administration's response to the crisis over the summer and fall of 2008 had seemed chaotic and ill-coordinated, lacking a coherent theory or even a convincing rationale.

The decisiveness of the electoral victory of Obama and the Democratic Party was in large part attributable to the economic chaos that finance had unleashed. But any reforms a new administration brought about had to go well beyond finance. The Obama Administration had its work cut out for it.

Notes

1. The New Financial Capitalism

1. Bell (1973: 15). Employment figures for agriculture: Carolyn Dimitri, Anne Effland, and Neilson Conklin, *The Twentieth Century Transformation of U.S. Agriculture and Farm Policy*. United States Department of Agriculture Economic Research Service, Electronic Information Bulletin 3 (2005). For other sectors and industries: Bureau of Labor Statistics http://data.bls.gov/PDQ/outside.jsp?survey=ce and http://www.bls.gov/news.release/ecopro.t01.htm. For mortgage brokers: "With Mortgages, Instant Wealth for Middlemen." Jeff Bailey, *New York Times* (10/8/05). For real estate agents: "Endangered Species." Stephen J. Dubner and Steven D. Leavitt, *New York Times* (3/5/06). For Wal-Mart: Wal-Mart form 10-K for 2007. "Largest manufacturers" includes firms deriving most of their revenues from manufacturing—see Chapter 3 for details. *Fortune* quote: cited in Mills (1956: 169).

2. Ownership in 1952: Kimmel (1952). Statistics on share ownership in subsequent years: from triennial Federal Reserve Board Survey of Consumer Finances, reported in Kennickell and Shack-Marquez (1992); Bucks, Kennickell, Moore (2006); Duca (2001); Joint Economic Committee, United States Congress, *The Roots of Broadened Stock Ownership*, April 2000. Statistics on mutual fund numbers and assets: Investment Company Institute, 2005, *Investment Company Factbook*, forty-fifth edition. "A New Game at the Office: Many Young Workers Accept Fewer Guarantees," Steve Lohr, *New York Times* (12/5/05).

3. According to the 2006 *Economic Report of the President*, the problem was not that Americans saved too little, but that foreigners saved too much. Unlike their American counterparts, foreign savers lacked attractive domestic investment opportunities and thus ended up buying American securities with their surplus. Bush second inaugural speech: http://www.whitehouse.gov/news/releases/2005/01/20050120-1.html. Economic Report of the President: http://www.gpoaccess.gov/eop/index.html.

4. See Espeland and Stevens (1998) and Carruthers and Stinchcombe (1999) on commensuration in financial and other markets.

5. For histories of the rise of the large-scale corporation, see Chandler (1977); Fligstein (1990); Roe (1994); Roy (1997); Perrow (2002).

6. History of Rouge plant: "The Rouge Plant—the Art of Industry." Vivian Baulch and Patricia Zacharias, Detroit News Online (7/11/98).
7. Vogel (1978: 58–59).
8. Kaysen (1957: 312; 313–314; 318). Mills (1956: 125).
9. Drucker's analysis was first presented in *Harper's Magazine* in "The New Society I: Revolution by Mass Production" (September 1949, pp. 21–30).
10. See Rivoli (2005).
11. On vertical outsourcing: "Is This the Factory of the Future?" Saul Hansell, *New York Times* (7/26/98). "Some U.S. Manufacturers Prosper by Easing Rise of 'Virtual' Firm." Scott Thurm, *Wall Street Journal* (8/18/98). "Ignore the Label, It's Flextronics Inside." John Markoff, *New York Times* (2/15/01). "With Some Help From Solectron, Sony Learns to Love Outsourcing." Peter Landers, *Wall Street Journal* (7/14/01). For an academic treatment, see Sturgeon (2002).
12. "The Long-Distance Journey of a Fast-Food Order." Matt Richtel, *New York Times* (4/11/06).
13. "At PartyGaming, Everything's Wild." Kurt Eichenwald, *New York Times* (6/26/05).
14. "Boom and bust at sea." *The Economist* (8/18/05). "How Savannah Brought New Life to its Aging Port: Georgia Lures Big Retailers, Expands Docks, Rail Yards; Imports Spur U.S. Boom." Daniel Machalaba, *Wall Street Journal* (8/22/05).
15. "If You Can Make It Here . . ." Louis Uchitelle, *New York Times* (9/4/05). "Factory Employment Is Falling World-Wide: Study of 20 Big Economies Finds 22 Million Jobs Lost; Even China Shows Decline." Jon E. Hilsenrath and Rebecca Buckman, *Wall Street Journal* (10/20/03).
16. Shiller (2003*a*: 81).
17. "How a Formula Ignited Market that Burned Some Big Investors: Credit Derivatives Got a Boost From Clever Pricing Model." Mark Whitehouse, *Wall Street Journal* (9/12/05).
18. See Duca (2001); Investment Company Institute, *Investment Company Factbook* (available at www.ici.org).
19. Hill (1996) gives an informative primer on securitization for distressed companies.
20. Board of director memberships from *Standard and Poor's Directory of Corporations, Directors, and Executives* (1982). See Davis, Yoo, and Baker (2003).
21. Reed quoted in Mayer (1997: 34). Kovacevich quoted in James and Houston (1996: 8). For an analysis of the consequences of the decline of corporate lending for banks and their boards, see Davis and Mizruchi (1999).
22. For a brief history of bank consolidation in the US, see Neuman, Davis, and Mizruchi (2008).
23. Savings accounts: Avery, Elliehausen, and Canner (1984); Kennickell and Shack-Marquez (1992). Mutual funds: Investment Company Institute, *Investment Company Factbook*, forty-fifth edition (2005).

24. Davis (2008) describes trends in the concentration of ownership positions held by mutual funds.

25. "Fidelity Pushes beyond Funds to Manage Payroll, Benefits: Diversifying Its Business, Fidelity Sees Fast Growth in Back-Office Management." John Hechinger, *Wall Street Journal* (1/3/03). Davis and Kim (2007) analyze how the largest mutual funds vote in annual corporate elections.

26. "Former WorldCom CEO Built an Empire on Mountain of Debt." Susan Pulliam, Deborah Solomon, and Carrick Mollenkamp, *Wall Street Journal* (12/31/02). "Salomon Made IPO Allocations Available to its Favored Clients: At World-Com, Ebbers Got Nearly a Million Shares; Two Dozen Other Telecom Officials Got Thousands." Charles Gasparino, Tom Hamburger, and Deborah Solomon, *Wall Street Journal* (8/28/02). "Ebbers Made $11 Million on 21 Stock Offerings." Gretchen Morgenson, *New York Times* (8/31/02). "Banks Give Wall Street a Run for its Money: Using Low-Cost Loans as a Teaser, They Seek Stock, M&A Business; Companies Learn to Play the Game." Jathon Sapsford, *Wall Street Journal* (1/5/04). "Executives See Rise in 'Tying' Loans to Other Fees: Survey Says Banks Press Clients to Expand Services; Fed is Weighing New Rules". Jathon Sapsford, *Wall Street Journal* (6/9/04).

27. See Fligstein (1990) on the rise of the conglomerate and Davis, Diekmann, and Tinsley (1994) on the bust-up takeovers of the 1980s.

28. "Sara Lee Contracts Out Work, Underscoring a Trend in U.S." Robert L. Rose and Carl Quintanilla, *Wall Street Journal* (9/17/97). "Remember When Companies Actually Created Products?" *Wall Street Journal* (9/18/97).

29. "Merger Wave Spurs More Stock Wipeouts." Nikhil Deogun, *Wall Street Journal* 11/29/99. See Davis (2005) for a critique.

30. North (1990: 6) describes the "central puzzle of human history." "Super Model: Asia's Financial Foibles Make American Way Look Like a Winner—IMF Comes Round to View that Short-Term Focus Has its Virtues After All." Alan Murray, *Wall Street Journal* (12/8/97).

31. "Admitting Error, Calpers Plans to Reinvest in the Philippines." Craig Karmin and James Hookway, *Wall Street Journal* (5/13/02).

32. "Bush talks, stocks fall." Alexandra Twin, CNN/Money online (7/9/02). See also Fraser (2005).

33. Roy (1997).

34. Royal Caribbean's 2005 proxy statement, including ownership information, is available from the SEC at http://www.sec.gov/Archives/edgar/data/884887/000095014405004218/g94397def14a.htm. Ship registries: "Landlocked Bolivia is Making Some Waves on the High Seas." Marc Lifsher, *Wall Street Journal* (10/23/02); Langewiesche (2004).

35. Branding: "When Nations Need a Little Marketing." Jim Rendon, *New York Times* (11/23/03); "A City Seeks to Sell Itself." Stuart Elliott, *New York Times* (12/10/04). Bermuda: "In Bermuda, AIG Helped Shape a Legendary Corporate Haven: Big Insurer Shifted Liabilities to Island Firms it Set Up." Glenn R. Simpson and Theo Francis, *Wall Street Journal* (9/20/05); "A New Twist in Tax Avoidance: Firms Send Best Ideas Abroad." Glenn R. Simpson, *Wall Street Journal* (6/24/02). Contracting: "In Washington, Contractors Take on Biggest Role Ever." Scott Shane and Ron Nixon, *New York Times* (2/4/07). "The Reach of War: Intelligence Collection; Army Policy Bars Interrogations by Private Contractors." Joel Brinkley, *New York Times* (6/12/04).

36. "Where Wall St. and Main St. Meet." *New York Times* (3/20/98). "Beardstown Ladies Confess to Having Made a Big Goof." Calmetta Y. Coleman, *New York Times* (3/18/98). For an academic discussion of investment clubs, see Harrington (2008). Declining portfolio size: Bucks, Kennickell, and Moore (2006).

37. Foreign ownership: "Housing-Bubble Talk Doesn't Scare Off Foreigners: Global Investors Gobble Up Mortgage-Backed Securities, Keeping Prices Strong." Ruth Simon, James R. Hagerty, and James T. Areddy, *Wall Street Journal* (8/24/05). Refinancing: Bucks, Kennickell, and Moore (2006).

38. DiPasquale and Glaeser (1999); Green and White (1997). "Buy a Home, and Drag Society Down." Eduardo Porter, *New York Times* (11/13/05).

39. Presidential quotes from Dreier (1982). On thrifts: quoted in Haveman and Rao (1997: 1612).

40. "Triple-A Failure." Roger Lowenstein, *New York Times* (4/27/08).

41. "Against the Political Bears: The Investor Class is Alive and Well—and Growing." Richard Nadler, National Review Online (3/1/05). "In Bush's 'Ownership Society,' Citizens Would Take More Risk." Jackie Calmes, *Wall Street Journal* (2/28/05). " 'Ownership' Swindle." David Moberg, *The Nation* (4/4/05).

42. American National Election Studies: http://www.umich.edu/~nes/

43. Robert Putnam's (2000) book *Bowling Alone* is the most influential analysis of the alleged decline of "social capital" in the US.

2. Financial Markets and Corporate Governance

1. For a general discussion of bank- and market-based systems, see Zysman (1983) and Hall and Soskice (2001). Evans (1995) describes the approaches of "developmental states" such as South Korea.

2. Weber, Davis, and Lounsbury (2008) analyze the spread of stock exchanges around the world after 1980 as well as the factors that made for more or less successful market implementation.

3. Giddens (2000: 27). Davis and Marquis (2005) analyze the governance practices of companies from Germany, France, Japan, the UK, Chile, and Israel that list their shares on US stock markets, typically through "American Depository Receipts" (ADRs).

4. Nomura launched the new business at a party for entertainment industry players at which Ozzy Osbourne—former lead singer for Black Sabbath, best known for biting the heads off live bats onstage—sang a duet of "Born to be wild" with the president of the new Nomura unit. One suspects the hand of Marcel Duchamp when a purported Satan worshipper is employed by a Japanese investment bank to induce entertainers in Los Angeles to follow the lead of an orange-haired former drug addict in selling their oeuvres to insurance companies. "Ziggy Stardust Hopes Investors Will Sing the Praises of This Issue." Jill J. Barshay and Cecile Gutscher, *Wall Street Journal* (12/5/96). "Prudential Insurance Buys Entire Issue of Bowie Bonds." *Wall Street Journal* (2/11/97). "Wall Street Makes Bets on Idols' Earning Power." Bruce Orwall, *Wall Street Journal*, (9/26/97). "Rock 'n' Roll Bonds Depend on Investors' Faith in Royalties." Patrick McGeehan, *Wall Street Journal* (2/10/98).

5. "J.G. Wentworth Offers Lump Sum In Exchange for Monthly Payments." Vanessa O'Connell, *Wall Street Journal* (2/25/98).

6. Malkiel (1996) is an accessible discussion of the efficient market hypothesis. Shiller (2003b) provides a convincing critique.

7. Surowiecki (2004) gives an informative overview of prediction markets.

8. Wolfers and Zitzewitz (2004).

9. Jensen (1988: 26).

10. *Wall Street Journal* (8/2/99).

11. Other analysts argued that the calculation of lost shareholder value was fundamentally flawed, and in any event did not merit such a lengthy sentence. "Dismal Science, Dismal Sentence." *The Economist* (9/7/06).

12. Berle and Means (1932: 7, 8). Section 13 of the Exchange Act of 1933 defines a beneficial owner as "any person who, directly or indirectly, through any contract, arrangement, understanding relationship, or otherwise has or shares: (1) voting power which includes the power to vote, or to direct the voting of such security; and/or (2) investment power which includes the power to dispose, or to direct the disposition, of such security." "Person" in this case means a person under the law, which can include companies or mutual funds.

13. Davis and Useem (2002) review the literature on shareholders and corporate governance. Blair (1995) gives an exceptionally lucid overview of corporate governance in the US. See also Useem (1996).

14. Manne (1965: 113).

15. Jensen and Meckling (1976: 311).

16. Jensen and Meckling (1976: 352).
17. North (1990: 3).
18. Fama (1980) describes competitive managerial labor markets in terms analogous to financial markets.
19. Fama and Jensen (1983) theorize the functions of boards of directors and other aspects of the modern corporation.
20. Easterbrook and Fischel (1991) apply the political science notion of "rational ignorance" to shareholder voting and, more generally, analyze the voluntary efforts of share price-oriented managers to create wealth-maximizing governance structures.
21. Demsetz and Lehn (1985).
22. Davis and Useem (2002) provide a critique of this model.
23. Romano (1993). The "race to the top/bottom" debate is discussed in more detail in Chapter 5.
24. Coffee (2001) gives a brief account of the New York Stock Exchange listing as a guarantee of quality for distant investors. Rao, Davis, and Ward (2000) analyze the competition for listings between Nasdaq and NYSE. Davis and Marquis (2005) examine the practices of US-listed foreign companies.
25. Consider J. Peter Grace II, scion of the family that founded WR Grace and CEO from the late 1940s until the late 1980s: under his leadership, the company moved into banking, chemicals, packaging, kidney dialysis, Western wear, Mexican restaurants, and sports teams, among others. Owning only a tiny fraction of equity, Grace used company resources to build an empire of unrelated units, set up his children in business, and buy luxurious apartments in New York staffed at company expense. "W.R. Grace's CEO, Bolduc, Resigns from his Positions," Thomas M. Burton, *Wall Street Journal* (3/3/95). "W.R. Grace Says Bolduc Resigned Because of Sex-Harassment Claim." Richard Gibson and Thomas M. Burton, *Wall Street Journal* (3/31/95). "Fight to the Death: How the Two Top Officials of Grace Wound Up in a Very Dirty War." Thomas M. Burton and Richard Gibson, *Wall Street Journal* (5/18/05).
26. Gilson (1981).
27. Easterbrook and Fischel (1991: 19).
28. Shiller (2003a).
29. Carruthers (1996).
30. Hargadon and Douglas (2001).
31. Insurers also play an unheralded role in shareholder capitalism by underwriting "dead peasants insurance"—policies that corporations take out on employees, often without their knowledge, naming the corporation as the beneficiary. These policies, in turn, can provide tax-free investment gains when the policies

increase in value or ultimately pay benefits—even after the employee has left the company—while also providing an asset against which the company can borrow. Wal-Mart took out such policies on about 350,000 of its employees in the 1990s for expected tax benefits, although it subsequently dropped the program. "Companies Profit on Workers' Deaths through 'Dead Peasants' Insurance." Ellen E. Schultz and Theo Francis, *Wall Street Journal* (4/19/02).

32. Davis and Robbins (2008) contrast the reasons for takeovers in the 1980s and 1990s.

33. "Triple-A Failure." Roger Lowenstein, *New York Times* (4/27/08).

34. Vise and Coll (1991) give a lively account of how this played out at the SEC. For a rebuttal, see Jarrell (1992). See also Davis and Stout (1992) for an account of changing regulation around takeovers.

35. Jensen and Meckling (1976); Fama and Jensen (1983). Jensen (1993) describes the place of takeovers in effecting large-scale industrial transformation.

36. "Pennsylvania's Anti-Takeover Law was Intended to Derail Greenmailers. It Does. It Also Leaves Management ... Cast in Concrete." Patty Tascarella, *Executive Report* (9/1/90). "Harvard Profs Make Good." Eric Schmuckler, *Forbes Magazine* (3/5/90). State Representative Marvin Miller introduced a "Motion of Censure for Unethical Conduct" to the Committee on Business and Commerce due to the perceived conflicts of interest in Jensen's actions: see "Miller of the Pennsylvania State House of Representatives Releases Statement on Anti-Hostile Raider Legislation," *PR Newswire* (2/15/90). The legislation was ultimately passed and the Belzbergs' bid failed, but Jensen was elected to the Armstrong board and served for several years.

37. "How Harvard Lost Russia." David McClintick, *Institutional Investor* (1/13/06). Wedel (2001) gives a more detailed account of Harvard's entanglement with Russia.

3. From Institution to Nexus

1. "State Attorney General Seeks to Block Hershey Foods Sale." *Wall Street Journal* (8/23/02). "Nestle Offers $11.5B for Hershey." Thor Valdmanis, *USA Today* (8/25/02). "Orphans' Court Ruling Expected this Week." Judy Etschmaier, *Hershey Chronicle* (9/4/02). "Hershey Trust asks Court to Lift Ban on Sale of Company." Andrew Ross Sorkin, *New York Times* (9/12/02). For a general history of Hershey and an analysis of the economic consequences of the aborted sale, see Klick and Sitkoff (2008).

2. The classic reference here is Selznick (1957).

3. Sewell (1981) provides an account of the legal and social metaphysics of the guilds in pre-Revolutionary France. The quote is from Sewell (1981: 36). For a more

general and accessible history of the corporation, see Micklethwait and Woolridge (2003).

4. Carruthers (1996: 132–133).

5. Berle and Means (1932) and Roy (1997) give accounts of the evolution of state corporate law in the 1800s.

6. For an accessible discussion of legal pragmatism, see Menand (2001) on Oliver Wendell Holmes and his prediction theory of the law.

7. Allen (1992). Allen's article provides an informative account of the tension between the "contractual" and "entity" views of the corporation in the law.

8. Alfred Chandler (1977) provides the now-standard story of the rise of the large corporation during this time period. Roy (1997) gives an alternative interpretation congenial to the arguments here. Roy (1983) and Roy and Bonacich (1988) describe the emergence and structure of communities of interest.

9. For analyses of the decline of finance capitalism, see DeLong (1991) and Simon (1998). Davis (2008) provides a contrast between twentieth- and twenty-first-century finance capitalism in the US.

10. See Jacoby (1997) for a discussion of the history of welfare capitalism in the US.

11. Quoted in Marchand (1998: 20). The definition of the nation as an imagined community comes from Benedict Anderson (1983).

12. Marchand (1998: 74). The history of AT&T's public relations campaign, and excellent reproductions of several of its advertisements, appears in Marchand (1998: ch. 2).

13. Statistics on ownership taken from Cox (1963) and Kimmel (1952). Figures for AT&T come from Berle and Means (1932).

14. Berle and Means (1932: 46).

15. Berle and Means (1932: 313).

16. Drucker's analysis was presented in a three-part series: "The New Society I: Revolution by Mass Production" (September 1949, pp. 21–30); "The New Society II: Is Management Legitimate?" (October 1949, pp. 74–79); and "The New Society III: The Insecurity of Labor Unions" (November 1949, pp. 86–92). The quotes are from the first article, pp. 22, 28, 29.

17. Drucker, "Revolution by Mass Production": 27.

18. Drucker, "Is Management Legitimate?": 76.

19. Quotes are from Kaysen (1957), 312; 313–314; 318.

20. March and Simon (1958: 4).

21. Marris (1964: 39–40).

22. See Dahrendorf (1959). Sociologist Maurice Zeitlin (1974) provides a pointed critique of the evidence and logic behind these claims.

23. Quotes are from Mills (1956: 125, 294). For a discussion of the board inter-lock network and its evolution, see Mizruchi (1982), Useem (1984), Mintz and Schwartz (1985), and Davis, Yoo, and Baker (2003). For an analysis of the political consequences of interlocks, see Mizruchi (1992).

24. For a discussion of the Celler–Kefauver Act and its effect on corporate strategies of diversification, see Fligstein (1990). For Harold Geneen's insider assessment, see Geneen (1997).

25. See Jacoby (1997) for a discussion of the origins and spread of welfare-capitalist practices among large firms.

26. Davis, Whitman, and Zald (2008) describe the linkage between notions of corpo-rate welfare capitalism and Federal policy.

27. William H. Whyte's *The Organization Man* (1956) is the classic critique. Sennett (2006) provides a surprising revisionist appreciation.

28. Manne (1965: 113).

29. Manne (1965: 113).

30. Jensen and Meckling (1976: 330-331).

31. Jensen and Meckling (1976: 310-311).

32. See Fligstein (1990) and Davis, Diekmann, and Tinsley (1994) for histories of the conglomerate.

33. Davis and Stout (1992) and Davis, Diekmann, and Tinsley (1994) analyze the antecedents and consequences of the 1980s takeover wave. LeBaron and Speidell (1987) describe the "chop shop" model.

34. Davis and Robbins (2008) analyze US conglomerates in the 1990s. Diversification in Figure 3.1 is calculated using the entropy measure $DT=\Sigma P_i \ln(1/P_i)$, where Σ means "sum," Pi is the proportion of a firm's sales made in industry segment I, as reported on annual 10Ks, and ln means "natural logaritham." See Davis, Diekmann, and Tinsley (1994) for a discussion of this measure.

35. Ford CEO quote: "Ford Motor Plans Spinoff of Associates First Capital." Valerie Reitman, *New York Times* (10/9/97). Sara Lee CEO quote: "Remember When Companies Actually Created Products?" *Wall Street Journal* (9/18/97).

36. Bebchuk and Fried (2004) provide a history of recent changes in executive com-pensation practices and critique the use or, perhaps, abuse of stock options. The Greenspan quote is from "Bosses' Pay: How Stock Options Became Part of the Problem." Mark Maremont and Charles Forelle, *Wall Street Journal* (12/27/06).

37. "Westinghouse Electric Seeks Bids for Struggling Industrial Firms." Timothy Appel and Steven Lipin, *Wall Street Journal* (10/28/97). "Westinghouse Plans to Focus on Broadcasting Business: Plans to Sell Industrial Lines, Change its Name to CBS." Kyle Pope, *Wall Street Journal* (11/17/97). "CEO Personalities Play Role as New Mergers Take Shape." Bernard Wysocki, Jr., *Wall Street Journal* (12/31/97).

38. Data come from the Compustat database, *Fortune Magazine*, and corporate 10-K statements for various years.

39. Most large firms break out their US and foreign employment in their annual reports. IBM reported having 387,000 employees in 2007, of whom fewer than one-third (120,000) were based in the US. Only 160,000 of Citigroup's 380,000 employees were US-based, along with 155,000 of GE's 327,000 workers, 110,000 of GM's 266,000 employees, and 94,000 of Ford's 246,000 employees. McDonald's, Federal Express, Berkshire Hathaway, and Bank of America did not provide employment breakdowns, but all have significant operations outside the US. The twelve largest manufacturing employers (i.e. those deriving most of their revenues from manufacturing), based on my estimates, were (in descending order): Boeing, Northrop Grumman, GM, Lockheed Martin, Tyson Foods, Ford, Altria Group, United Technologies, General Dynamics, Coca-Cola Enterprises, Johnson Controls, and Emerson Electric, which collectively employed roughly 1.12 million Americans, compared to Wal-Mart's 1.42 million.

40. Quoted in "Jack Welch Class Day Interview—Jack Welch to HBS Grads: 'Don't Be a Jerk.'" Martha Lagace, *Harvard Business School Working Knowledge* (6/11/01). Accessed at http://hbswk.hbs.edu/archive/2310.html.

41. Alchian and Demsetz (1972: 777).

42. "GM's Decision to Cut Pensions Accelerates Broad Corporate Shift." David Wessel, Ellen E. Schultz, and Laurie McGinley, *Wall Street Journal* (2/8/06). "Delphi as a Case Study for a Global Problem." Joseph Schuman, *Wall Street Journal* (10/11/05).

43. Fast Company's contributing editor Daniel Pink captured this zeitgeist in his 2001 book *Free Agent Nation*.

44. Sara Lee quote: "Remember When Companies Actually Created Products?" *Wall Street Journal* (9/18/97). HP quote: "Is This the Factory of the Future?" Saul Hansell, *New York Times* (7/26/98).

45. This story is described by Baker (2000: 32). A general account of using affiliations to establish status in markets comes from Podolny (2005).

46. Potemkin Villages were fake villages supposedly erected and staffed with happy "extras" by Grigori Potemkin in order to impress Catherine the Great on her visits to the Crimea.

47. See Davis and Robbins (2005) for evidence on corporate boards and their efforts at recruiting for reputation.

48. This section adapted from Gerald F. Davis, "American Cronyism: How Executive Networks Inflated the Corporate Bubble," *Contexts*, 2(3) (summer 2003): 34–40. Copyright 2003 American Sociological Association and the University of California Press.

49. See Westphal and Zajac (2001) on stock buybacks; Westphal and Zajac (1998) on descriptions of compensation plans. See Davis (2005) for a review of recent work on the rhetoric of corporate governance.

50. Davis (1991) and Davis and Greve (1997) analyze the spreads of the "poison pill" takeover defense and the golden parachute severance package. Vogus and Davis (2005) describe the effect of well-connected elites on state legislation.

51. "Ties to Two Tainted Firms Haunt Top Doctor in Houston." Geeta Anand, *Wall Street Journal* (12/24/02).

52. "Grubman Attended 10 Board Meetings." Patrick McGeehan, *New York Times* (8/10/02). "Salomon Made IPO Allocations Available to its Favored Clients." Charles Gasparino, Tom Hamburger, and Deborah Solomon, *Wall Street Journal* (8/22/02). "Salomon's Deals Prod Congress to Consider Expanding Probes." Tom Hamburger, Susan Pulliam, and Susanne Craig, *Wall Street Journal* (8/29/02). "Former WorldCom CEO Built an Empire on Mountain of Debt." Susan Pullman, Deborah Solomon, and Carrick Mollenkamp, *Wall Street Journal* (12/31/02). Telecom executives were not the only ones to benefit from IPO allocations. eBay CEO Meg Whitman, who served on the Goldman Sachs board, received shares in more than 100 Goldman-managed IPOs, typically selling them for an immediate payoff after the public offering. "EBay CEO Quits Goldman Board on IPO Concerns." Nick Wingfield, *Wall Street Journal* (12/20/02). William Clay Ford, Chairman of Ford Motor Company, personally received 400,000 shares of Goldman Sachs stock when it went public. Goldman was Ford's long-time investment bank, and Goldman's president (a prep school acquaintance of William Ford) served on Ford's board.

53. O'Reilly and Pfeffer (2000) describe several successful US companies that continue to follow a welfare-capitalist approach to employee relations.

54. Davis, Whitman, and Zald (2008) analyze the effects of globalization and "placelessness" on conceptions of corporate social responsibility.

55. "Statement by Hershey Trust." *Wall Street Journal* (10/9/07). "At Hershey, Sweetness is in Perilously Short Supply." Julie Jargon, *Wall Street Journal* (10/10/07). "Bitter Times at Hershey." The Economist (11/15/07). "Can Hershey Survive Candy Wars?" Julie Jargon, *Wall Street Journal* (6/18/08).

4. From Banks to Markets

1. "U.S. Credit Crisis Adds to Gloom in Arctic Norway." Mark Landler, *New York Times* (12/2/07). "As Oil Prices Swing, Gas-Station Owners Try Futures Market." George Anders, *Wall Street Journal* (6/21/05). "From Australia, Money Chases Roads, Airports around Globe." Patrick Barta and Mary Kissel, *Wall Street Journal* (12/6/05). The *Wall Street Journal*'s David Wessel describes the Federal Reserve

as trying to use a toolkit for a Model T on a twenty-first-century computer-controlled hybrid. "Crisis Tests Fed Chairman's Toolbox." David Wessel, *Wall Street Journal* (8/23/07).

2. "Two Weeks that Shook the Titans of Wall Street." Robin Sidel, Minoca Lengley, and David Enrich, *Wall Street Journal* (11/9/07).

3. The *Wall Street Journal* kept a tally of losses at http://online.wsj.com/public/resources/documents/infro-retro-subpar20070925.htm?&s=2&ps=false&a=up.

4. "Alternative Lenders Buoy Economy; Will Easy Terms End Hard Times?" Greg Ip, *Wall Street Journal* (6/10/02).

5. For a brief history of bank consolidation, see Neuman, Davis, and Mizruchi (2008). The Federal Reserve Board's listing of the assets of large commercial banks is available at http://www.federalreserve.gov/releases/lbr/.

6. *Wall Street Journal* (6/10/96).

7. "When It Goes Wrong . . ." *The Economist* (9/20/07).

8. "Regulators Scrutinized in Mortgage Meltdown." Greg Ip and Damian Paletta, *Wall Street Journal* (3/22/07).

9. On securitization for firms in financial distress, see Hill (1996). On mortgages, see "Triple-A Failure." Roger Lowenstein, *New York Times* (4/27/08).

10. Neuman, Davis, and Mizruchi (2008) give a brief account of recent changes in bank regulation. Roe (1994) provides a more detailed history of US bank regulation.

11. Mintz and Schwartz (1985) describe the position of commercial banks in the network of shared directors among corporate boards during the 1960s. Davis and Mizruchi (1999) analyze changes in bank boards during the 1980s and 1990s.

12. For the effect of local banks on corporate philanthropy, see Marquis, Glynn, and Davis (2007). For the political impact of shared directors, see Mizruchi (1992).

13. Mizruchi and Davis (2004) analyze the global expansion of US banks in the 1960s and 1970s.

14. Reed described Citibank's situation in Anne Sigismund Huff, "Citigroup's John Reed and Stanford's James March on Management Research and Practice." *Academy of Management Executive*, 14(1): 52–64.

15. Reed quoted in Mayer (1997: 34).

16. "Alternative Lenders Buoy Economy; Will Easy Terms End Hard Times?" Greg Ip, *Wall Street Journal* (6/10/02).

17. Data and publications from the Survey of Consumer Finances are available from the Federal Reserve at http://www.federalreserve.gov/PUBS/oss/oss2/scfindex.html. Data on mutual funds available at http://www.icifactbook.org/. Bank deposits: "Banks' Cry: 'Give Us Your Cash!'" Clint Riley, *Wall Street Journal* (1/12/07).

18. Quoted in James and Houston (1996: 8).

19. Information on board memberships in 1982 from *Standard and Poor's Directory of Corporations, Directors, and Executives* and *Moody's Bank & Finance Manual* (1982). See Davis and Mizruchi (1999) for documentation of the link between corporate lending and bank board composition. 2007 board data from proxy statements for JP Morgan Chase and Bank of America, available at http://www.sec.gov/edgar.shtml. Neuman, Davis, and Mizruchi (2008) analyze changes in bank boards due to the consolidation of the 1990s and 2000s.

20. "Behind Buyout Surge, a Debt Market Booms." Serena Ng and Henny Sender, *Wall Street Journal* (6/26/07).

21. "Bank Group Opposes Bill that Would Allow Financial Services Mergers." Timothy L. O'Brien, *New York Times* (3/26/98).

22. "The Birth of a Bureaucratic Mastodon?" Ron Chernow, *Wall Street Journal* (4/9/98).

23. Marquis and Lounsbury (2007) analyze the growth in community-based banking in the wake of the bank consolidation movement.

24. "Banks' Cry: 'Give Us Your Cash!'" Clint Riley, *Wall Street Journal* (1/12/07). "Domesticity Helping Bank Take On Citi." Conrad de Aenlle, *New York Times* (12/9/06).

25. Roe (1994) describes the history of populist concerns about concentrated financial power in the US. The text of Jackson's veto is available at http://www.yale.edu/lawweb/avalon/presiden/veto/ajveto01.htm.

26. "Executives see Rise in 'Tyings' Loans to Other Fees." Jathon Sapsford, *Wall Street Journal* (6/9/04).

27. The fifth major investment bank in the US was Bear Stearns until its collapse and forced sale to JP Morgan Chase in March 2008.

28. Golding (2003) is an accessible guide to the contemporary financial services industry.

29. "The Firm with a Shadow that Extends Far Past Wall Street." Michael J. de la Merced, New York Times (11/15/07).

30. All quoted in DeLong (1991).

31. For a discussion of the advantages of the partnership model for a long-term orientation, see "Best Bet Against Risk Further Down the Road may be Wall Street Gig." Dennis K. Berman, *Wall Street Journal* (7/31/07).

32. "Pioneer Helped Merrill Move Into CDOs." Serena Ng and Carrick Mollenkamp, *Wall Street Journal* (10/25/07).

33. "When It Goes Wrong..." *The Economist* (9/20/07).

34. "UBS Helped Guide HealthSouth in Years Leading up to Scandal." Carrick Mollenkamp and Robert Frank, *Wall Street Journal* (5/14/03). "Grubman Attended 10 Board Meetings." Patrick McGeehan, *New York Times* (8/10/02).

35. IPO figures from Ghosh (2006).

36. Shiller (2003*a*).

37. "Salomon Made IPO Allocations Available to its Favored Clients." Charles Gasparino, Tom Hamburger, and Deborah Solomon, *Wall Street Journal* (8/28/02). "IPO 'Spinning' is Under Fire; Securities Firms are Charged." Randall Smith, *Wall Street Journal* (8/29/03). "Ebbers made $11 Million on 21 Stock Offerings." Gretchen Morgenson, *New York Times* 8/31/02. "Ebbers, Nacchio, Others are Sued over Hot IPOs." Charles Gasparino, *Wall Street Journal* (10/1/02).

38. See Malkiel (1996) and Rao, Greve, and Davis (2001) for a discussion of analysts. On why analysts rarely give "Sell" recommendations on client firms, see "Today, Delivering Good News is a Way to Ensure Good Business Relationships." Michael Siconolfi, *Wall Street Journal* (5/18/98).

39. "Merrill is Ordered to Reform Way its Analysts Rate Corporate Clients." Charles Gasparino, *Wall Street Journal* (4/9/02). "Wall Street Firms Settle Charges over Research in $1.4 Billion Pact." Randall Smith, Susanne Craig, and Deborah Solomon, *Wall Street Journal* (4/29/03).

40. "Biotech Firm Claims Piper Jaffray Halted Coverage of it as Payback." Randall Smith and Geeta Anand, *Wall Street Journal* (4/16/02).

41. "Overstock's Campaign of Menace." Joe Nocera, *New York Times* (2/25/06).

42. "Wall Street Firms Settle Charges over Research in $1.4 Billion Pact." Randall Smith, Susanne Craig, and Deborah Solomon, *Wall Street Journal* (4/29/03).

43. Robert B. Avery, Glenn B. Canner, Gregory E. Elliehausen, and Thomas A. Gustafson, "Survey of Consumer Finances 1983." *Federal Reserve Bulletin* (September 1984: 688).

44. Statistics on mutual funds available at http://www.icifactbook.org/. Fraser (2005: 583).

45. Hall (2000) gives a general account of the sources of the rising prevalence of stock ownership. Duca (2001) describes how lower fees corresponded to higher ownership of mutual funds.

46. Bogle (2005) provides an astute insider analysis of the growth and structure of the mutual fund industry and its implications for corporate capitalism. For an analysis of the growing concentration of corporate ownership through mutual funds, see Davis (2008).

47. Zitzewitz (2006). "How Merrill, Defying Warnings, let 3 Brokers Ignite a Scandal." Susanne Craig and Tom Lauricella, *Wall Street Journal* (3/27/06). "Cleaning Up the Fund Industry." Karen Damato and Judith Burns, *Wall Street Journal* (4/5/04).

48. "As Scandals Mount, Boards of Mutual Funds Feel the Heat." George Anders, *Wall Street Journal* (3/17/04).

49. "Cleaning Up the Fund Industry." Karen Damato and Judith Burns, *Wall Street Journal* (4/5/04).

50. Davis (2008) and Davis and Yoo (2003) analyze the large-block shareholdings of Fidelity.

51. "Fidelity Pushes Beyond Funds to Manage Payroll, Benefits." John Hechinger, *Wall Street Journal* (1/3/03). "Fidelity Shuffles Top Management amid Challenges." John Hechinger, *Wall Street Journal* (5/3/05). "Fidelity Plans Reorganization in Effort to Capture Boomers' 'Rollover' Market." Jennifer Levitz, *Wall Street Journal* (9/28/07).

52. Bogle (2005). See Davis and Kim (2007) on conflicts of interest created by mutual funds' pension management business and how it affects their proxy voting.

53. "Companies Profit on Workers' Deaths through 'Dead Peasants' Insurance." Ellen E. Schultz and Theo Francis, *Wall Street Journal* (4/19/02).

54. Quinn (2007) gives a history of the viatical industry and the moral debates it raised.

55. "Late in Life, Finding a Bonanza in Life Insurance." Charles Duhigg, *New York Times* (12/17/06).

56. "101 Brand Names, 1 Manufacturer." Ellen Byron, *Wall Street Journal* (5/9/07).

57. The safety of Fannie and Freddy's business changed dramatically during the mortgage meltdown, requiring a government of potentially vast proportions in 2008. "Rescue Plan Is Latest In a Series of Risks Taken on by Taxpayers." Deborah Solomon, *Wall Street Journal* (7/18/08).

58. "Regulators Scrutinized in Mortgage Meltdown." Greg Ip and Damian Paletta, *Wall Street Journal* (3/22/07). "No. 1 Company in Mortgages Faces Turbulence." James R. Hagerty and Serena Ng, *Wall Street Journal* (8/11/07). "Behind Bank of America's Big Gamble." Valerie Bauerlein and James R. Hagerty, *Wall Street Journal* (1/12/08).

59. "At a Mortgage Lender, Rapid Rise, Faster Fall." James R. Hagerty, Ruth Simon, Michael Corkery, and Gregory Zuckerman, *Wall Street Journal* (3/12/07).

60. "With Mortgages, Instant Wealth for Middlemen." Jeff Bailey, *New York Times* (10/8/05).

61. Quote from "With Mortgages, Instant Wealth for Middlemen." Jeff Bailey, *New York Times* (10/8/05). On offshoring mortgage broking: "Home and Away: India Moves in on the West's Mortgages." *The Economist* (10/5/06).

62. "U.S. Mortgage Crisis Rivals S&L Meltdown." Greg Ip, Mark Whitehouse, and Aaron Lucchetti, *Wall Street Journal* (12/10/07).

63. "GE Capital: Jack Welch's Secret Weapon." John Curran, Fortune (11/10/97). "Alternative Lenders Buoy Economy; Will Easy Terms End Hard Times?" Greg Ip, *Wall Street Journal* (6/10/02).

64. "Hedge Funds are Taking Role of Jekyll and Hyde in Markets." Steve Liesman, *Wall Street Journal* (5/27/05).

65. "Hedge Funds Nip at Wall Street." Henny Sender, *Wall Street Journal* (5/26/05).

66. Dingell quoted in Barth, Brumbaugh, and Litan (1992: 54).

67. "Citicorp Plans $70 Billion Merger with Travelers Group." Timothy O'Brien and Joseph B. Treaster, *New York Times* (4/7/98). "The Birth of a Bureaucratic Mastodon?" Ron Chernow, *Wall Street Journal* (4/9/98).

68. "Salomon Made IPO Allocations Available to its Favored Clients." Charles Gasparino, Tom Hamburger, and Deborah Solomon, *Wall Street Journal* (8/28/02). "Ebbers made $11 Million on 21 Stock Offerings." Gretchen Morgenson, *New York Times* (8/31/02). "Ebbers, Nacchio, Others are Sued over Hot IPOs." Charles Gasparino, *Wall Street Journal* (10/1/02). "Former WorldCom CEO built an Empire on Mountain of Debt." Susan Pulliam, Deborah Solomon and Carrick Mollenkamp, *Wall Street Journal* (12/31/02).

69. "Grubman Attended 10 Board Meetings." Patrick McGeehan, *New York Times* (8/10/02).

70. "New York Widens Salomon Probe to Look at Citigroup CEO's Role." Charles Gasparino, *Wall Street Journal* (8/23/02). "Grubman Boast: AT&T Rating had Altogether Different Goal." Charles Gasparino, *Wall Street Journal* (11/13/02). "Why Grubman was So Keen to get his Twins into the Y." Emily Nelson and Laurie P. Cohen, *Wall Street Journal* (11/15/02). "New York Preschool's Link to Citigroup is Investigated." Charles Gasparino, *Wall Street Journal* (11/18/02).

71. "Wall Street Firms Settle Charges over Research in $1.4 Billion Pact." Randall Smith, Susanne Craig, and Deborah Solomon, *Wall Street Journal* (4/29/03).

72. "Citigroup Agrees to a Settlement over WorldCom." Gretchen Morgenson, *New York Times* (5/11/04).

73. "Banks give Wall Street a Run for its Money." Jathon Sapsford, *Wall Street Journal* (1/5/04).

74. Gilson and Milhaupt (2008) give a brief history of recent investments by sovereign wealth funds in US businesses, particularly banks. SWFs are also discussed in Chapter 5.

5. From Sovereign to Vendor-State

1. "At PartyGaming, Everything's Wild." Kurt Eichenwald, *New York Times* (6/26/05). Unfortunately for PartyGaming, the US Congress passed a law in late 2006 explicitly banning revenues from "unlawful Internet gambling," in spite of the fact that the World Trade Organization had previously ruled that the US cannot ban online gambling housed in other countries. The lesson learned by the countless other online gambling sites: avoid publicizing the illegality of your business plans if and when you go public.

2. "I.R.S. Says Offshore Tax Evasion Is Widespread." David Cay Johnston, *New York Times* (3/26/02). "Laundering Queries Focus on Delaware." Glenn R. Simpson, *Wall Street Journal* (9/30/04). Kentucky also hosted corporations allegedly used by money launderers from Russia, Iran, and Libya. "How Top Dutch Bank Plunged into World of Shadowy Money." Glenn R. Simpson, *Wall Street Journal* (12/30/05).

3. See Davis and Marquis (2005) for an analysis of US-listed foreign corporations. The 25 largest corporations taken from Fortune Magazine's "Global 500" list; dates of US listing from http://www.nyse.com/about/listed/lc_ny_region.html. On SEC's reach, see "New Role for SEC: Policing Companies Beyond U.S. Borders." Michael Schroder and Silvia Ascarelli, *Wall Street Journal* (7/30/04).

4. "101 Brand Names, 1 Manufacturer." Ellen Byron, *Wall Street Journal* (5/9/07). "Filler in Animal Feed is Open Secret in China." David Barboza and Alexei Barrionuevo, *New York Times* (4/30/07). "U.S. Identifies Tainted Heparin in 11 Countries." Gardiner Harris, *New York Times* (4/22/08). "House Panel Criticizes F.D.A. Role in Drug Cases." *New York Times* (4/23/08).

5. Bush quote from *Fox News Sunday* (2/10/08). Transcript available at http://www.foxnews.com/printer_friendly_story/0,3566,330234,00.html. Another example from 2004 is available at http://www.whitehouse.gov/news/releases/2004/08/20040809-3.html.

6. "In Washington, Contractors Take on Biggest Role Ever." Scott Shane and Ron Nixon, *New York Times* (2/4/07). "Iraq Contractor in Shooting Case Makes Comeback." James Risen, *New York Times* (5/10/08).

7. Beard (1913: 12); Stinchcombe (1997: 3).

8. "Irish Subsidiary Lets Microsoft Slash Taxes in U.S. and Europe." Glenn R. Simpson, *Wall Street Journal* (11/7/05). Royal Caribbean 10-K available at http://www.sec.gov/Archives/edgar/data/884887/000008488708000067/final10k07.htm. "U.S. Companies File in Bermuda to Slash Tax Bills." David Cay Johnston, *New York Times* (2/18/02).

9. Reich (1991). Logitech mouse: "As China Surges, It Also Proves A Buttress to American Strength." Andrew Higgins, *Wall Street Journal* (1/30/04).

10. The grey goo scenario was originally described in Drexler (1986).

11. Bobbitt (2002: 178–179).

12. Anderson (1983: 6).

13. Bobbitt (2002: 219).

14. The *lex mercatoria* (merchant law), governing contracts and disputes among merchants and traders during the Middle Ages, was essentially a non-state business operated through private courts in port cities and along trade routes, analogous to contemporary alternative dispute resolution. England ultimately absorbed *lex mercatoria* into its common law during the late seventeenth century, as the volume

of commercial litigation business from international trade expanded. See Carruthers (1996: 129-130).

15. Tiebout (1956). Ironically, the vendor-state responds to traditional criticisms of the state on both the left and the right. From the right, the critique suggests that states are overly expansive and that the appropriate role for governments is tightly circumscribed. States become monopolists over the services they provide, leading to inefficiency through a lack of competition. In response, to the extent possible, government services should be privatized, e.g. through school vouchers to create competition among providers. Bush's unrealized vision of an "ownership society" was in some sense the extreme version of this, with private accounts taking the place of government guarantees of economic security. The critique from the left indicates that states are too easily captured by economic elites. Economic power translates readily into political power through a variety of mechanisms that put the wealthy in the driver's seat. The model of the vendor-state answers both of these criticisms. First, governmental bodies are in competition whether they like it or not: with mobile consumers among citizens and business, governments have no choice but to respond to their (actual or potential) customers. Moreover, competing states need not be dominated by elites for them to serve elite interests. If "profit-maximizing" governments spontaneously provide the products demanded by their corporate consumers, then the need for shadowy backroom deals is mitigated. The invisible hand of the market for law replaces the visible hand of elites—as sociologist Fred Block put it in 1977, "the ruling class does not rule" because it does not have to in order for its interests to be served.

16. The most compelling positive case for interstate competition in corporate law is made in Romano (1993). Easterbrook and Fischel (1991) analyze the consequences of state competition for corporate governance. On the prospect of interstate competition in the EU, see Kirchner, Painter, and Kaal (2004).

17. Kahan and Kamar (2002) argue that state competition in corporate law is a myth due to the low stakes involved—only Delaware and, to a lesser extent, Nevada are actually racing. LeRoy (2005) exposes the more destructive forms of interstate competition for business locations.

18. "A Tax Maneuver in Delaware Puts Squeeze on Other States." Glenn R. Simpson, *Wall Street Journal* (8/9/02). "The Case against Delaware: Rogue State." Jonathan Chait, *New Republic* (8/2/02).

19. See Kirchner, Painter, and Kaal (2004) on prospects for interstate competition in corporate law within the EU.

20. Davis, Whitman, and Zald (2008) describe the "responsibility paradox" facing "placeless" multinational corporations that are called on to demonstrate their social responsibility. On a US Supreme Court case upholding applications of the

Alien Tort Claims Act to multinational corporations, see "US High Court Allows Apartheid Claims against Multinationals." Warren Richey, *Christian Science Monitor* (5/13/08).

21. Polanyi (1944: 15).
22. Mizruchi and Davis (2004) describe the expansion and contraction of US commercial banks abroad from the 1960s through the 1980s.
23. Weber, Davis, and Lounsbury (2008) analyze the factors leading countries to open stock exchanges after 1980 and the sources of their subsequent success or failure.
24. Davis and Marquis (2005) analyze the ownership, governance, and investor recognition of US-listed firms from Chile, Israel, and elsewhere.
25. Langewiesche (2004) gives an alarming account of the competition among flags of convenience.
26. "Landlocked Bolivia Is Making Some Waves on the High Seas." Marc Lifsher, *Wall Street Journal* (10/23/02).
27. Langewiesche (2004: 6).
28. "In Bermuda, AIG Helped Shape a Legendary Corporate Haven." Glenn R. Simpson and Theo Francis, *Wall Street Journal* (9/20/05).
29. "A New Twist in Tax Avoidance: Firms Send Best Ideas Abroad." Glenn R. Simpson, *Wall Street Journal* (6/24/02). "How Merck Saved $1.5 Billion Paying Itself for Drug Patents." Jesse Drucker, *Wall Street Journal* (9/28/06).
30. "Tax Break Brings Billions to U.S., But Impact on Hiring Is Unclear." Timothy Aeppel, *Wall Street Journal* (10/5/05). "Tax Break Used by Drug Makers Failed to Add Jobs." Alex Berenson, *New York Times* (7/24/07).
31. "U.S. Companies File in Bermuda to Slash Tax Bills." David Cay Johnston, *New York Times* (2/18/02). "Companies Use Ex-Lawmakers in Fight on Offshore Tax Break." Alison Mitchell, *New York Times* (8/10/02).
32. "Companies Use Ex-Lawmakers in Fight on Offshore Tax Break." Alison Mitchell, *New York Times* (8/10/02). "Pricewaterhouse's Spinoff Finds Bermuda Tax-Penalty Loophole." John D. McKinnon, *Wall Street Journal* (5/9/02).
33. "Tiny Pacific Island Is Facing Money-Laundering Sanctions." Agence France Presse (12/6/01).
34. Data from Compact Disclosure.
35. "Forget the Call of the Wild: In Montana, the R.V. Set is Drawn by the Words 'No Taxes'." Jim Robbins, *New York Times* (8/17/05).
36. "Irish Subsidiary Lets Microsoft Slash Taxes in U.S. and Europe." Glenn R. Simpson, *Wall Street Journal* (11/7/05).
37. Carruthers (1996: 90). Carruthers (1996) is an excellent account of the financial revolution in England around the turn of the 18th century.

38. "As Banks Bid for City Bond Work, 'Pay to Play' Tradition Endures." Mark White-house, *Wall Street Journal* (3/25/05).

39. On PIMCO: "A Fund Chief Flexes Muscles When Countries Need a Loan." Craig Karmin, *Wall Street Journal* (10/26/04). Indonesia quote: "Washington's Tilt to Business Stirs a Backlash in Indonesia." Peter Waldman, *Wall Street Journal* (2/11/04).

40. Clinton quoted in *New York Times* (1/98). Speechwriter quote from Birnbaum (1996).

41. *New York Times* (3/13/99). *Wall Street Journal* (7/16/99). "Indian Stocks Surge after Recent Plunge." Saritha Rai, *New York Times* (5/19/04).

42. Davis and Zald (2005) analyze Estrada's ouster. For a contemporary account, see "Herd on the Street: For Corporate Leaders In Manila, Economy Can't Survive Estrada—President's Scandals Compel Businessmen to Adopt a Risky Activist Stance—For the Poor, Only Déjà vu." Robert Frank, *Wall Street Journal* (12/6/00).

43. "Admitting Error, Calpers Plans to Reinvest in the Philippines." Craig Karmin and James Hookway, *Wall Street Journal* (5/13/02).

44. "Kings, Elections, Polls, the Stock Market." Holman Jenkins, *Wall Street Journal* (7/29/98).

45. "Clinton's Support Remains Strong When Viewed as Successful CEO." Dennis Farney, *Wall Street Journal* (2/6/98). Keynes biographer: "Playing the Election Market." Jonathan D. Glater, *New York Times* (2/1/04).

46. "Big Stakes in Ailing Airlines Raise Questions for U.S. Pension Agency." Michael Schroeder, *Wall Street Journal* (11/3/05). See also the discussion of pensions in Chapter 3.

47. Chapter 4 gave an account of SWF purchases of shares in financial institutions. Gilson and Milhaupt (2008) provide a description of the size, holdings, and investment strategies of SWFs. Buffett's letter available at http://www. berkshire-hathaway.com/letters/2004.html.

48. "To Cut Costs, Cities Ponder Mergers With Counties." Kris Maher, *Wall Street Journal* (2/22/05).

49. Naomi Klein, "Disaster Capitalism: The New Economy of Catastrophe." *Harper's Magazine* (October 2007): 47–58.

50. "When Nations Need a Little Marketing." Jim Rendon, *New York Times* (11/23/03). Placebrands website at http://www.placebrands.net/. There are also, of course, sub-national brands as well, with their own consultancies, focus groups, and ad campaigns, often timed to coincide with events like the Olympics or the Super Bowl. "A City Seeks to Sell Itself." Stuart Elliot, *New York Times* (12/10/04).

51. Corporate and state brands are often intermingled, for better or worse. American multinationals discovered that the Iraq war had besmirched "brand America" and

sought to rectify the extensive collateral damage to their own brands through better foreign policy. Evidently bungled invasions, massive civilian casualties, and state-sanctioned torture had taken some of the shine off of Marlboro, Barbie, and McDonald's. "Erasing the Image of the Ugly American." William J. Holstein, *New York Times* (10/23/05).

52. The text of the FAIR Act, and its definition of "inherently governmental," are available at http://www.whitehouse.gov/omb/procurement/fairact.html.

53. "In Washington, Contractors Take on Biggest Role Ever." Scott Shane and Ron Nixon, *New York Times* (2/4/07).

54. Definition of "inherently governmental" from Office of Management and Budget Policy Letter 91–92 (9/23/02).

55. "The Reach of War: Intelligence Collection; Army Policy Bars Interrogations by Private Contractors." Joel Brinkley, *New York Times* (6/12/04). "Iraq Contractor in Shooting Case Makes Comeback." James Risen, *New York Times* (5/10/08).

56. "Some Abroad Praise the SEC For Governance-Law Retreat." Craig Karmin and Kevin Delaney, *Wall Street Journal* (1/13/03). "Corn Flakes Clash Shows the Glitches In European Union." G. Thomas Sims, *Wall Street Journal* (11/1/05).

57. Davis and Marquis (2005) describe the legal situation facing foreign firms listed on US stock markets. On SEC actions outside the US, see "New Role for SEC: Policing Companies Beyond U.S. Borders." Michael Schroder and Silvia Ascarelli, *Wall Street Journal* (7/30/04). On de-listing from the US, see "A Different Sort of Exit Strategy." Daniel Epstein, *Wall Street Journal* (2/9/05).

58. "Europe's New High-Tech Role: Playing Privacy Cop to World." David Scheer, *Wall Street Journal* (10/10/03). Quote from GE CEO: "Cops of the Global Village." Marc Gunther, *Fortune Magazine* (6/27/05). Davis, Whitman, and Zald (2008) describe the new role of EU standards in multinational business.

59. "Sarbanes–Oxley Makes Running a Corporation Like Campaigning for Elective Office." Michael Weiser and Jeff Zilka, *Barron's Online* (1/27/03). Fiorina quote: "When CEOs Have Tea With Tony Blair." Alan Murray, *Wall Street Journal* (2/2/05).

60. Articles on ATCA cases available at the Global Policy Forum website http://www.globalpolicy.org/intljustice/atca/atcaindx.htm.

61. See Davis and Anderson (2008) on the limited response of US multinationals to the AIDS epidemic.

6. From Employee and Citizen to Investor

1. Cox (1963); Berle and Means (1932).

2. Jacoby (1997).

3. Perrow (1991: 725-726).

4. On changes in aggregate concentration, see White (2001). On GM: "Fight over Jobs, Cost Cuts Spurs Walkout at GM." John D. Stoll and Jeffrey McCracken, *Wall Street Journal* (9/25/07). "GM Offers Buyouts to 74,000." Chris Isidore, CNN-Money.com (2/12/08). US employment figures for Wal-Mart and others from 10K statements, available at www.sec.gov. See also Chapter 3. Bell (1973: 26).

5. On the "free agent nation," see Pink (2001). Agnew (1986) describes the role of the theater in making sense of market society around the time of Shakespeare.

6. "Stocks Tarnished by 'Lost Decade'" E. S. Browning, *Wall Street Journal* (3/26/08).

7. "Keeping Families above Water." David Wessel, *Wall Street Journal* (5/8/08).

8. Reich (1991) coined the term "symbolic analyst." Friedman (2005) describes the notion of a flat world. Blinder (2006) analyzes the types of occupations most amenable to offshoring.

9. "Debt Collection Done from India Appeals to U.S. Agencies." Heather Timmons, *New York Times* (4/24/08).

10. Berle and Means (1932: 3). Jacoby (1997).

11. Whyte (1956) is the classic journalistic account of the "organization man." Sennett (2006) describes the lost virtues of a bureaucratic career. Weber (1958) describes the link between careers and virtue under capitalism.

12. Kaysen (1957). Marquis, Glynn, and Davis (2007) describe how community norms and networks encourage local charity. Galaskiewicz (1985) provides a detailed portrayal of the Minneapolis-St. Paul non-profit community and its links to business.

13. Davis, Diekmann, and Tinsley (1994) examine the shift from the conglomerate to the network form during the 1980s and 1990s.

14. Friedman (2005).

15. "Outsourcing Your Life." Ellen Gamerman, *Wall Street Journal* (6/2/07). "The Baby-Name Business." Alexandra Alter, *Wall Street Journal* (6/22/07). Naomi Klein's *No Logo* is the classic contemporary critique of branding.

16. Blinder (2006). Mankiw's response is at his blog at http://gregmankiw. blogspot.com/2007/05/blinder-on-offshoring.html.

17. Textile manufacturing has been a keystone industry in the process of industrialization from England's industrial revolution onward, and China achieved a commanding market share early on, making 17% of the world's clothes by 2005. But China's vast textile industry has been a mixed blessing, as the cost demands of multinationals have created environmental havoc in China. In one city, locals said that you could tell what color was in style by what color the river is, as the massive local textile manufacturer poured toxic dyes directly into the local water supply to save costs. High-minded OEM firms routinely have programs to monitor their suppliers, but they commonly go only one step back in the supply chain ("China Pays Steep Price as Textile Exports Boom." Jane Spencer,

Wall Street Journal 8/22/07.) The potential dangers of offshoring can run in both directions. India's call centers used to wait for you to call them, but now some have expanded into debt collection, seeking payments from those overdue on their credit cards and having on-screen access to delinquent borrowers' Social Security and credit information ("Debt Collection Done from India Appeals to U.S. Agencies." Heather Timmons, *New York Times* 4/24/08.)

18. "Arriving in London: Hotels Made in China." Fred A. Bernstein, *New York Times* (5/11/08). "Ogre to Slay? Outsource it to Chinese." David Barboza, *New York Times* (12/9/05). "The Life of the Chinese Gold Farmer." Julian Dibbell, *New York Times* (6/17/07). US labor statistics from the Bureau of Labor Statistics at www.bls.gov.

19. Langewiesche (2004). "Will a Floating Tech Factory Fly?" Reed Tucker, *Fortune Magazine* (8/22/05).

20. "At I.B.M., a Smarter Way to Outsource." Steve Lohr, *New York Times* (7/5/07). "When Foreigners Buy Factories: 2 Towns, 2 Outcomes." Peter S. Goodman, *New York Times* (4/7/08). See Marquis, Glynn, and Davis (2007) on the local orientation of corporate philanthropy.

21. "High Hopes: Conditions are Ideal for Starting an Airline, And Many are Doing it." Scott McCartney, *Wall Street Journal* (4/1/96). "Picture Shift: U.S. Upstart Takes on TV Giants in Price War." Christopher Lawton, Yukari Iwatani Kane, and Jason Dean, *Wall Street Journal* (4/15/08). "Off-the-Shelf Parts Create New Order In TVs, Electronics." Evan Ramstad and Phred Dvorak, *Wall Street Journal* (12/16/03). "As Barriers Fall in Auto Business, China Jumps in." Gordon Fairclough, *Wall Street Journal* (11/7/06).

22. Kaysen (1957); Peter F. Drucker, "The New Society I: Revolution by Mass Production" (*Harper's Magazine*, September 1949, pp. 21–30).

23. Hacker (2006), chapter 1.

24. See Cobb (2008) for an analysis of the shift from DB to DC plans in the 1980s. *Wall Street Journal* (3/8/06), "The debt bubble..."

25. "A New Game at the Office: Many Young Workers Accept Fewer Guarantees." Steve Lohr, *New York Times* (12/5/05).

26. "Dynamic Capitalism." Edmund S. Phelps, *Wall Street Journal* (10/10/06).

27. A summary of several of these new books is contained in "They're Micromanaging Your Every Move." Simon Head, *New York Review of Books* (8/16/07).

28. "Companies Profit on Workers' Deaths through 'Dead Peasants' Insurance." Ellen E. Schultz and Theo Francis, *Wall Street Journal* (4/19/02). Similar mixed motives plague those that participate in the "life settlement" industry by selling the pay-offs to their life insurance policies to investors, as Larry King did. His attorney worried that the investor purchasing King's policy could turn out to be a Mafia

don with the capacity to facilitate the payoff. "An Insurance Man Builds a Lively Business in Death." Liam Pleven and Rachel Emma Silverman, *Wall Street Journal* (11/26/07).

29. Bernhardt et al. (1999). "Promotion Track Fades for Those Starting at Bottom." Joel Millman, *Wall Street Journal* (6/6/05).

30. "Haves and Have-Nots of Globalization." William J. Holstein, *New York Times* (7/8/07). "A New Game at the Office: Many Young Workers Accept Fewer Guarantees." Steve Lohr, *New York Times* (12/5/05).

31. Hacker (2006); "Incomes Suffer More Volatility." Greg Ip, *Wall Street Journal* (6/22/07). "Shifting Sands." *The Economist* (1/4/07).

32. Corak (2004); Corak (2006). "As Rich–Poor Gap Widens in the U.S., Class Mobility Stalls." David Wessel, *Wall Street Journal* (5/13/05).

33. "Income-Inequality Gap Widens." Greg Ip, *Wall Street Journal* (10/12/07). Rauh and Kaplan (2007) document the extreme pay of hedge fund managers.

34. "GM's Decision to Cut Pensions Accelerates Broad Corporate Shift." David Wessel, Ellen E. Schultz, and Laurie McGinley, *Wall Street Journal* (2/8/06). "A Turning Point for Health Care." Chad Terhune and Laura Meckler, *Wall Street Journal* (9/27/07). The Pension Benefit Guarantee Corporation maintains a website with data and press releases on its corporate pension obligations at http://www.pbgc.gov.

35. Economic Report of the President for 2006: http://www.gpoaccess.gov/eop/index.html "Report Plays Down Economic Woes." Greg Ip, *Wall Street Journal* (2/14/06). "Shifting Sands." *The Economist* (1/4/07).

36. Text of second inaugural: http://www.whitehouse.gov/news/releases/2005/01/20050120-1.html

37. "In Bush's 'Ownership Society,' Citizens Would Take More Risk." Jackie Calmes, *Wall Street Journal* (2/28/05).

38. Presidents quoted in Dreier (1982); Green and White (1997).

39. On the effects of home ownership on good citizenship: DiPasquale and Glaeser (1999). On outcomes for children of homeowners vs. renters: Green and White (1997).

40. Di Tella, Galiani, and Schargrodsky (2008) describe the effects of titling on attitudes. "Barrio Study Links Land Ownership to a Better Life." Matt Moffett, *Wall Street Journal* (11/9/05).

41. Shiller (2006).

42. Smith's quote is from *The Wealth of Nations*. The quotes on thrift are taken from Haveman and Rao (1997: 1612).

43. "Homeowners Abroad Take Currency Gamble in Loans." Craig Karmin and Joellen Perry, *Wall Street Journal* (5/29/07).

44. Kimmel (1952) reports a large-scale survey of stock ownership in the early 1950s. Cox (1963) surveys research on ownership over the first half of the twentieth century. More recent summaries based on the Federal Reserve's Survey of Consumer Finances are provided in Hall (2000) and Duca (2001).

45. Fraser (2005: 583). Davis (2008); Duca (2001). Individual ownership figures come from the Federal Reserve's triennial Survey of Consumer Finances. Corporate ownership by financial institutions compiled from the Spectrum 13F database.

46. Figures on household ownership of homes and stocks reported in Bucks, Kennickell, and Moore (2006).

47. Cox (1963), Bertaut (1996).

48. "A Lesson for Social Security: Many Mismanage their 401(k)s." Tom Lauricella, *Wall Street Journal* (12/1/04). Annual surveys of 401(k) plans are conducted jointly by the Employee Benefit Research Institute (EBRI) and the Investment Company Institute (ICI) and are available at the ICI website www.ici.org.

49. "Lopsided 401(k)'s, All Too Common." Gretchen Morgenson, *New York Times* (10/5/03). "Enron's 401(k) Calamity." Michael W. Lynch, *Reason Magazine* (12/27/01). "SEC Finds Retirement-Fund Issues." Deborah Solomon, *Wall Street Journal* (5/16/05).

50. Shiv et al. (2005). "Lessons from the Brain-Damaged Investor." Jane Spencer, *Wall Street Journal* (7/21/05).

51. Thaler and Sunstein (2008).

52. "Chinese Investors Crunching Numbers are Glad to See 8s." James T. Areddy, *Wall Street Journal* (5/24/07). "China's Stock Surge Raises Fundamental Questions." James T. Areddy, *Wall Street Journal* (10/16/07).

53. The text of *The Federalist #10* is available at http://www.constitution.org/fed/federa10.htm

54. Richard Nadler, "The Rise of Worker Capitalism." Cato Institute Policy Analysis #359 (1999). Richard Nadler, "Portfolio Politics: Nudging the Investor Class Forward." *National Review* (12/4/00).

55. Ramesh Ponnuru, "Investor Class, Investor Nation: America is Becoming an 'Ownership Society,' a Seismic Development." *National Review Online* (2/9/04). "In Bush's 'Ownership Society,' Citizens Would Take More Risk." Jackie Calmes, *Wall Street Journal* (2/28/05).

56. Davis and Cotton (2007) provide statistical analyses of time-series data on party identification and stock ownership. Data from the American National Election Studies are available at http://www.electionstudies.org.

57. "Affluent Voters Switch Brands." John Harwood, *Wall Street Journal* (11/16/07).

58. Thomas Frank's *One Market under God* provides an acute analysis of how markets have been substituted for democracy in much contemporary discourse.

59. "Trading on the Wisdom of Crowds." L. Gordon Crovitz, *Wall Street Journal* (4/28/08).

60. And perhaps the running of government functions could be handed over to someone who would do it well: Wal-Mart. The firm's CEO stated in an address to employees, "We live in a time when people are losing confidence in the ability of government to solve problems . . . But Wal-Mart does not wait for someone else to solve problems." Those comparing Wal-Mart's performance to that of FEMA after Hurricane Katrina could hardly disagree. "Wal-Mart: The New Washington." Michael Barbaro, *New York Times* (2/3/08).

61. "Probe Widens on Inflated Home Appraisals." James R. Hagerty and Ann Carrns, *Wall Street Journal* (11/8/07).

62. "Payback Time." Stephen J. Dubner and Steven D. Levitt, *New York Times* (6/10/07).

63. "Wall Street Wizardry Amplified Credit Crisis." Carrick Mollenkamp and Serena Ng, *Wall Street Journal* (12/27/07).

64. "The United States of Subprime." Rick Brooks and Constance Mitchell Ford, *Wall Street Journal* (10/11/07). "Subprime Debacle Traps Even Very Credit-Worthy." Rick Brooks and Ruth Simon, *Wall Street Journal* (12/3/07).

65. "Behind Subprime Woes, A Cascade of Bad Bets." Carrick Mollenkamp and Ian McDonald, *Wall Street Journal* (10/17/07). "Housing Bust Fuels Blame Game." Greg Ip, James R. Hagerty, and Jonathan Karp, *Wall Street Journal* (2/27/08).

66. Quotes and other material on rating agencies in this section are drawn from an outstanding article by Roger Lowenstein. "Triple-A Failure." Roger Lowenstein, *New York Times* (4/27/08).

67. Hume describes the problem of induction in *An Enquiry Concerning Human Understanding*. The problem, as he describes it, is that our knowledge of laws of nature are induced from prior experience, but prior experience is not logically sufficient to conclude that the laws will continue to hold in the future. As Hume put it, "all inferences from experience suppose, as their foundation, that the future will resemble the past, and that similar powers will be conjoined with similar sensible qualities. If there be any suspicion that the course of nature may change, and that the past may be no rule for the future, all experience becomes useless, and can give rise to no inference or conclusion."

68. "Speculators Helped Fuel Florida's Housing Boom." Michael Corkery and James R. Hagerty, *Wall Street Journal* (1/8/07). "Online, Some Home Buyers Find a House of Cards." Katie Hafner, *New York Times* (3/11/06).

69. "Fraud Seen as a Driver in Wave of Foreclosures." Michael Corkery, *Wall Street Journal* (12/21/07).

70. Brian K. Bucks, Arthur B. Kennickell, and Kevin B. Moore (2006). "Recent Changes in U.S. Family Finances: Evidence from the 2001 and 2004 Survey of Consumer Finances." Federal Reserve Bulletin, A1–A38. Greenspan and Kennedy (2008). "Home Truths." *The Economist* (10/12/06). "Homeowners' Reduced Equity Raises Fear of Slow Spending." Peter S. Goodman, *New York Times* (11/8/07).

71. For mortgage brokers: "With Mortgages, Instant Wealth for Middlemen." Jeff Bailey, *New York Times* (10/8/05). For real estate agents: "Endangered Species." Stephen J. Dubner and Steven D. Leavitt, *New York Times* (3/5/06). For other industries, see the Bureau of Labor Statistics at www.bls.gov.

72. "A Fable, Adapted From Aesop." Eduardo Porter, *New York Times* (9/17/06). "As Housing Prices Cool, Americans Keep Spending." Christopher Conkey, *Wall Street Journal* (10/2/06).

73. "Housing-Bubble Talk Doesn't Scare off Foreigners." Ruth Simon, James R. Hagerty, and James T. Areddy, *Wall Street Journal* (8/24/05).

74. "Signs of Lean Times for Home Equity, the American Piggy Bank." Floyd Norris, *New York Times* (12/9/06). "Housing, Bank Troubles Deepen." Sudeep Reddy and Sara Murray, *Wall Street Journal* (3/7/08).

75. " 'Subprime' Aftermath: Losing the Family Home." Mark Whitehouse, *Wall Street Journal* (5/30/07).

76. "Reports Suggest Broader Losses from Mortgages." Vikas Bajaj and Edmund L. Andrews, *New York Times* (10/25/07).

77. "U.S. Credit Crisis Adds to Gloom in Arctic Norway." Mark Landler, *New York Times* (12/2/07).

78. "Now, Even Borrowers with Good Credit Pose Risks." George Anders, *Wall Street Journal* (12/19/07).

79. "Debt Collection Done from India Appeals to U.S. Agencies." Heather Timmons, *New York Times* (4/24/08).

80. "Rescues for Homeowners in Debt Weighed." Edmund L. Andrews and Louis Uchitelle, *New York Times* (2/22/08).

81. "Buyers' Revenge: Trash the House After Foreclosure." Michael M. Phillips, *Wall Street Journal* (3/28/08).

82. "Keeping Families Above Water." David Wessel, *Wall Street Journal* (5/8/08). "Housing Bust Fuels Blame Game." Greg Ip, James R. Hagerty, and Jonathan Karp, *Wall Street Journal* (2/27/08). "Mortgage-Relief Plan Divides Neighbors." Jonathan Karp, *Wall Street Journal* (12/17/07).

83. Elizabeth Warren, "Unsafe at Any Rate." *Democracy: A Journal of Ideas* (summer 2007).

84. "Pinched Consumers Scramble for Cash." Eleanor Laise, *Wall Street Journal* (6/2/08). "High-Interest Lenders Tap Elderly, Disabled." Ellen E. Schultz and Theo Francis, *Wall Street Journal* (2/12/08). "Needing Cash, Veterans Sign Over Pensions." Diana B. Henriques, *New York Times* (12/29/04).

7. Conclusion

1. Gray (1999) also describes parallels between Polanyi's analysis of mid-Victorian Britain and late twentieth-century free marketism.
2. "Japan's Companies Gird for Attack." Andrew Morse and Sebastian Moffett, *Wall Street Journal* (4/30/08).
3. See Piore and Sabel (1984) for an account of alternative paths of industrialization.
4. Jameson (1991) wrote some of the most thoughtful early works on postmodernism and its link to capitalism economic organization.
5. Harvey (1990) analyzes the link between postmodernism and the shift from mass production to a flexible regime of accumulation and flexible or network forms of production, along the lines described by Piore and Sabel (1984). Harvey further offers an insightful view of the constitutive role of finance in postmodernism: "What does seem special about the period since 1972 is the extraordinary efflorescence and transformation in financial markets... it is not so much the concentration of power in financial institutions that matters, as the explosion in new financial instruments and markets, coupled with the rise of highly sophisticated systems of financial coordination on a global scale. It is through this financial system that much of the geographical and temporal flexibility of capital accumulation has been achieved... I am therefore tempted to see the flexibility achieved in production, labor markets, and consumption more as an outcome of the search for financial solutions to the crisis-tendencies of capitalism, rather than the other way round. This would imply that the financial system has achieved a degree of autonomy from real production unprecedented in capitalism's history, carrying capitalism into an era of equally unprecedented financial dangers" (1990: 192-4). And: "if we are to look for anything truly distinctive (as opposed to 'capitalism as usual') in the present situation, then it is upon the financial aspects of capitalist organization and on the role of credit that we should concentrate our gaze" (1990: 196).
6. Menand (2001: 355). Oliver Wendell Holmes articulated a similar view in his "prediction theory of the law": "it is not the law that determines the outcome in a particular case; it is what judges *say* is the law" (Menand, 2001: 343).
7. McCloskey (1985: 47).
8. Podolny (2005) analyzes how affiliations can lead to perceptions of status in IPOs and other markets.

9. "Without a Doubt." Ron Suskind, *New York Times* (10/17/04).

10. "At Medical Journals, Writers Paid by Industry Play Big Role." Anna Wilde Mathews, *Wall Street Journal* (12/13/05). "Merck's Publishing Ethics are Questioned by Studies." Ron Winslow and Avery Johnson, *Wall Street Journal* (4/16/08). "Report Says Merck Vioxx Study Aimed at Marketing." Ron Winslow and Jacob Goldstein, *Wall Street Journal* (8/19/08).

11. "Study Tied Pollutant to Cancer; Then Consultants Got Hold of it." Peter Waldman, *Wall Street Journal* (12/23/05).

12. "US Investors Face an Age of Murky Pricing." Susan Pulliam, Randall Smith, and Michael Siconolfi, *Wall Street Journal* (10/12/07).

13. "In Bear Stearns Case, Question of an Asset's Value." Louise Story, *New York Times* (6/20/08).

14. "Bankers Cast Doubt on Key Rate Amid Crisis." Carrick Mollenkamp, *Wall Street Journal* (4/16/08). "Study Casts Doubt on Key Rate." Carrick Mollenkamp and Mark Whitehouse, *Wall Street Journal* (5/29/08).

15. "Numbers Racket: Why the Economy is Worse than We Know." Kevin Phillips, *Harper's Magazine* (May 2008) 43–47. See also Phillips (2008: chapter 3).

16. Several recent popular books also address some of these problems. Jacob Hacker analyzes the decline of corporate pensions and health care in *The Great Risk Shift*. Kevin Phillips discusses finance gone wild in *Bad Money: Reckless Finance, Failed Politics, and the Global Crisis of American Capitalism*. Naomi Klein describes the outsourcing of core government services in *The Shock Doctrine: The Rise of Disaster Capitalism*. And Thomas Frank portrays a concerted effort to render the Federal government incompetent in *The Wrecking Crew: How Conservatives Rule*.

References

Agnew, J.-C. 1986. *Worlds Apart: The Market and the Theater in Anglo-American Thought, 1550–1750*. New York: Cambridge University Press.

Alchian, A. & Demsetz, H. 1972. Production, Information Costs, and Economic Organization. *American Economic Review*, 92: 777–795.

Allen, W. T. 1992. Our Schizophrenic Conception of the Business Corporation. *Cardozo Law Review*, 14: 261–281.

Anderson, B. 1983. *Imagined Communities: Reflections on the Origin and Spread of Nationalism*. London: Verso.

Applebaum, E., Bernhardt, A. D., & Murnane, R. J. 2003. *Low-Wage America: How Employers are Reshaping Opportunity in the Workplace*. New York: Russell Sage.

Avery, R. B., Elliehausen, G. E., & Canner, G. B. 1984. Survey of Consumer Finances 1983. *Federal Reserve Bulletin*: 679–692.

Baker, W. E. 2000. *Achieving Success through Social Capital*. San Francisco: Jossey-Bass.

Barth, J. R., Brumbaugh, R. D., & Litan, R. E. 1992. *The Future of American Banking*. Armonk, NY: M. E. Sharpe.

Beard, C. A. 1913. *An Economic Interpretation of the Constitution of the United States* (1935 edition of the 1913 original edn.). New York: Macmillan.

Bebchuk, L. & Fried, J. 2004. *Pay without Performance: The Unfulfilled Promise of Executive Pay*. Cambridge, MA: Harvard University Press.

Bell, D. 1973. *The Coming of Post-Industrial Society*. New York: Basic Books.

Berle, A. A. & Means, G. C. 1932. *The Modern Corporation and Private Property* (repr. 1991). New Brunswick, NJ: Transaction.

Bernhardt, A. D., Morris, M., Handcock, M. S., & Scott, M. A. 1999. *Job Instability and Wages for Young Adult Men*. Pennsylvania State University Working Paper 99–01.

Bertaut, C. C. 1996. Stockholding Behavior of U.S. Households: Evidence from the 1983–89 Survey of Consumer Finances. Federal Reserve System International Finance Discussion Papers.

Birnbaum, J. H. 1996. *Madhouse: The Private Turmoil of Working for the President*. New York: Crown.

Blair, M. M. 1995. *Ownership and Control: Rethinking Corporate Governance for the Twenty-First Century*. Washington: Brookings Institution.

Blinder, A. S. 2006. Offshoring: The Next Industrial Revolution? *Foreign Affairs*, 85(2): 113–128.

Block, F. 1977. The Ruling Class Does Not Rule. *Socialist Revolution*, 7(3): 6–28.

Bobbitt, P. 2002. *The Shield of Achilles: War, Peace, and the Course of History*. New York: Alfred A. Knopf.

Bogle, J. C. 2005. *The Battle for the Soul of Capitalism*. New Haven: Yale University Press.

Brandeis, L. D. 1914. *Other People's Money: And How the Bankers Use It*. New York: Frederick A. Stokes Company.

Bucks, B. K., Kennickell, A. B., & Moore, K. B. 2006. Recent Changes in U.S. Family Finances: Evidence from the 2001 and 2004 Survey of Consumer Finances. *Federal Reserve Bulletin*: A1–A38.

Carruthers, B. G. 1996. *City of Capital: Politics and Markets in the English Financial Revolution*. Princeton: Princeton University Press.

_____ & Stinchcombe, A. L. 1999. The Social Structure of Liquidity: Flexibility, Markets, and States. *Theory and Society*, 28: 353–382.

Chandler, A. D. 1977. *The Visible Hand: The Managerial Revolution in American Business*. Cambridge, MA: Belknap Press.

Coase, R. 1937. The Nature of the Firm. *Economica*, 4: 386–405.

Cobb, J. A. 2008. The Employment Contract Broken? The Deinstitutionalization of Defined Benefit Retirement Plans. Unpublished, Ross School of Business, University of Michigan.

Coffee, J. C. 2001. The Rise of Dispersed Ownership: The Roles of Law and the State in the Separation of Ownership and Control. *Yale Law Journal*, 111: 1–82.

Corak, M. (ed.). 2004. *Generational Income Mobility in North America and Europe*. Cambridge, UK: Cambridge University Press.

_____ 2006. *Do Poor Children Become Poor Adults? Lessons from a Cross Country Comparison of Generational Earnings Mobility*. Bonn, Germany: IZA.

Cox, E. B. 1963. *Trends in the Distribution of Stock Ownership*. Philadelphia: University of Pennsylvania Press.

Dahrendorf, R. 1959. *Class and Class Conflict in Industrial Society*. Stanford, CA: Stanford University Press.

Davis, G. F. 1991. Agents without Principles? The Spread of the Poison Pill through the Intercorporate Network. *Administrative Science Quarterly*, 36(4): 583–613.

_____ 1996. The Significance of Board Interlocks for Corporate Governance. *Corporate Governance*, 4: 154–159.

_____ 2003. American Cronyism: How Executive Networks Inflated the Corporate Bubble. *Contexts*, 2(3): 34–40.

_____ 2005. New Directions in Corporate Governance. *Annual Review of Sociology*, 31: 143–162.

_____ 2008. A New Finance Capitalism? Mutual Funds and Ownership Re-concentration in the United States. *European Management Review*, 5: 11–21.

_____ & Anderson, P. J. J. 2008. Social Movements and Failed Institutionalization: Corporate (Non)Response to the AIDS Epidemic. In R. Greenwood, C. Oliver, K. Sahlin, & R. Suddaby (eds.), *The SAGE Handbook of Organizational Institutionalism*: 371–388. London: Sage.

_____ & Cotton, N. C. 2007. Political Consequences of Financial Market Expansion: Does Buying a Mutual Fund Turn You Republican? Presented at the American Sociological Association Annual Meetings, New York.

_____ Greve, H. R. 1997. Corporate Elite Networks and Governance Changes in the 1980s. *American Journal of Sociology*, 103(1): 1–37.

_____ & Kim, E. H. 2007. Business Ties and Proxy Voting by Mutual Funds. *Journal of Financial Economics*, 85: 552–570.

_____ & Marquis, C. 2005. The Globalization of Stock Markets and Convergence in Corporate Governance. In V. Nee & R. Swedberg (eds.), *The Economic Sociology of Capitalism*: 352–390. Princeton: Princeton University Press.

_____ & Mizruchi, M. S. 1999. The Money Center Cannot Hold: Commercial Banks in the U.S. System of Corporate Governance. *Administrative Science Quarterly*, 44(2): 215–239.

_____ & Robbins, G. E. 2005. Nothing but Net? Networks and Status in Corporate Governance. In K. Knorr-Cetina & A. Preda (eds.), *The Sociology of Financial Markets*: 290–311. Oxford: Oxford University Press.

_____ _____ 2008. The Fate of the Conglomerate Firm in the United States. In W. W. Powell & D. L. Jones (eds.), *How Institutions Change*. Chicago: University of Chicago Press.

_____ & Stout, S. K. 1992. Organization Theory and the Market for Corporate Control: A Dynamic Analysis of the Characteristics of Large Takeover Targets, 1980–1990. *Administrative Science Quarterly*, 37(4): 605–633.

_____ & Thompson, T. A. 1994. A Social Movement Perspective on Corporate Control. *Administrative Science Quarterly*, 39(1): 141–173.

_____ & Useem, M. 2002. Top Management, Company Directors, and Corporate Control. In A. Pettigrew, H. Thomas, & R. Whittington (eds.), *Handbook of Strategy and Management*: 233–259. London: Sage.

_____ & Yoo, M. 2003. Le Monde Toujours Plus Petit des Grandes Entreprises Américaines: Participations Communes et Liens dans les Conseils d'Administration (1990-2001). *Gérer et Comprendre*, 74: 51–62.

_____ & Zald, M. N. 2005. Social Change, Social Theory, and the Convergence of Movements and Organizations. In G. F. Davis, D. McAdam, W. R. Scott, & M. N. Zald (eds.), *Social Movements and Organization Theory*: 335–350. New York: Cambridge University Press.

Davis, G. F. Diekmann, K. A., & Tinsley, C. H. 1994. The Decline and Fall of the Conglomerate Firm in the 1980s: The Deinstitutionalization of an Organizational Form. *American Sociological Review*, 59(4): 547–570.

——— Whitman, M. v., & Zald, M. N. 2008. The Responsibility Paradox. *Stanford Social Innovation Review*, 6(1): 30–37.

——— Yoo, M., & Baker, W. E. 2003. The Small World of the American Corporate Elite, 1982–2001. *Strategic Organization*, 1(301–326).

DeLong, J. B. 1991. Did JP Morgan's Men Add Value? An Economist's Perspective on Financial Capitalism. In P. Temin (ed.), *Inside the Business Enterprise: Historical Perspectives on the Use of Information*: 205–236. Chicago: University of Chicago Press.

Demsetz, H. & Lehn, K. 1985. The Structure of Corporate Ownership: Causes and Consequences. *Journal of Political Economy*, 93: 1155–1177.

DiPasquale, D. & Glaeser, E. L. 1999. Incentives and Social Capital: Are Homeowners Better Citizens? *Journal of Urban Economics*, 45: 354–384.

DiTella, R., Galiani, S., & Schargrodsky, E. 2008. The Formation of Beliefs: Evidence from the Allocation of Land Titles to Squatters. *Quarterly Journal of Economics*.

Dreier, P. 1982. The Status of Tenants in the United States. *Social Problems*, 30: 179–198.

Drexler, K. E. 1986. *Engines of Creation: The Coming Era of Nanotechnology*. New York: Anchor.

Duca, J. V. 2001. The Democratization of America's Capital Markets. *Federal Reserve Bank of Dallas Economic and Financial Review* (Second Quarter): 10–19.

Easterbrook, F. H. & Fischel, D. R. 1991. *The Economic Structure of Corporate Law*. Cambridge, MA: Harvard University Press.

Espeland, W. N. & Stevens, M. L. 1998. Commensuration as a Social Process. *Annual Review of Sociology*, 24: 313–343.

Evans, P. 1995. *Embedded Autonomy: States and Industrial Transformation*. Princeton: Princeton University Press.

Fama, E. 1980. Agency Problems and the Theory of the Firm. *Journal of Political Economy*, 88: 288–307.

——— & Jensen, M. C. 1983. Separation of Ownership and Control. *Journal of Law and Economics*, 26: 301–325.

Fligstein, N. 1990. *The Transformation of Corporate Control*. Cambridge, MA: Harvard University Press.

Frank, T. 2000. *One Market under God: Extreme Capitalism, Market Populism, and the End of Economic Democracy*. New York: Doubleday.

Fraser, S. 2005. *Every Man a Speculator: A History of Wall Street in American Life*. New York: HarperCollins.

Friedman, M. 1970. The Social Responsibility of Business is to Increase its Profits. *New York Times Magazine*, September 13.

Friedman, T. L. 2005. *The World is Flat: A Brief History of the Twenty-First Century*. New York: Farrar, Straus, and Giroux.

Galaskiewicz, J. 1985. *Social Organization of an Urban Grants Economy: A Study of Business Philanthropy and Nonprofit Organizations*. Orlando: Academic Press.

Geneen, H. 1997. *The Synergy Myth: And Other Ailments of Business Today*. New York: St. Martin's.

Ghosh, A. 2006. The IPO Phenomenon in the 1990s. *Social Science Journal*, 43: 487–495.

Giddens, A. 2000. *Runaway World: How Globalization is Reshaping Our Lives*. New York: Routledge.

Gilson, R. J. 1981. A Structural Approach to Corporations: The Case against Defensive Tactics in Tender Offers. *Stanford Law Review*, 33: 819–891.

—— & Milhaupt, C. J. 2008. *Sovereign Wealth Funds and Corporate Governance: A Minimalist Response to the New Mercantilism*. Stanford University Law and Economics Olin Working Paper 355.

Golding, T. 2003. *The City: Inside the Great Expectation Machine*, 2nd edn. London: Pearson.

Gray, J. 1999. *False Dawn: The Delusions of Global Capitalism*. New York: New Press.

Green, R. K. & White, M. J. 1997. Measuring the Benefits of Homeowning: Effects on Children. *Journal of Urban Economics*, 41: 441–461.

Greenspan, A. & Kennedy, J. 2008. Sources and Uses of Equity Extracted from Homes. *Oxford Review of Economic Policy*, 24(1): 120–144.

Hacker, J. S. 2006. *The Great Risk Shift: The Assault on American Jobs, Families, Health Care, and Retirement—And How You Can Fight Back*. New York: Oxford University Press.

Hall, J. 2000. The Roots of Broadened Stock Ownership: Report to the Joint Economic Committee of the US Congress, April 2000. *Washington: US Congress, Joint Economic Committee*.

Hall, P. A. & Soskice, D. 2001. *Varieties of Capitalism: The Institutional Foundations of Comparative Advantage*. Oxford: Oxford University Press.

Hargadon, A. B. & Douglas, Y. 2001. When innovations meet institutions: Edison and the design of the electric light. *Administrative Science Quarterly*, 46: 476–501.

Harrington, B. 2008. *Pop Finance: Investment Clubs and the New Investor Populism*. Princeton: Princeton University Press.

Harvey, D. 1990. *The Condition of Postmodernity: An Enquiry into the Origins of Cultural Change*. Cambridge, MA: Blackwell.

Haveman, H. A. & Rao, H. 1997. Structuring a Theory of Moral Sentiments: Institutional and Organizational Coevolution in the Early Thrift Industry. *American Journal of Sociology*, 102(6): 1606–1651.

Hill, C. A. 1996. Securitization as a Low-Cost Sweetener for Lemons. *Washington University Law Quarterly*, 74: 1061–1126.

Jacoby, S. M. 1997. *Modern Manors: Welfare Capitalism Since the New Deal*. Princeton: Princeton University Press.

James, C. & Houston, J. 1996. Evolution or Extinction: Where are Banks Headed? *Journal of Applied Corporate Finance*, 9(2): 8–23.

Jameson, F. 1991. *Postmodernism, or, the Cultural Logic of Late Capitalism*. Duram, NC: Duke University Press.

Jarrell, G. A. 1992. The 1980s Takeover Boom and Government Regulation. *Regulation: The Cato Review of Business & Government*, 15(3).

Jensen, M. C. 1988. Takeovers: Their Causes and Consequences. *Journal of Economic Perspectives*, 2: 21–48.

——— 1993. The Modern Industrial Revolution, Exit, and the Failure of Internal Control Systems. *Journal of Finance*, 48(3): 831–880.

——— 2002. Value Maximization, Stakeholder Theory, and the Corporate Objective Function. *Business Ethics Quarterly*, 12: 235–256.

——— & Meckling, W. H. 1976. Theory of the Firm: Managerial Behavior, Agency Cost and Ownership Structure. *Journal of Financial Economics*, 3: 305–360.

Kahan, M. & Kamar, E. 2002. The Myth of State Competition in Corporate Law. *Stanford Law Review*, 55: 679–749.

Kaplan, S. N. & Rauh, J. 2007. *Wall Street and Main Street: What Contributes to the Rise in the Highest Incomes?* Cambridge, MA: National Bureau of Economic Research.

Kaysen, C. 1957. The Social Significance of the Modern Corporation. *American Economic Review* (Papers and Proceedings), 47(2): 311–319.

Kennickell, A. & Shack-Marquez, J. 1992. Changes in Family Finances from 1983 to 1989: Evidence from the Survey of Consumer Finances. *Federal Reserve Bulletin* (January): 1–18.

Kimmel, L. H. 1952. *Share Ownership in the United States: A Study Prepared at the Request of the New York Stock Exchange*. Washington: Brookings Institution.

Kirchner, C., Painter, R. W., & Kaal, W. 2004. *Regulatory Competition in EU Corporate Law after Inspire Art: Unbundling Delaware's Product for Europe*. University of Illinois College of Law, Law and Economics Working Paper 17.

Klein, N. 1999. *No Logo*. New York: Picador.

Klick, J. & Sitkoff, R. H. 2008. Agency Costs, Charitable Trusts, and Corporate Control: Evidence from Hershey's Kiss-Off. *Columbia Law Review*, 108: 749–838.

Langewiesche, W. 2004. *The Outlaw Sea: A World of Freedom, Chaos, and Crime*. New York: North Point Press.

LaPorta, R., Lopez-de-Silanes, F., Shleifer, A., & Vishny, R. W. 1998. Law and Finance. *Journal of Political Economy*, 106: 1113–1155.

LeBaron, D. & Speidell, L. S. 1987. Why Are the Parts Worth More than the Sum? "Chop Shop," a Corporate Valuation Model. In L. E. Brown & E. S. Rosengren (eds.), *The Merger Boom*. Boston: Federal Reserve Bank of Boston.

LeRoy, G. 2005. *The Great American Jobs Scam*. San Francisco: Berrett-Koehler.

Malkiel, B. G. 1996. *A Random Walk down Wall Street*. New York: Norton.

Manne, H. G. 1965. Mergers and the Market for Corporate Control. *Journal of Political Economy*, 73: 110–120.

March, J. G. & Simon, H. A. 1958. *Organizations*. New York: Wiley.

Marchand, R. 1998. *Creating the Corporate Soul: The Rise of Public Relations and Corporate Imagery in American Big Business*. Berkeley: University of California Press.

Marquis, C. & Lounsbury, M. 2007. Vive la Résistance: Consolidation and Community-Level Professional Counter-Mobilization in US Banking. *Academy of Management Journal*, 50: 799–820.

_____ Glynn, M., & Davis, G. F. 2007. Community Isomorphism and Corporate Social Action. *Academy of Management Review*, 32: 925–945.

Marris, R. 1964. *The Economic Theory of "Managerial" Capitalism*. New York: Free Press.

Mayer, M. 1997. *The Bankers: The Next Generation*. New York: Truman Talley.

Menand, L. 2001. *The Metaphysical Club: A Story of Ideas in America*. New York: Farrar, Straus, and Giroux.

Micklethwait, J. & Woolridge, A. 2003. *The Company: A Short History of a Revolutionary Idea*. London: Phoenix.

Mills, C. W. 1956. *The Power Elite*. New York: Oxford University Press.

_____ 1959. *The Sociological Imagination*. New York: Oxford University Press.

Mintz, B. & Schwartz, M. 1985. *The Power Structure of American Business*. Chicago: University of Chicago Press.

Mizruchi, M. S. 1982. *The American Corporate Network: 1904–1974*. Beverly Hills, CA: Sage.

_____ 1992. *The Structure of Corporate Political Action: Interfirm Relations and their Consequences*. Cambridge, MA: Harvard University Press.

_____ & Davis, G. F. 2004. The Globalization of American Banking, 1962–1981. In F. Dobbin (ed.), *The Sociology of the Economy*: 95–126. New York: Russell Sage.

Neuman, E. J., Davis, G. F., & Mizruchi, M. S. 2008. Industry Consolidation and Network Evolution in U.S. Global Banking, 1986–2004. *Advances in Strategic Management*, 25: 213–248.

North, D. C. 1990. *Institutions, Institutional Change and Economic Performance*. New York: Cambridge University Press.

O'Reilly, C. & Pfeffer, J. 2000. *Hidden Value: How Great Companies Achieve Extraordinary Results with Ordinary People*. Boston: Harvard Business School Press.

Perrow, C. 1991. A Society of Organizations. *Theory and Society*, 20: 725–762.

Perrow, C. 2002. *Organizing America: Wealth, Power, and the Origins of Corporate Capitalism*. Princeton: Princeton University Press.

Phillips, K. 2008. *Bad Money: Reckless Finance, Failed Politics, and the Global Crisis of American Capitalism*. New York: Viking.

Pink, D. H. 2001. *Free Agent Nation: How America's New Independent Workers are Transforming the Way We Live*. New York: Warner Books.

Piore, M. J. & Sabel, C. F. 1984. *The Second Industrial Divide: Possibilities for Prosperity*. New York: Basic.

Podolny, J. 2005. *Status Signals: A Sociological Study of Market Competition*. Princeton: Princeton University Press.

Polanyi, K. 1944. *The Great Transformation*. Boston: Beacon.

Putnam, R. 2000. *Bowling Alone: The Collapse and Revival of American Community*. New York: Touchstone.

Quinn, S. 2008. The Transformation of Morals in Markets: Death, Benefits, and the Exchange of Life Insurance Policies. *American Journal of Sociology*, 114.

Rao, H., Davis, G. F., & Ward, A. 2000. Embeddedness, Social Identity and Mobility: Why Firms Leave the NASDAQ and Join the New York Stock Exchange. *Administrative Science Quarterly*, 45(2): 268–292.

_____ Greve, H. R., & Davis, G. F. 2001. Fool's Gold: Social Proof in the Initiation and Abandonment of Coverage by Wall Street Analysts. *Administrative Science Quarterly*, 46(3): 502–526.

Rauh, J. D. & Kaplan, S. N. 2007. *Wall Street and Main Street: What Contributes to the Rise in the Highest Incomes*. CRSP Working Paper 615.

Reich, R. B. 1991. *The Work of Nations: Preparing Ourselves for twenty-first-Century Capitalism*. New York: Alfred A. Knopf.

Rivoli, P. 2005. *The Travels of a T-Shirt in the Global Economy: An Economist Examines the Markets, Power, and Politics of World Trade*. Hoboken, NJ: John Wiley & Sons.

Roe, M. J. 1994. *Strong Managers, Weak Owners: The Political Roots of American Corporate Finance*. Princeton: Princeton University Press.

Romano, R. 1993. *The Genius of American Corporate Law*. Washington: American Enterprise Institute.

Roy, W. G. 1983. The Unfolding of the Interlocking Directorate Structure of the United States. *American Sociological Review*, 48: 248–257.

_____ 1997. *Socializing Capital: The Rise of the Large Industrial Corporation in America*. Princeton: Princeton University Press.

_____ & Bonacich, P. 1988. Interlocking Directorates and Communities of Interest among American Railroad Companies, 1905. *American Sociological Review*, 53: 368–379.

Selznick, P. 1957. *Leadership in Administration*. New York: Harper & Row.

Sennett, R. 2006. *The Culture of the New Capitalism*. New Haven: Yale University Press.

Sewell, W. H., Jr. 1981. *Work and Revolution in France: The Language of Labor from the Old Regime to 1848*. New York: Cambridge University Press.

Shiller, R. J. 2003a. *The New Financial Order: Risk in the twenty-first Century*. Princeton: Princeton University Press.

—— 2003b. From Efficient Market Theory to Behavioral Finance. *Journal of Economic Perspectives*, 17(1): 83–104.

—— 2006. Long-Term Perspectives on the Current Boom in Home Prices. *Economists' Voice*, 3(4): 1–11.

Shiv, B., Loewenstein, G., Bechara, A., Damasio, H., & Damasio, A. R. 2005. Investment Behavior and the Negative Side of Emotion. *Psychological Science*, 16: 435–439.

Simon, M. C. 1998. The Rise and Fall of Bank Control in the United States, 1890–1939. *American Economic Review*, 88: 1077–1093.

Smith, R. C. 1989. *The Global Bankers*. New York: Dutton.

Stinchcombe, A. L. 1997. On the Virtues of the Old Institutionalism. *Annual Review of Sociology*, 23: 1–18.

Sturgeon, T. J. 2002. Modular Production Networks: A New American Model of Industrial Organization. *Industrial and Corporate Change*, 11: 451–496.

Surowiecki, J. 2004. *The Wisdom of Crowds*. New York: Anchor.

Thaler, R. H. & Sunstein, C. R. 2008. *Nudge: Improving Decisions about Health, Wealth, and Happiness*. New Haven: Yale University Press.

Tiebout, C. M. 1956. A Pure Theory of Local Expenditures. *Journal of Political Economy*, 64: 416–424.

Useem, M. 1984. *The Inner Circle*. New York: Oxford University Press.

—— 1996. *Investor Capitalism: How Money Managers are Changing the Face of Corporate America*. New York: Basic.

Vise, D. A. & Coll, S. 1991. *Eagle on the Street*. New York: Scribners.

Vogel, D. 1978. Why Businessmen Distrust their State: The Political Consciousness of American Corporate Executives. *British Journal of Political Science*, 8: 45–78.

Vogus, T. J. & Davis, G. F. 2005. Elite Mobilizations for Antitakeover Legislation, 1982–1990. In G. F. Davis, D. McAdam, W. R. Scott, M. N. Zald (eds.), *Social Movements and Organization Theory*: 96–121. New York: Cambridge University Press.

Weber, K., Davis, G. F., & Lounsbury, M. (forthcoming). Policy as Myth and Ceremony? The Global Spread of Stock Exchanges, 1980–2005. *Academy of Management Journal*.

Weber, M. 1958. *The Protestant Ethic and the Spirit of Capitalism*. New York: Scribners. (Original 1904–1905.)

Wedel, J. R. 2001. *Collision and Collusion: The Strange Case of Western Aid to Eastern Europe* (Updated). New York: Palgrave Macmillan.

Westphal, J. D. & Zajac, E. J. 1998. The Symbolic Management of Stockholders: Corporate Governance Reforms and Shareholder Reactions. *Administrative Science Quarterly*, 43: 127–153.

————— 2001. Decoupling Policy from Practice: The Case of Stock Repurchase Programs. *Administrative Science Quarterly*, 46: 202–228.

White, L. J. 2001. *What's Been Happening to Aggregate Concentration in the United States? (And Should We Care?)*. New York: Department of Economics, New York University.

Whyte, W. H. 1956. *The Organization Man*. New York: Doubleday.

Wolf, M. 2004. *Why Globalization Works*. New Haven: Yale University Press.

Wolfers, J. & Zitzewitz, E. 2004. Prediction Markets. *Journal of Economic Perspectives*, 18(2): 107–126.

World Bank. 1997. *Private Capital Flows to Developing Countries: The Road to Financial Integration*. Oxford: Oxford University Press.

Zeitlin, M. 1974. Corporate Ownership and Control: The Large Corporation and the Capitalist Class. *American Journal of Sociology*, 79: 1073–1119.

Zitzewitz, E. W. 2006. How Widespread is Late Trading in Mutual Funds? *American Economic Review* (Papers and Proceedings), 96.

Zysman, J. 1983. *Governments, Markets, and Growth: Financial Systems and the Politics of Industrial Change*. Ithaca, NY: Cornell University Press.

INDEX